The Sincere Veneer

The Sincere Veneer

*What Drives the Development Industry off the Rails
and How to Get It Back on Track*

Geoffrey Ferster, Ph.D.

Dr Keeley,

Enjoy the read. Perhaps you will get some new ideas.

With Appreciation,

Geoffrey

30 March 2018

Copyright © 2012, 2014, Geoffrey Ferster, all rights reserved. No portion of this book may be reproduced in any form, printed or electronic, without the written consent of the author.

cover photos:
top: © Avava | Dreamstime.com
bottom: © africa924 / Shutterstock.com

*To my many mentors in villages, academia, colleagues in
bureaucracies and friends worldwide who provided me
the tools and experiences—and for the concerned citizens,
enlightened bureaucrats and students who will 'put a shoulder
to the wheel' to transform the development industry.*

Contents

Preface	9
Introduction	14
In Praise of Working in the Field	18
Centroid Power: The Other Side of the Coin	25
My Own Story	31
A Brief History of the Development Industry	98
The Barriers to Change	113
The Challenges of Decentralization	131
Six Practical Lessons for Decentralization	143
Millennium Villages Project (MVP)	156
The Five Levers of the Development Industry (and what we can do to make them work better)	171
Inaugurating a Pilot Project	197
How will the New Dynamic Approach be Sustained?	218
Appendix	233
Acknowledgements	238
Notes	249

Preface

My name is Geoffrey Ferster. I have spent the better part of my adult life in the field, in Indonesia and other parts of the world, working to alleviate poverty. During this time I have worked with university-educated technical experts, tribal chiefs, and humble villagers; elected officials and bureaucrats, governmental aid organizations and mid-level apparatchiks too numerous to count. In the course of my career I have learned that the design, funding, and management of programs to improve the living standards and economic welfare of citizens in developing nations is seldom as straightforward as one might expect. On the contrary, such efforts are invariably complex, and they're also prone to waste and mismanagement, largely because funding is seldom linked to results. Armed with the generous donations of taxpayers, foundations, and NGOs, a growing cadre of experts has, in the course of time, brought into being an entity that we might well call the Development Industry. Regardless of the specific agency or program involved, this industry's guiding principle, above and beyond any ameliatory effect it might have in the developing world, is to perpetuate itself.

In fact, I have come to the distressing conclusion that the individuals who decide which development programs to fund, which courses of action to pursue, which pockets of local poverty to attack, do a far better job of delivering profits and exceptional rewards to themselves. Though I began work on this book in sadness and anger, my researches have given me greater hope that a reorganization of the current system can bring greater prosperity to those billions of individuals who currently live on $2.50 a day or less.

Such a task requires that we first understand how the current system is organized. And I'd like to make clear from the onset that the type of aid I'm referring to is not the humanitarian aid we hear so much about when a tsunami or an earthquake hits. The industry I'll be examining is the one that administers official developmental assistance (ODA).

The Organization for Economic Cooperation and Development defines such assistance as follows:[1]

> *Flows of official financing administered with the promotion of the economic development and welfare of developing countries as the main objective, and which are concessional in character with a grant element of at least 25 percent... By convention, ODA flows comprise contributions of donor government agencies, at all levels, to developing countries ("bilateral ODA") and to multilateral institutions.*

Such transfers of developmental funds really became big business after World War II when the United States used its economic resources to help rebuild Europe in the gloomy atmosphere of the nascent Cold War. Since that time, official "foreign aid" has been sent in many directions and used in many ways in pursuit of a variety of measurable goals. And almost from the first, a cadre of aids experts has been part and parcel of the process, espousing theories, developing and administrating programs and projects, applying for and distributing grants. For almost as long, other theorists and economists have challenged the effectiveness of official developmental aid, often suggesting that such efforts produce a result quite different from the one intended. The history of such criticisms extends from the pioneering work of Hungarian economist Paul Thomas Bauer to the latest best-sellers by Dambisa Moyo, William Easterly, and Paul Collier.[2]

These folks have a point. It has been estimated that since 1960, nearly $4 trillion (in constant 2013 $US) in public funds has passed through the development industry. Yet today more than half of the world's populations still live on $2.50 a day or less. The UN established Millennium Developmental Goals (MDG) in 1990, targeting those who live on *half* that amount daily, but two decades later they are they are still a significant distance from reaching their targets.

In documents published by the UN prior to the 2010 September Summit, the decline in the number of people living in extreme poverty was attributed entirely to economic progress in China between 1990 and 2005.[3] The report goes on to state:

> *The number of people living in extreme poverty actually went up between 1990 and 2005 by about 36 million… The number of "$1 a day poor" went up by 92 million in sub-Saharan Africa and by 8 million in West Asia during the period 1990 to 2005.*

The report adds that when other dimensions of poverty such as deprivation, social exclusion, and lack of participation are considered, the situation becomes still more dire.

New estimates suggest that the percentage of the world's population experiencing extreme hunger declined during the early years of the new century.[4] And in February 2012 the World Bank's Development Research Group released estimates suggesting that 'extreme poverty' (< $1.25 per day at 2005 prices) had declined in all 'six developing regions' from 2005 to 2008, with 1.1 billion of the 1.28 billion people within that category living outside China.[5]

Are we to conclude that the Development Industry is doing its job well? I don't think so. Experts attribute most of the improvement in people's livelihoods over the last ten years not to the impact of official development assistance but to economic growth within the developing world. And the triumph of lifting millions above the $1.25 per day threshhold ought to be tempered by the fact that so many remain beneath that level.[6] In October 2013 the United Nation's Food and Agriculture Organization determined that one in eight people worldwide (842 million) still suffer from chronic hunger.[7] And the likelihood of reaching a $2.50 per day income, meager though that may be, remains a distant dream for billions worldwide.

In the appendix I present estimates and forecasts for nutrition, maternal and infant mortality, HIV/AIDS, and water and sanitation—confirming that key MDG targets are unlikely to be reached for decades. The estimates for sub-Saharan Africa are especially dire.[6]

In short, after more than fifty years of effort and trillions of dollars filtering through international and domestic bureaucracies, daily grinding poverty remains a scourge on half of the world's humanity (more than 3 billion people). By any legitimate objective measure, the Development Industry has failed to produce results commensurate with its goals or its budgets.

> What is needed is…a deeper commitment on the district and local levels to programs that address the varied issues faced by struggling communities and economies in an integrated way.

Why has so much expenditure had so little effect? No one said it would be easy. The hurdles facing those who would dispense aid in the best ways and in the most appropriate places are many.

But as I intend to show in the pages that follow, the very structures of the organizations that administer the aid too often stand at odds to the desired results. The existing operating system—its architecture, institutions, operations, and above all the ingrained mindset of the individuals at its helm—will never lead to sustained poverty reduction or local economic growth.

The reason things don't work, in a nutshell, is that too much money is being spent at the top of the pyramid among well-heeled executives, program administrators, and government agency workers, and too little is being spent in the field. And the money that *does* trickle down to the people who need it is dispersed in the service of a plethora of fragmented schemes that too often lack the breadth or follow-through to be effective in the long term. What is needed is a serious reduction in smoozing and a deeper commitment on the district and local levels to programs that address the varied issues faced by struggling communities in an integrated way.

Can it be done? Can the pyramid be returned to a solid foundation? Can the multi-dimensional labyrinth of official development aid, with its mysterious sinkholes, cul-de-sacs, and distorting mirrors, be converted into an effective force for fighting poverty?

I think it can. And I'm going to show you how.

Introduction

"Shocked, shocked, I am absolutely shocked!' came the cry from a chorus of diplomats and foreign affairs experts in the Middle East as events unfolded during the New Arab Awakening of Spring 2011. In countries stretching in an ark from the Persian Gulf through the Middle East and on to the Maghreb region of North Africa, ordinary people—men, women, and children of all ages and from all strata of society—were demonstrating and defending their personal and common interests, often putting their lives and those of their families in real danger. Why were all these experts and diplomats and Gucci elites so profusely shocked at the sight? A likely reason is that they themselves had been hard at work for decades developing an intricate web of collusion among international organizations, transnational corporations, academic institutions, and national governments to insure that as few developmental resources as possible made their way to places where they would benefit the segments of a given country's population for whom they were intended. With the passage of time, this skein of fiscal diversion and misdirection had hardened, year after year, though postcolonial and neocolonial periods.

However, to a few intrepid field-oriented experts, such as World Affairs correspondent John Simpson and his seasoned colleagues, Jonathan Head and Owen Bennett-Jones with BBC, various Al Jazeera reporters, and selected academics who have spent time in the villages and on the city's streets, the events weren't much of a mystery. These individuals may have come from Oxbridge or Yale, but they have since been pickled by field experience. As a result, they could fully appreciate how tyrannical governments, in league with international organizations and transnational corporations, engage in a wide spectrum of corrupt practices, often in the name of preserving "stability." The promise of the Arab Spring has not been fulfilled, and events have underscored the fact that stability is a marvelous thing, but the price is often high. In many nations, stability has been achieved by maintaining a vice grip on the inequality and poverty that plagues at least half of the world's population.

As a field-oriented applied economist myself, I, too, have witnessed the *collusion of corruption* for more than four decades, and have created an expression for it. I call it Centroid Power, though it might with equal rationale be termed the *Collusion of Elites*. I discuss the concept more fully in Chapter 2 and later in the book, but for now it may suffice to say that Centroid Power differs from mere autocracy in that it functions at the level of self-serving elites who cooperate with one another across nations and institutions. In the case of developmental aid, these elites work to maintain a façade of social betterment while making sure, first and foremost, that their own large piece of the pie remains intact. I have seen Centroid Power at work in sub-Saharan Africa, the Middle East, and several Asian countries at both the central and field levels. But more about that later.

Though the schemes of Centroid Power continue to be implemented by battalions of civilian and military apparatchiks across the developing world, recent events have shown once again that there is an innate sense of social justice and humanity in even the most downtrodden people that no amount of nationalistic rhetoric can obliterate entirely. At the risk of over-generalizing, I think it's safe to say that the "keg finally blew" in the Middle East when autocrats, at the behest of international organizations, began investing in education over the last generation, but then willfully failed to develop concomitant opportunities for employment. Eventually pent-up frustration exploded.

Much of the talk, at first, was of "democracy." Can it work in the region? Is it practical? Can such institutions be sustained? Who will ultimately take control? In the Arab world these questions are still very much up in the air and the situation is far from hopeful. My background in the field leads me to raise a different set of questions, for example: will it be possible, as a result of demonstrations and "regime change," to reorient the resources and monies that are already being spent by the international development industry, so that they don't continue to disappear into the sand, but rather, are applied, as they were intended, toward building the physical and systems infrastructure required to deliver essential services and create opportunities for local economic growth?

The two sets of questions may or may not be related. Democracies can be wildly corrupt, after all, and autocracies can sometimes (though rarely) set massive social development programs in motion effectively. (China may perhaps be taken as an example.) What I try to do, in the pages that follow, is describe what a more effective system of developmental aid disbursement would look like, how it would be organized and managed, and what the likely fruits of such an effort might be. I have come to believe that no system of developmental aid is likely to be effective unless attention (and money) is directed away from the self-serving bureaucracies that write the progress reports and grant-renewal requests, toward those field-workers who manage programs on a day-to-day basis.

Throughout the pages that follow I call this shift 're-righting' the Pyramid. I focus my attention, for the most part, on the poorer sub-Saharan and Asian countries. However, the plan I set out offers a strategic framework that, with some modifications, can also provide an operational blueprint for nations with higher economic potential that are currently plagued by Centroid Power.

I hope you enjoy the read, during which I share some personal experiences in several developing countries as well as more general constructs and prescriptions for a thorough transformation.

As you reflect on benefits that might accrue to your own country through the reforms I'm suggesting, my advice is to view the principles I advance in the light of your personal knowledge of the local landscape, and devise solutions that fit the circumstances at hand. Flexibility and adaptability are of the essence—though both comcepts run counter to the rigid, top-heavy tastes of the Centroid elite.

1
In Praise of Working in the Field

In 2005 I was recruited by a senior UN official to be a team leader on a World Bank project in Turkey. My role, should I be chosen for the position, would involve strengthening the management of the project and integrating the infrastructure within the Turkish Ministry of Health. I was asked, during the recruitment process, why postgraduate degrees in agricultural economics would qualify me for such a position. The question gave me the opportunity to explain that anyone who does *not* understand the rigors of rural life and farming—an understanding that can only come from experience—would be ill-equipped to give advice at the central level on any policy decision relating the health, education, or economic development of the rural poor within a nation or community. Furthermore, the multiple-linkage among agriculture and health were recognized by professionals and people, particularly poor households residing in communities and urban slums. Yes, I did get this position and enjoyed working with my Turkish colleagues on the project, which, upon completion, was deemed highly successful, even by the World Bank's standards.

An Introduction to Field Work Close to Home

It has occurred to me that my interest in applied economics has always been part and parcel of a greater interest in the "nitty-gritty" realities of daily life in the fields. During the initial year of my graduate study in the Economics Department of the University of Minnesota, I was fortunate to meet, quite literally, 'farm boys' doing their graduate studies in the Department of Agricultural Economics. One student most generously made introductions for me with the head of the Department of Agricultural Economics, and he, unbeknownst to me, set the wheels in motion for a research assistantship in his department, which I was more than happy to accept.

The U of Minnesota is a large land-grant institution with a rich tradition of contributions to specialties within agricultural economics, conducting important research and promoting farming and agribusiness both within the state and around the world. Fortunately, these were the times in which substantial research monies were made available for that purpose. Indeed, as the Cold War was raging contacts to the Soviet Union and obviously to Europe and Asia continued to germinate between the nations' academic communities, government officials, and selective business and corporate interests.

The field project which I was appointed to conduct was in fact a follow-up study. I was to inquire into the land tenure and business arrangements of a sample of farmers in fourteen southwestern counties who had first been interviewed about fifteen years previously. The purpose of the inquiry was to determine how stable the farm population was and how their farming enterprises has changed during the interval. Other departmental and college studies indicated that farm production had increased in this region, with corn and soybean yields rising dramatically as new fertilizers, herbicides, and pesticides were adopted. At the same time, investments in storage and livestock facilities had boosted hog and beef production. I was given the previous questionnaires and asked to update and expand it. During the approximately four months of fieldwork I drove all the back roads in these prosperous agricultural counties, meeting and interviewing most all of the farmers who had participated in the initial sample. Though the farmers were cordial, many of the questions I was asking involved the sensitive topic of farm income and wealth, and I'm sure some of these gnarled and savvy farmers, who spent their time dealing with bankers, machinery mechanics, and seed and fertilizer reps, wondered what a young graduate student from the city was doing asking such questions. Furthermore, while some of the farmers thought highly of the university's College of Agriculture, others did not—and spoke openly of the bad advice they received from academic "experts."

That summer—it was in the early 1960s—gave me a far better understanding of vibrancy of the rural community than I ever would have gotten from books. I met not only with farmers, but with Agricultural Extension Officers and agribusiness owners; I attended farm auctions, sat in local restaurants and coffee houses, attended county fairs, church harvest dinners, and similar social settings, and was impressed by the people whose hard work, risk-taking, and diligent attention to detail were often coupled with an inquisitiveness regarding new technology and economic relationships extending far beyond the borders of the state. Obviously the reality that these farmers and communities were dealing with was far more 'real' than anything I'd met up with hitherto at the university. The experience didn't undermine my interest in large-scale economic issues, but it heightened my appreciation of the links between these issues and the practical ones that farmers and rural communities face on a daily basis.

In the late 1960s, after further years of coursework in economic theory, statistics, research techniques, and water resources (among other things) I was given the opportunity, once again, to conduct research in the field—this time at Cornell University in upstate New York. I once again interviewed farmers in an effort to understand the local land (including agronomic) and water resources, as part of a feasibility study regarding supplemental irrigation on a stretch of the New York State Barge Canal. The study focused not only on the land and water resources, but also on the market potential of the supposed production increase that would accompany supplemental irrigation, and the legal arrangements that would have to accompany such a program, including investments from the government and those directly from the farmers who were to benefit. This 'study zone' had a more complex farm economy than that of southwestern Minnesota, though many of the sociocultural elements of the community were strikingly similar. One pronounced difference lay in the different aims of the two studies themselves. The Midwestern work focused on what changes had transpired over the previous fifteen years, while the New York work framed questions with a forward focus: from the current situation, what would have to take place, by whom, and if it did, change, how would the outlook for the farming and agribusiness interests change as a result?

Further and Further Afield

With this background (and PhD) in hand, I began a career that initially entailed many years in the tropics. Many of the tools and techniques I used conducting fieldwork in Minnesota and New York State proved to be just as effective, with adaptations for local conditions, to more remote and exotic environments. As it happened, I contracted a nasty case of hepatitis during a field project in Tanzania and I decided to spend five years out of the Tropics due to an opportunity that arose in the UK. During that time I worked for a British university conducting applied field level research on maternity/obstetric care that was linked to biostatistical analyses, health care administration and policies, and other facets, of the National Health Service (NHS). Working with NHS doctors, including senior university-based medical specialists, general practitioners, nurses, midwives, and administrators, got me up to speed in various aspects of maternity/obstetric care, and also in how the NHS worked, and I will forever be indebted to those academic and healthcare professionals for the time they spent with me. This intensive yet informal 'postdoctoral' training in maternity/obstetric services in a real health system complemented my training in regional agricultural economic development, since maternal and child health were (and remain) key focal determinants for project initiatives in poor tropical countries and communities in Africa and Asia.

A further dimension was added to my education when I took up a WHO position with the Indonesian Ministry of Health's Planning

Bureau. This position gave me the opportunity to sit at 'central level' with Indonesian and international colleagues. I learned many things about tropical diseases, public health, the Indonesian health care and related public finance systems in the course of this assignment, and also about WHO's early primary health care initiatives. Our three-person WHO team supported various Indonesian health agencies in policy formulation, statistical analyses, planning and budgeting of government resources along with foreign aid projects, at the central and provincial levels. I also visited many provinces, districts, sub-districts villages to follow-up on various subjects of concern to the Ministry of Health and WHO. These experiences provided a 'ring side' seat on how humongous international and domestic bureaucracies work and for whose benefit, and gave me a deeper understanding of the differences between central-level planning and field-level implementation of a program.

> To bureaucrats safely ensconced in their respective international agencies, any work done at country level is considered 'field level.'

I ought to point out before we go any further that the expression "field level" means different things to different people. To bureaucrats safely ensconced in their respective international agencies, any work done at country level is considered 'field level.' The perspective I'm offering within the pages of this book more closely resembles common speech. I consider working with a nation's central government to be 'central level,' while doing work on the provincial, district, and community levels is 'field level.' I have worked at all of these levels and am convinced that those who transverse them with ease are more likely to make viable, pragmatic policy decisions—decisions that have a likelihood of achieving the desired result—than academics, theoreticians, and bureaucrats who know little of about the lives of the people they're trying to serve.

When Indonesia won independence from the Dutch in August 1945, the country faced major challenges. Though it possesses ample natural resources, it was large both in extent and population, and culturally complex. The country found it necessary to develop the public administration almost from scratch. Training the 'best and most promising' students for public service was a huge investment, and the task of designing and implementing legal, financial and institutional infrastructure was formidable. Preventive health programs and medical care were scarce and erratic, though these services were essential to every family and community. Therefore, the medical profession played an important role in the government's development strategy. It subsidized medical education highly, with the proviso that all medical and public health professionals would serve several years (usually five) in underserved and remote rural communities and cities throughout the archipelago. Virtually all Indonesian colleagues (the men and women) I met over the decades relished with fondness their service and contributions in regional capitals, smaller cities and rural areas to families and communities, as a major cornerstone of Indonesia's national development. And this background established and esprit de corps among medical and public health professionals, which in turn, led to the basis of the policy decisions of primary health care—accompanied by domestic and international donor projects, significant funding, implementation and management—as discussed in these chapters.

I was most fortunate to benefit personally from these programs, receiving direct tutelage by two generations of doctors and public health specialists whose formative training had been at field level. I was also impressed to see how the pragmatic field level experiences of these Indonesian medical and public health colleagues of mine were so easily integrated into policy, planning, budgeting, and implementation work within the Ministry of Health. Both at large meetings and in one-on-one discussions with Indonesian colleagues with considerable field level experience, I often heard disagreements voiced regarding the naiveté of the representatives of international health and development agencies, and also of

Indonesian colleagues who had risen to prominent central level with little or no field experience.

I regret to add that during the several decades during which I had the privilege of working in Indonesia, genuine field level experiences played a role in central-level decisions with decreasing frequency. Why?

First, fewer professionals had personal experience in underserved communities, for reasons we'll take up shortly.

Second, as the nation's nascent institutions began to coalesce into a classic example of what I will be describing as Centroid Power, a pattern emerged whereby even the most field-oriented professionals responded to the allure of joining a bureau, directorate, or ministry, where most of the resources allocated for any particular project are spent.

Third, this trend toward bureaucracy and away from field work was further reinforced by the fact that development agencies find it easier and more attractive to work at the country level, which allows it to maintain a veneer of impeccable professionalism. Though allocations administered at this level are likely to be self-serving and unproductive, with little budgeting for physical and systems infrastructure or implementation they grow ever more popular with the passing years.

These, in brief, are a few of the experiences upon which my rather severe and critical diagnosis of the industry is based. In the chapters that follow I will explore in greater detail how entrenched Centroid Power has become in every 'cranny' of the development industry, present a series of examples from my fieldwork and studies in different parts of the world of how sclerotic the aid and development industry has become as a result, and propose some practical reforms.

2

Centroid Power: The Other Side of the Coin

I am using the term Centroid Power to describe a sociopolitical and economic phenomenon that differs somewhat in its structure and ethos from authoritarianism pure and simple. Centroid Power is the premeditated consolidation of political and economic power in the hands of an elite of executives, bureaucrats, and/or military leaders. Far from being a new thing, Centroid Power has been the norm in political and economic life since the days of the pyramids. In the political sphere, there has seldom been a need to mask the relations of power linking central authorities to disparate regions and communities. On the contrary, the *perception* of power was one (among many) elements employed to maintain order and manage resources efficiently. What is unique about the human and cultural component of the development industry is how advanced and disparate the network of power relations it sustains, and how effectively it uses (or abuses) knowledge, technology and manipulative communication to successfully obfuscate it's real agenda, which is to maintain its own power, while also doing as much as it can to advance the suggestion that it's on the *verge* of making real breakthroughs in poverty reduction and other well-defined goals that have inspired donors, both private and public, to continue contributing so generously to its coffers.

Centroid Power is typically supported by both institutions and family connections, and its *reason d'être* is to ensure stability and continuity within government and the community at large, for the purpose of delivering an unending stream of wealth and prestige to those who are a part of it. It's important to note that these benefits are often extended beyond the confines of a nation or principality to include a wide circle of elite personages internationally, many of which may be executives and professionals of international aid organizations, for example. For this reason, the phenomenon I'm calling Centroid Power might with equal justification be called the Collusion of Elites.

The benefits of Centroid Power flow far less often in the other direction, toward the larger community over which it rules and whom it is ostensibly obliged to serve. An important source of its strength, considering the perversity of this arrangement, is its tireless production of doctrines, policies, and ideological assertions, statements designed to justify its position of pre-eminence and to glorify its accomplishments. Such doctrines and assertions often undergird high-profile projects that have ostensibly been designed to serve the betterment of the nation. Whether they actually do produce such benefits I will examine in detail in coming chapters.

> ...despite refined protestations to the contrary, Centroid Power bears striking similarities to neocolonialism in its mindset, strategy, and tactics.

This *multidimensional labyrinth of interwoven international and domestic systems* affects virtually all decisions regarding the accumulation, exploitation, and distribution of wealth. As such, and despite refined protestations to the contrary, Centroid Power bears striking similarities to neocolonialism in its mindset, strategy, and tactics. Needless to say, it's inimical to democratic institutions and processes, though it may sponsor 'mock' elections, a 'free' press, and an 'independent' academia. The loyal military, Secret Service, apparatchiks, 'busybodies', and communication experts in all government departments work together to *feign* participation in ameliorative programs, sometimes in partnership with the private sector, while mostly insuring that the 'revolving door' between the government and private sector continues to keep the lion's share of resources within its own elite sphere.

With respect to the development industry in particular, practitioners of Centroid Power have become adept at massaging bilateral and multilateral treaties, laws, and institutions to their own benefit. They also willingly enter into arrangements with transnational corporations (TNC) in development initiatives which are usually, though not always, related to the exploitation of basic resources. The budgets of these deals are almost invariably rigged so the financial allocations remain overwhelmingly under Centroid control, with only a relative pittance being delivered to districts and at local levels for grass-roots social and economic development initiatives.

Despite decades of honing laws to weed out corruption, both international and domestic, it remains the "code" of many realms. As long as Centroid Power arrangements continue to provide stability, international development agencies and TNC will find it convenient to make them. The military *coups d'état* that erupt from time to time, replacing the leadership and its minions, merely rearranges the 'deck chairs' while keeping the power structures intact.

Differences may be noted, to be sure, between regimes that maintain the power structures I'm describing here, some being 'hard-line' while others project a softer image. But all authoritarian regimes have virtually the same accoutrements of oppression, either present or on standby, to insure that the general public never loses sight of the instruments of control which can be brought to bear upon them individually or as family and social groups. This makes protest difficult and dangerous, and seldom fruitful. Meanwhile, those in power at the district and social levels often have had that power delegated (or franchised) via arrangements both written and unwritten. The system of descending links of patronage and fealty have a distinctly feudal ring to them. In many instances, local families in positions of power, already wealthy due to land and resource ownership, increase their hold on the local community by assuming leadership roles and cornering the contracts doled out in development projects. Such local power centers are an integral component of Centroid Power no less than the elites in the capitol.

All development initiatives face the challenge of dealing with such elites, and the problem is compounded by a similar accretion of cozy ties and self-serving arrangements that almost invariably develop *within* the agencies that administer the funds and design the programs. It's only natural that with the passage of time, these two components of the development industry learn to work well together, like hand in glove.

This assessment of the Development Industry may sound rather cynical, but the facts bear out my analysis. Of course, merely to carp about the waste, corruption, rampant nest-feathering and endless campaigns of self-serving disinformation won't get us anywhere. What we need is a new operating system for the Development Industry. That's why I'm writing this book.

In the pages that follow, I make the case that success in alleviating poverty is tied to efforts to strengthen the district level systems, empower members of the communities the programs are seeking to help, and integrate programs more fully, so economists, agrarians, teachers, physicians, and public health officials can contribute more efficiently to an improvement of livelihoods, rather than working in isolation and leaving one another unexpectedly in the lurch.

A less glamorous aspect of the re-orientation I'm proposing involves improvement in the ways projects are monitored. The UN and other agencies are good at establishing goals but less successful at seeing if they're being met, *and at what cost*. Many programs are self-evaluated, and few "insiders" are motivated to critique themselves out of lucrative positions by pointing out how top-heavy and ineffective their programs have been. Part of this initiative would concern itself with coordinating the statistical standards and outputs of Millennium Development Goals (MDG) with Local Economic Growth (LEG) project initiatives. I'll say a word about the relation between these two sets of measurements, and how misleading it can be to focus exclusively on MDG criteria, in later chapters.

Meanwhile, there is enormous room for improvement in how agencies harness and exploit the information available from programs in other parts of the world. When the right hand doesn't know what the left hand is doing, things don't get done very well. It often happens that programs with a narrow focus even fail to tap resources that are available nearby. I'm proposing the establishment of knowledge and technology centers that would reduce the duplication of services and facilitate the sharing of information related to common problems and innovative technologies. Societies of poor farmers and livestock owners are adroit at adopting new technologies which fit their approach to the land and don't cost much. Cell phones have had an impact in some parts of the world, but the relevant technologies extend beyond the digital revolution to low-cost tools and techniques that increase productivity, improve water quality, reduce post-harvest losses and lead to sustained improvements in the standard of living in countless other ways.

> The Centroid Power structures currently in place have one big advantage from an administrative point of view—they're far easier to manage than any de-centralized scheme would be. Their glaring drawback is that they simply don't work.

Yet another area requiring attention is that of exposing corruption within developmental agencies. It would be possible, for example, making use of techniques developed to combat terrorism, to track the flow of funds between developmental agencies and powerful individuals within recipient nations and communities. Such heightened oversight would insure that less of a given project's funding ends up in Swiss bank accounts and more in the field.

It should be obvious, even from these brief remarks, that the challenges associated with turning the development industry on its head are immense. The Centroid Power structures currently in place have one big advantage from an administrative point of view—they're far easier to manage than any decentralized scheme would be. Their glaring drawback is that they simply don't work. Some strides have been made in improving the welfare and future prospects of *some* of the world's poorest people. All the same, the problem of grinding poverty remains enormous.

3

My Own Story

Tanzania

As a 'Green PhD,' I was 'poured' onto my first transatlantic flight from New York to Heathrow in January 1969. In those days, flights to postcolonial African capitals were few and far between, and BOAC had arranged hotel accommodation in the Charing Cross area of London for the three days I'd have to wait for my connection. This gave me a fine opportunity (the frisky January weather notwithstanding) to retrace paths and revisit sites that stirred happy memories from a decade earlier, when I had been privileged to spend an undergraduate academic year at the famed London School of Economics and Political Science (LSE).

Returning to Heathrow on the appointed day and going through the formalities, I was soon on the long overnight BOAC flight to Dar es Salaam. After sleeping for some hours I lifted the shade and peered down 30,000 feet to see the remnants of tanks and military equipment in the Sinai that had been abandoned during the recent Six-Day War. Then thousands of miles of desert, which finally gave way to the lush tropics. Hours later the plane made a wide circle over Lake Victoria, dropping all the while, and soon we could see villagers doing their daily morning chores.

We landed in Entebbe shortly thereafter. It was a Sunday morning. As I walked down the steps I noted the heavy tropical mist enveloping the coconut trees. I gathered my bags at the terminal and checked through customs. I had arrived in an environment known to me only vaguely through reading. Indeed, outside of hearing some English spoken, it was an entirely new world!

Still overdressed and already sweating in a rumpled long-sleeve shirt, I set out from Entebbe with a driver, gazing out the window at the lush multi-cropped farmlands and the occasional roadside village. The driver pointed out proudly how his fellow Ugandan farmers, who were blessed with productive soil and plenty of rain throughout the year, used an efficient inter-cropping system of their own devising, with cropped cassava, bananas and beans interspersed across the same land. The taxi sped down the empty new macadam road for nearly an hour before it reached the outskirts of the still-sleeping environs of Makerere University.

Post-Colonial Independent East African academia

Within a few minutes of arriving at the university, two Brits—a man and a woman, both recent under-graduates—introduced themselves, and at tea I met the gent's wife and a Ugandan and his American wife. A week later, after attending the conference, the six of us would be driving the department's Land Rover back to Dar es Salaam.

During the periods of heavy socializing at the conference, I was able to glean hints of the struggle that would soon ensue between a new batch of neocolonialists and the sometimes starry-eyed cadre of East African academics, who would, in turn, enter soon enough into a long struggle with their own new countries' leaders to spur development in villages like the one's I'd glimpsed on my arrival. Indeed, these African academics showed great enthusiasm, albeit tinged with naiveté, in their efforts to enunciate how a new pragmatic approach drawing upon both 'European' and East African scholarship and traditions would 'show the light' to local politicians in Kenya, Tanzania, and Uganda. The same air of enthusiasm was also extended to Americans and some academics from the Nordic countries.

As a neophyte I learned a lot that week from some gnarled old Brits who had worked in the colonies most of their careers, and, looking back across decades of subsequent expensive "development," the judgment of these experienced tropical practitioners seems more prescient to me than ever!

Initial and Genuine Safari: Kampala to Dar

At the end of the conference we drove the Land Rover in what I still consider the 'Safari journey of a lifetime.' We were most fortunate in having Albert, our Ugandan Bureau colleague, along on the journey. Albert generously shared his knowledge and insights in the most brotherly spirit—always calm, always in good humor, never showing the slightest annoyance as he fielded the most elementary questions from his 'European' colleagues. For me, having Albert with us was the best part of the journey.

From Kampala, we drove some hours and spent the night in a very lively bar complex offering a range of nocturnal enticements, as would be expected in a country known as the 'social center of East Africa'. At Queen Victoria Game Park the following day, we found ourselves at one point surrounded by a pride of fifteen lions. Albert advised us to keep the engine running, calmly explaining that the exhaust fumes blunted the lions' keen sense of smell and made it easier to make a quick getaway!

We pitched our tents that night on a grassy sward a few hundred yards away from a small pond. It was a wonderful moonlit night, during which I was awakened by the 'oinking' sound of the hippopotamuses in the pond. I viewed them from the window of the tent for quite some time, admiring these enormous herbivores while remaining anxious about whether they would trample us as they proceeded on their nocturnal path.

The next morning we encountered a truly dreadful sight on the side of the road: a decapitated body! This was two years before Idi Amin's January 25, 1971, coup d'état. Albert calmly gave us some background, and we asked a passing local to notify the authorities.

Two years later, during my final months in Tanzania, I learned that Albert was actively involved in the resistance movement against Idi Amin and had been killed. He had given no hint of such involvement to me, and why would he have? This was my first close awareness of the 'high stakes - winner takes all' coup d'état politics in African and other countries—though not my last.

The rest of the week's journey took us through the incomparable Serengeti National Park, Ngorongoro Crater, Lake Manyara to view nature's finest wildlife in and the natural habitat was indelibly etched in my subconscious, to be awoken with occasional *National Geographic* magazines or *History Channel* specials on 'the box.' And who could ever forget the majesty of Mount Kilimanjaro on a crystal clear morning? (Fortunately, I was able to climb it just before I finished my assignment in Tanzania). Along the way it became obvious to me that I would have little need for my winter coat in Tanzania. A few months later I gave it to the houseboy I shared with a British couple from the department. The boy's family lived in the higher, cooler altitudes of Moshi, near to Mount Kilimanjaro.

Field study in Nzega District

My new job at University es Salaam focused on agriculture and water development at a locale two days drive from the Indian Ocean in the center of Tanzania. I was put in charge of the fieldwork conducted with university students in the Study Zone and was also responsible for completing the subsequent reports, which would have wide distribution within the university and government. The ministries of Agriculture and Water and Irrigation had decided to invest in infrastructure to expand cotton production south of Lake Victoria, since 'king cotton' had become Tanzania's major export earner. The plan was to construct two dams and sufficient underground pipelines to distribute the water within the Mwambiti and Wembere Plains (M&W Plains) of North East Nzega. The water would be used both for livestock grazing and for human consumption, satisfying the needs of a population base that was expected to grow along with expanding cotton production. I found my initial briefings with government officials very interesting, "green" as I was, but they contained precious few specifics regarding this huge project, which at 40 million Tanzanian Shillings (perhaps $5.7 million dollars) was the largest capital expenditure of this kind in Tanzania to date. We were provided with a very basic map showing elevation lines, and the hydro-engineer's grid laid out the two dams, the distribution systems, the large tanks for livestock, and the standpipes for villagers. One part of the scheme, the Bulenya Hills Dam, had already been completed, though it comprised only a fifth of the total system.

We made an introductory trip to the site to discuss the project with local officials and make arrangements for my return with students in April to begin fieldwork that would last about six months. The roads in the region were hard 'wash-board' surfaces, there was no electricity to be had anywhere nearby, and the availability of kerosene was not assured. Buses ran on the main road and the petrol station was about 35 miles (56km) away.

Key Features of the Fieldwork

The M&W Plains is a 700-square-mile area at 3500 feet elevation, give or take a few hundred feet—a 'comfortable tropical highland' area. It has a dry season from June through November and a rainy season from November to May, with the heaviest rains typically falling at the end of that period. About 40,000 people lived in the Plains when I was there, including a large contingent of Sumba people who had moved southwards from Lake Victoria to take up cotton farming on land hitherto for livestock grazing. Clearly, the potential for land-use conflict in the region was considerable, and it was likely to be exacerbated by the new water project.

During that first visit I was introduced to two local men, one was the local village executive officer, who would become key local colleagues, accompanying me and my students daily throughout our interviews, offering valuable insights, and paving the way for us to meet the local farmers, herdsmen, and villagers. The purpose of our information-gathering was to determine the economic potential of the water project and the utilization patterns that were already well underway. You might say that we were conducting a feasibility study—after the decision had already been made to invest. This arrangement seemed odd to me at the time, and in retrospect it may serve as a graphic example of how politicians and engineers who are removed from the realities on the field can make expensive mistakes.

Among the things we were eager to ascertain was how the new water source would most likely affect livestock, cotton production and human settlement in the plain. In the course of our investigations I was pleased to find that the graduate courses I'd taken in land and regional development, abstract and statistical, though focused on practicalities, had equipped me with some great tools to address the complex issues involved.

Some of the most important technical contribution made by our team was to provide more detailed and accurate information about the soil-types that would determine productivity, and water utilization patterns. During the dry season women with some boys from their settlement daily chores included journeying up to twenty kilometers overnight to fetch tins of brackish water from the dry riverbeds. Hence, a reliable piped supply of water would add productivity, food and income for families and greatly reduce the drudgery of water collection for nearly six-months a year. Sampling data on water utilization of the current underground piped system by 'blocked-hours' over the day included: filling containers for household use, washing clothes and bathing children at the village sites, and at the large tanks for livestock, the numbers of different kind of livestock at types of usage by the people, which leads to spreading of numerous diseases. Obviously it is extremely difficult to have convincing 'messaging' to stop people from mixing their water usage practices. This water utilization data was subsequently used by the engineers and in further planning for settlements in the M&W Plain. In regards to land productivity, with the keen knowledge of the local herdsman and farmers we eventually came up with a map delineating fourteen 'Performance Zones,' some better for farming and others for grazing. As far as I know, this map was not used by the engineers in designing their pipeline system, though it answered the question we'd been asked, and shed light on the return on investment that might be expected and the probable limits to settlement in the area in the coming two or three decades.

One of the most important things we discovered was that the soil of the Mbuga type was composed of heavy clay and shale that contracted significantly in the dry season. This process often squeezed and broke the Italian asbestos pipe carrying the water, thus cutting off the supply. We were disturbed to find that such soils were common in precisely the areas where the proposed expansion of the underground water system would take place. As a result of our investigations, the engineers in Tabora changed the distribution systems and tightened the specs on the underground pipes to ensure they wouldn't break with seasonal changes in the weather.

MORE ASPECTS OF TANZANIA AND FIELD-LEVEL DEVELOPMENT

The years I spent in the region were the early, heady years of Tanzania's independence (Tanganyika 1961; Tanzania 1967). Only two years before (1969) President Nyerere had issued the Arusha Declaration emphasizing self-reliance and African socialism, the dominant policy themes for his vision of Tanzania. Indeed there was much enthusiasm for agricultural and economic development at the time, though the country largely lacked both the human skills and the infrastructure to bring such development about. Tanzania had a Centroid Power structure at the time, controlled from Dar es Salaam, though President Nyerere did make an effort to strengthen competency at the regional and district levels. During my years there I found discussions with technical staff at all government levels to be open and the staff-members eager for a healthy exchange of views and information.

A key concept of President Nyerere's vision for rural development was *Ujamaa*, which is based on a Swahili word for familyhood. Unfortunately, in practice, *ujamaa* became a blanket justification for the collectivization of agriculture and the widespread forced relocation of large groups of people. All of that took place after my departure. But I would like to think that our work in North East Nzega offered a better model for empowering people in their communities with facts and information for real 'bottom-up' planning.

In any case, my experience in Tanzania working with farmers, livestock owners, and residents of small communities, including businessmen, reinforced my belief that to be effective, such projects must a) empower local people and communities and b) integrate planning, management, and investments among the relevant sectors, especially agriculture, water, health, and education, and c) keep sight of the goal—to improve the human condition, reduce poverty, and spur sustainable economic growing in local areas. These are some of the central themes of this book.

> **Unfortunately, in practice, *ujamaa* became a blanket justification for the collectivization of agriculture and the widespread forced relocation of large groups of people.**

I have found that such beliefs don't square very well with the Centroid Power structures that often arise in the areas most in need of developmental aid. I was more surprised to discover, however, as the decades sped by, that they were not widely shared by my colleagues working in the emerging development field either.

Indeed, it was during this late 1960s and early 1970s period that the World Bank was formulating and then perfecting its preferred 'project cycle'. Whilst in the early days the systematic accumulation and analyses of data at the field level was paramount in the process, the fact that the incentives proffered to project managers were all skewed to the short-term—toward 'getting the money out the door' rather than arriving at a satisfactory result. It did not take long for these managers to 'game' the activities within the project cycle in such a way as to deemphasize systematic evidence accumulation and analysis while feeding the appetite of the industry for the latest 'fall and winter fashions' in policy instead. It was, and remains today, relatively rare to meet up with a program that moves beyond convenient assumptions about how things are supposed to work and statistical slights-of-hand that create an illusion of success. In the Bulenya Hills Dam project I've just described, for example, the engineers who designed and located the large water distribution tanks for animals failed to separate them adequately from the sources the villagers used. As a result, with new people arriving from the Southern side of Lake Victoria, where schistosomiasis was endemic, to participate in the cotton expansion in the M & W Plain; the newly piped water expanded the spread of diseases such as schistosomiasis rampantly. This project provided me early example of the 'negative effects' of development investments in local communities.

I recall interviewing some traditional herdsman during my fieldwork to understand their operations. This livestock farmer with his whole family, including his sons' families totaling about twenty people, welcomed us. Although his operations were traditional (similar to the Masai) and the male members of the family did go on grazing tracks with the livestock during the dry season due to shortage of grass, his base of operation and adjacent land area served their needs for most of the year. They had also begun to cultivate cotton and a variety of vegetables for their household consumption. When the interview was completed, the herdsman invited our team of university students for lunch. Fifteen of us sat on the ground eating together and discussing, in Kiswahili, the problems faced by this herding family. At one point the gentleman excused himself, went to the house, and returned ten minutes later with a Japanese transistor radio. We should listen to Radio Tanzania, he said, because the recent American moon shot was following a trajectory directly overhead and towards Dar es Salaam! This was in 1969. To me it was crystal clear these herdsmen and villagers craved and would adapt and incorporate knowledge transfer and appropriate technologies to improve the lives of their families and communities. The recognition for the quest for knowledge and how local people could adapt it for their own betterment was demonstrated in all field endeavors I have participated in and is main theme in the recommendations you will read about in following chapters. Some decades later 'appropriate technology and knowledge transfer' has been made a 'subsection' of the development industry.

It should have been quite straightforward to integrate agriculture, water, health, education and local development programs in places like this. Yet under Centroid Power systems, two generations of professionals have manipulated virtually all organs of the development industry to serve their personal needs while giving short shrift to those of the farmers, villagers, and urban slum-dwellers they are ostensibly dedicated to serve and empower.

Tanzanian Livestock Market

I was the guest of a government official who was buying local livestock on behalf of the government one afternoon. The marketplace was replete with merchants selling a variety of goods, including colorful Katanga's and supplies for the local farmers. The livestock waiting their call were kept in large pens about 200 feet from the structure for the auction. The screening system conducted before and in the pens would allow only healthy animals to reach the auction ring—an enclosed, circular space surrounded by benches, newly built by the government.

My experienced Tanzania host, a gentleman in his 50s and over 6 feet tall informed me that, in addition to himself (buying for the government) the buyers included private dealers who, in turn, sold the livestock to private herdsman and to the abattoir (livestock processing company) about 100 miles away in Tabora, the regional capital. There were few farmers or livestock owners in the stands.

My host told me that his presence with government money would make it difficult for private buyers, acting in collusion, to squeeze livestock owners and drive down prices. It was the government's policy to encourage the livestock industry and benefit the herdsman whilst shifting their traditional values and practices of having their 'four hoofs' become their bank and 'walking' storehouse of value. Just as the water project benefitted cotton production as an export earner, the government was also trying to foster livestock ownership as part of a wider rural economic development program accelerating the 'multiplier effect' to benefit families, catalyze agribusiness and, in turn, the communities—a proactive usage of Centroid Power perhaps unique to Tanzania under President Nyerere.

Tanzanian health systems

During my time in Tanzania I had frequent opportunities to see clinics that provided rudimentary care to the villagers, particularly women with children tied onto their backs who queued patiently to receive medicines and other forms of care. And it struck me that such local health systems, even with water piped from the new dam, had a largely negative impact to the villagers' health. One morning I was awoken early with the request for my pocket knife. The villager's wife had just given birth and there was nothing with which to cut the umbilical cord. I handed the instrument over, advising the villager to have it sterilized before cutting the cord.

Many months later, after recovering from a terrible bout of hepatitis, I returned to the University of Dar es Salaam, to find that a dedicated British doctor was advising President Nyerere on a cost-effective preventive healthcare policy. I discussed the program with him at some length and became keenly interested in health systems and their linkages to agricultural systems. Who could not after experiencing how rural families and communities lived in Tanzania? As life is serendipitous I was moving in that direction; and after spending six years doing applied economics healthcare research in the UK's National Health System (NHS), largely focused on maternal and child health (MCH), I was invited to join the WHO team in Indonesia as the health economist.

By that time, some of the lessons I had learned in Tanzania were already being adopted in Indonesia, and through WHO, under the larger policy rubric of primary health care, attempts were being made to develop a cost-effective system of preventive and basic curative healthcare in several developing countries.

Indonesia

The Halcyon years

In many ways, the years from the mid-1970s until 1997, when the Asian Currency and Economic Crisis hit Indonesia, were halcyon ones for economic and social development in Indonesia. Yes, things worked well under President Soeharto, and if a program or ministry wasn't working, he would find out who was responsible and get it back on track again. It was a corrupt regime, to be sure, favoring the First Family and friends; but President Soeharto, perhaps unusual among autocrats, also felt a strong need to introduce policies beneficial to people living in villages, with the help of both government and donor funds, many of which were loans.

President Soeharto, a very keen strategist and tactician, surrounded himself with strong groups of largely Javanese technocrats and senior military officers, many of whom had been educated in Dutch, German, and US universities, to address the nation's issues, foremost of which was the skyrocketing population; a legacy of his predecessor, President Soekarno. Soeharto pursued a three-pronged strategy, addressing the issues of family planning, primary health care, and rice production, with impressive results. Through diligent investments in training programs, fertilizers, and irrigation systems, and the cultivation of new varieties of rice, Indonesia had achieved self-sufficiency in rice production by the early 1980s. This amazing advance improved the nutrition of hundreds of millions of people and also proved to be a net plus for the economy, notwithstanding the higher input costs. Meanwhile, over the next two decades the Indonesian Family Planning Program (BKKBN), with strong support from President Soeharto, pursued both 'top-down' and 'bottom-up' approaches, resulting in one of the great family-planning success stories worldwide. Professors and development specialist flocked to Indonesia to see how the program was actually run. Indeed, many of the development initiatives in population and Primary Health Care rebranded by WHO and the development agencies came from countries like Indonesia who had to finance and strengthen the institutions and operations at field level to get the results. (Of course, significant financing in fact came from the development agencies and donor projects; but we're getting a little ahead of ourselves.)

Among the keys to Soeharto's success was the creation of a National Family Planning Board separate from the Ministry of Health. It's interesting to note that the only paid employee of the central government at village level was the family planning worker. The family-planning data obtained was used to grade political appointees (i.e., provincial Governors, heads of districts and mayors of regencies (in rural areas and municipalities) on how well they met family-planning targets designed to lower birthrates.

By the mid-1970s, it was widely recognized in academic circles that even among low-income populations, birthrates would decline even as perinatal, neonatal, and infant mortality declined: as the likelihood of a baby surviving rose, couples voluntarily reduced their size of family. This relationship became even stronger as income levels increased. The Soeharto Indonesian family-planning motto became 'two [children] are enough.'

Dramatic changes to adopt Primary Health Care

The Dutch didn't leave the Indonesians with much economic or social infrastructure when they abandoned their five-hundred-year empire, but they did leave behind an elite class, largely Javanese, exemplified by the Royal Javanese court at Yogyakarta, President Soekarno, and later President Soeharto, and their respective minions. Soeharto, for all his failings, well understood how inadequate health services in poor communities would hurt families and eventually might even undermine his credibility. This may explain why, in the mid-1970s, the health sector began to both expand and to improve significantly.

The WHO, UNICEF, and donors such as USAID also played their part in implementing primary health care initiatives. By 1974 about 3,700 health centers and about 9,000 sub-health centers had been constructed in Indonesia. This was no mean accomplishment in a country with five major islands and nearly 600 smaller inhabited islands stretching in an archipelago spanning more than 3000 miles.

In the early 1980s I visited a district in Central Java where the avant-garde health center doctors were all ethnic Chinese Indonesians from wealthy families who were pioneering an independent, community-level approach to health care.

This approach was outside of the program structure of the Ministry of Health, Directorate General of Community Medicine, but with the 'blessings' of the DG and Minister. After several years of trials and assessments, it led to a village-based Posyandu's primary health care system combining medical, paramedic, and managerial support from the Ministry of Health, regional and district levels and health centers, together with support from the local women involved in their community—the local knowledge-base of these women being an essential ingredient. For example, the health center has to coordinate the logistics of the "cold chain" for the Expanded Program of Immunization (EPI) under tropical conditions. To make a village immunization program effective, the staffs, transport, and villagers needed to get the people out to the session, particularly families that might be reluctant for their children to be immunized. These women also helped in record-keeping, which is vital for such village-based public health efforts.

> To make a village immunization program effective, the staffs, transport, and villagers needed to get the people out to the session, particularly families that might be reluctant for their children to be immunized.

When visiting villages, I would ask if even the known ill family with their children would attend today's clinic. I understood it was not easy to stay away with the active women participating. Also, I would look at locally kept records and ask about the 'white out'; and invariably found that an error was corrected by the supervising lady as many women volunteers were not fully literate. In other villages I visited I spoke with the person (usually a mother) who was responsible for holding the basic medicines and diagnosing the simple illnesses, then supplying the medicines and collecting a small fee which she retained and then brought to the health center to resupply her local medicine kit. Invariably she was extremely dedicated and well received and supported by the community. She had been trained in simple diagnosis and referral to the health center, and this was a very popular part of the health center outreach services. However, this community health worker "position" was not universal and often fell vacate. (As an aside, the Chinese 'barefoot doctor' system had originated many of the elements of village and community support including the diagnosis and treatment including basic medicines for minor ailments and injuries. Additionally, the previous Chinese system made legendary contributions in environmental public health initiatives.)

As the Posyandu program matured, with empowered women together with their children genuinely participating and working with the visiting health center staff and specialists, the vibrancy was easy to discern.

In the Central Java district, which had also set an innovative program in place, the head of the district health office and various health-center doctors frequently held three-hour evening sessions with the community volunteers. The sessions included topics on various aspects of preventive and community medicine, usually ending at about 10 p.m. The participants were invariably farmers who would be back in the fields early the next morning. There was no payment involved and I recall community leaders voicing their concerns about the difficulties of holding similar training sessions about rice production and other agricultural issues.

Driving back from Central Java to Semarang to catch a plane to Jakarta, I asked a senior official who had also attended the evening meetings why it would not be possible to pay these community-based volunteer health-workers? He calmly replied that the government considered it their duty to promote their community. After all, the government was providing the technical support and building the infrastructure for the various systems; and considering how many thousands of villages and programs there were, to pay volunteers even a small amount would end up being exorbitantly expensive.

Though I held my peace, it was obvious to me that the battalion of bureaucrats I had been working with was also expensive. They often attended meetings, and got paid for each meeting during their working hours, though they were already getting monthly remuneration and various other perks. In fact, they would often arrive at a meeting, sign in, greet colleagues, utter an inane comment or two, pick up their payment envelope, and then leave for another meeting! Day after day I watched this well-organized 'parade of attendees' come and go like a recurring scene from the Indonesia Wayang (shadow puppet) theater, making me wonder how they were able to get anything done during their regular office hours. No doubt it was the responsibility of loyal staff-members to answer the complex questions and process requests. Yes indeed, this too is important reality check and also reflects the halcyon years in Indonesian social-economic development!

But the Centroid Power system was pleased to maintain these meeting schedules, and the international development agencies were complicit, making healthy contributions to cover the costs of hotels retreats and distributing packaged 'envelopes' usually after the last session.

I don't mean to suggest that the Indonesian Directorates did not possess well-trained, highly dedicated, skilled professionals and staff. Indonesians know their country exceedingly well and can find out anything they want to know quickly via both informal means and official information systems. Indonesia has invested heavily in IT and over the decades has repeatedly upgraded its technical and managerial capabilities. It seems to me that the information is both too much and too little, often quite overwhelming, and difficult to take fully into account when making managerial decisions.

Local empowerment: The issues surrounding local empowerment in Indonesia was made more difficult by the fact that Soeharto's overthrow of Soekarno in September 1965 had overtones of excessive community participation itself. For the Soeharto's stalwarts, to actively encourage community participation was considered to be the 'thin edge of the wedge' which might eventually undermine his authority. On the other hand, the realists in the Ministry of Health, and particularly the Directorates General of Community Health, perceived the benefits that would accrue to villages and villagers, including improvements in the key health status and indices that are now among the key Millennium Development Goals.

The overriding question in Indonesia, and at many other parts of the world, is whether decision-makers can relax their grip on the decision-making process, and transfer a degree of trust—and adequate reliable funding—to district and local leaders, leaving for themselves the still-considerable role of formulating overall strategy, integrating sectors and programs, and monitoring results. In Indonesia such a voluntary "re-righting" of the pyramid is unlikely. Generations of individuals have benefited personally in a big way from running the system in the standard, top-down way.

By the late 1970s the Soeharto regime had regularized planning and budgeting processes for annual development budget. As the WHO health economist in a three-person team that also included the senior public health specialist and a statistician, I found myself ensconced in the Ministry of Health's Bureau of Health Planning— one of the Bureaus in the Secretary-General's stable which gave me a unique perspective on how it worked. Here are a few overview thoughts.

First, Indonesia's annual and five-year planning and budgeting process was entirely necessary, considering the size and spread of the country and the lack of experience among those employed by the public administration, who were essentially learning "on the job" without much of a track record to guide them.

Second, President Soeharto opted to give the lead power to the National Planning Board (BAPPENAS); but this was pragmatically balanced with the 'real power' given to the Ministry of Finance. Further balancing was provided to ministries who were to be responsible for their programs. But the strong BAPPENAS, with Soeharto's backing, always led the way and 'adjudicated' all consensuses in their favor. Ministries such as Health, of course, had plenty of internal competition, most notably amongst the Directorates Generals fiefdoms and the powerful Directorates (usually technical units) within the DG, which received the lion's share of the funds distributed by foreign donors.

Third, once a multiyear foreign assistance/donor project was formally approved, it would become linked into each Directorate's development plan and budget. The complexities of the Indonesian public administration system were compounded by the fact that each international development agency had its *own* lengthy project formulation process, with multiple stages, some taking literally two years before being approved and integrated to the next annual budget. Indonesia accommodated the requests from the plethora of different donors, although this responsibility invariably fell mostly onto the shoulders of the hard-working civil servants in BAPPENAS, Ministry of Finance, and line ministries.

A Front Row Seat in the Ministry of Health and WHO

The Head of the Ministry of Health's Bureau of Health Planning at one point invited me and one the bureau staff to visit a few provinces to collect and analyze budget data from the multiple sources of budgets—data that was not easy to come by at the central level. It's important to note here that programs typically receive routine budget allocations from the central level, mostly for expenses related to personnel, but also from many other sources. For example, a health center might receive support in the form of personnel and drugs from fourteen different sources.

Here are a few of the conclusions we arrived at on the basis of the data we collected:

- The most dramatic discovery we made was that funds from the Ministry of Finance were subsidizing personnel at the provincial and district/regencies levels to the tune of 75 percent. This huge source of funding had been excluded from my earlier estimates of the health sector.

- Conversely, examining of budgets made it clear that the local areas themselves contributed very little toward developing their public health sector services.

- The 'city' districts received significantly higher percentage of both recurrent and development (investment) budgets than did the 'rural' districts, even though populations in the 'rural' districts where many times larger than in 'city' districts. This difference was attributable to numbers and class of hospitals based in the cities.

- Due to the central government's subsidized drugs through INPRES Drug Funds (discussed below), many rural districts did generate income, approximately half as much as the smaller number of city districts. We were unable to determine if that income was returned to the local treasury or used by the facility to offset other expenditure.

- The estimates from the fieldwork did not include the central government's budgeted expenditures for administration at the provincial level or infrastructure (facilities, equipment, and training) in the provinces and districts. Separately we had made estimates of public resources and the private sector supporting health development in Indonesia. Roughly these amounted to an average of $4/per capita from public resources and a further $8/per capita for private health/medical care (largely dominated by pharmaceuticals)—bringing the health sector to about 4.5 percent of GNP.

- Quite obviously it would be a herculean task to select priorities, plan, allocate budgets, implement, and manage public programs to increase the health status (the population in 1975 was 133 million, in May 2011 it was 237 million) on an average of $4 per person; even combined with multi-pronged multi-sectoral efforts, if they all functioned well. Hence, foreign assistance through donor aid projects was an integral part of Indonesia's strategy in the health related and all sectors to accelerate infrastructure, systems and economic development.

Collecting, analyzing and distilling public finance information in the health sector at field level provided a more cohesive understanding for central level administration to use in planning and budgeting health programs with the panoply of donor's knocking on the Ministry of Health's door with their projects. In view of Indonesian poor health status indices, particularly in rural locales throughout the archipelago, it was urgent to invest in health-related systems and the primary health care strategies. Alongside this push by international donors, which began during the late 1970s and early 1980s, Indonesia was awakening to its resources (including petrochemicals) which would serve as a source of added revenue to spur social-economic development. Hence, an urgent need arose for sound strategies coupled with an administrative and managerial infrastructure to put those programs and projects into effect. It is not surprising that an already strong centralized regime was further solidified at this time, thus increasing its already enormous influence on a fragmented system of provinces, districts, villages and villagers.

Since I was working with public finance, which included support through the lengthy and extensive budgeting process, it was essential to be totally open, even with the most ardent skeptics, who are certainly entitled to their opinions.

This attitude of openness is highly regarded in Indonesia, because it leads, they believe, to good relationships (*humbugan baik*) and the all-important concept of being in harmony (*cocok*). Yet a degree of suspicion nevertheless pervaded the Soeharto regime, with regard to potentially subversive agents, both local and foreign. Our team was the first to be located in the Bureau of Planning, one of the Bureaus within the Sectary General. The Bureau of Planning's central role included coordination with the Directorate Generals, BAPPENAS, Ministry of Finance to (i) formulate national health policy; (ii) prepare Five-Year and annual budgets, (iii) collect and analyze health related information; (iv) foreign assistance and donor projects, (iv) monitor and evaluate programs and projects; in reality less emphasis was put on the last function. Surely this pivotal role would have been prime territory for a 'foreign agent.'

During the early years of the project our team was tested repeatedly, but by virtue of our independent perspective and support for Indonesian policies and initiatives, we slowly broke down any remaining barriers. We were eventually invited to participate in numerous high-level meetings such as the weeklong conference I described a moment ago, where we met many Indonesian colleagues in different directorates generals and corners of the Ministry of Health and other ministries. Such interactions helped to spread the word that we could be constructive assets to various health sector initiatives. It was thus, after establishing personal credibility, that I was privileged to work with specifics in healthcare and health sector financing, both during my years with WHO and subsequently as an independent consultant.

You may discern, from the preceding remarks, that most of my activities in health care and systems financing in Indonesia were focused on 'macro'—strategic issues at the program level and broad development of budget allocations to expand and primary health care for Five-Year Plans and annual budgets. Although I did have interactions with Indonesian colleagues in such technical sub-Directorates as maternal and child health, family planning, nutrition; and the CDC (which included water and sanitation) I was not directly involved in formulating budgets for or prioritizing sets of activities, as these were done within the Directorates' Generals technical units.

And of course, I was aware there were detailed subprojects and activities within the Directorates Generals and Secretary-General's office, one of which was the Bureau of Health Planning. Indeed I well remember all of the work was done pre-computers on the tried-and-true IBM 'Selectric'—a very large carriage manual typewriter! All offices of the Ministry of Health had teams of assistants preparing all forms of documentation, including the different requirements for the annual health development and routine budgets. In fact, as I have noted elsewhere, the planning and budgeting process was a variable but unrelenting twelve-month cycle. I remember long, hectic days, nights, and weekends in February (prior to the end-of-March final approvals) during which the teams finalized the activities and projects to be sent to BAPPENAS and the Ministry of Finance for approval and the all-important signatures of senior officials.

On one occasion during this intensive wrap-up I happened to meet our head of the Bureau of Health Planning and a director general in the parking lot as I left the office. I greeted them both and we had a pleasant chat before they excused themselves and disappeared into the backseats of their cars. Sitting in the front passenger seats I noticed a pile of loose files stacked to the top of the back of the seat, each with a project, its detailed activities, and its budget requests—similar to the ones I had seen being prepared for weeks. It was these gentlemen's evening work, presumably, to go through each of the files and sign off on the project which should duly be delivered to their offices in the morning. Imagine this sequence carried out day after day in all Indonesian ministries and agencies!

While this was not the first time I had seen many people involved with great flurries of paper and process, I was struck once again by how odd it seemed. Why, I thought to myself, would a system use Directorates Generals' and the Secretary-General's precious time to look over literally thousands of numbers on hundreds of budget proposals? In a hierarchical structure such as Indonesia's, wouldn't the energies of senior decision-makers yield even greater rewards if they were directed toward mobilizing their technical teams in sub-directorates to improve infrastructure and delivering services? Wouldn't this result in higher performance and improved health status indices at the village level?

Later in my career, I was able to better articulate these heretical ideas to selective Indonesian and international colleagues, sometimes getting nods of approval. Yet most development agencies and consultants grew quiet when I brought up the subject, preferring the systems the way they were. The lessons I had learned in the field disposed me toward the opposite view. Clearly, I was out of step with the game, which was to 'get the money'—don't worry about performance and outcome measures, hopefully these will come if we continue to pour more money into the systems. Naïve as I may have been regarding the intricacies and nuances within the decision-making process of the Directorate General technical directorates, and the system of generating annual development budgets, I was shocked to learn from senior BAPPENAS officials that in some Ministry of Health offices the practice was to alter, 'tweak and game' the final agreed budget allocations just before sending the final copies to be signed. This resulted in far larger allocations for some projects and activities than had been agreed to by BAPPENAS and the Ministry of Finance.

Initial Consultancy: Managerial Audit with MOH's Inspector General

After finishing my WHO appointment in 1983, I was invited by the Ministry of Health's Inspector General to work with his Director of Development. Our task was to design, carry out, and then analyze a Managerial Audit on the INPRES Drugs Fund. My consultant fee and expenses were to be financed by USAID for three months. The whole project took six-months (though I was only paid for three).

The Ministry of Health's costs for this managerial audit were vastly higher than USAID's since Inspector General's team of inspectors would be going to the field for several months.*

After the initial design period, the Director of Development, Dr. Agus, reviewed each of the current regulations and procedures for each component of the INPRES Drug Fund system. We discussed each aspect in detail and then formulated sets of questions in a lengthy segmented questionnaire. The idea was that Dr. Agus and his 15-member team of inspectors would give the questionnaire to each decision-maker and responsible person in the program, including buyers, transport and storage executives, and health center managers. A second questionnaire was worked up for interviewing patients to determine what level of compliance they met when taking specific medicines. This was a serious Managerial Audit; and as a consultant I was asked to participate in creating each part of its methodology.

My discussions with Dr. Agus always were fully open, with 'no holds barred' with respect to potentially sensitive issues.

The initial proposal was to include two provinces in the

---

*A key element in primary health care operations was to provide basic medicines (drugs and pharmaceuticals) at highly subsidized prices to families and individuals, including civil servants and their families, using health centers. By the late 1970s advisers confirmed to President Soeharto what his field level intelligence had already indicated: either the drugs were insufficient for the increased demand due to expansion of health centers, or stocks were being poorly managed and hived off by staff along the supply chain.

The decision was made to increase by a third the Government of Indonesia health sector budget allocation specifically designed as a Presidential Instruction or INPRES Drug Fund for pharmaceuticals/drugs to each health center. [Note: The total Government of Indonesia health budgets were about one-third Development and included operational items, one-third Recurrent expenditure and one-third for the INPRES Drugs Fund (which was classed as investment/development but mainly included consumables and thus annually recurring expenditures). Most support from donor projects/foreign assistance projects was classed as Development.] The INPRES Drug Fund was highly promoted by the administration; thus most of the population throughout the archipelago knew the president was taking extra effort to meet their basic needs. And INPRES drugs became a popular component of community health. There were other specific INPRES funds for other sectors including agriculture and education.

study—one in Java and another in an Outer Island. Within each province, we planned to extend the study to ten health centers in each of several districts.

Dr. Agus and the Inspector's team began by testing the questionnaires at a small number of storage-distribution warehouses and health centers. Dr. Agus and I then refined and clarified the questions based on the responses he and his team had received. Once the revisions were in place the team was ready to go to the heavily populated Java province to conduct the formal fieldwork.

Second stage of fieldwork: Due to the sensitive nature and details of the subjects, including many site visits, I was kindly requested not to accompany the team to the field. About a month later, when the survey was half-complete, I was asked to come to the Ministry of Health guest-house for a week to discuss the findings, which Dr. Agus had begun to summarize. Essentially I was asked to help analyze the information and data without viewing it. Perhaps that was a new unique way of carrying out field research, but having been intimately connected with the design of the questionnaires, I had little difficulty listening to the Director of Development discuss the early findings. The team returned to the field to complete the survey, then returned to the Ministry of Health to compile the final "results"—a process done largely by hand, as in those days computers were a rarity!

The interim report to the IG: Dr. Agus wrote up reports on the findings, and the Inspector General, who was kept informed on our progress, also contributed insights, advice and guidance. It was clear that our methodology had been sound, and the IG's concluded that there was no need to survey the second "sample" province. We had produced enough evidence to expose both the weaknesses and the strengths of the INPRES Drug Fund regulations, through the steps of implementation and related management.

The Ministry of Health IG wanted to promote our Managerial Audit approach further, and he encouraged the Director of Development to prepare a background methodology report with field results and recommendations to present to senior members of the Supreme Audit Board. The Director of Development was delighted, if not ecstatic, with this news. Dr. Agus, who also relished the opportunity, set up the meeting. I was invited to accompany Dr. Agus.

The session was cordial and extremely professional. I discerned from the dialogue that members of the Supreme Audit Board and Dr. Agus had already met a few times. This was the first time, however, that they had seen such a serious and thorough managerial audit, and they were duly impressed. The managerial audit of a multi-year civil works project worth hundreds of millions of dollars would not approach the complexity outlined in the Ministry of Health IG's Managerial Audit for INPRES Drug Funds. Members of the Supreme Audit Board asked a variety of questions about all aspects of the program and were particularly interested in the short and mid-term recommendations.

> **We must ask why, with such effective tools available, major corruption scandals continued under President Soeharto and the administrations that succeeded him.**

I am confident senior Indonesian decision-makers in at least the Ministries of Health and Finance, and the Supreme Audit Board were able to make important change to the core procedures, implementation and managerial aspects of the INPRES Drug Fund program as a result of our report. It strengthened the capacity of the Ministry of Health's Inspectorate General, and other ministries and agencies inspectorates' generals may also have adopted the methods and techniques involved.

We must ask why, with such effective tools available, major corruption scandals continued under President Soeharto and the administrations that succeeded him. I don't know. One factor might be a warped incentive system, and the uneven level of competence available to ensure genuine transparency and oversight of public resources and decisions. Certainly Indonesia is not the only country with corruption.

During the Soeharto regime, I noticed a curious paradox

among professionals, and this might well be found in other countries with restrictive regimes as well. On the one hand there was (and is) a genuine thirst for knowledge, and the exchange of ideas is seemingly endless. Yet the existence of institutions rooted in 'Centroid Power' puts numerous often-unspoken limits on how far policies and projects can go that are designed to reduce poverty, improve health, extend educational opportunities and extricate people from the generational poverty trap. And a result, few professionals and leaders have the courage to buck this system, and throw in their lot with those attempting to re-right the Pyramid. *Such is the central dilemma of economic and political development for half of the world's population.*

In this, my first consultancy after leaving WHO, I must have pushed all the right buttons, for I was invited to participate in numerous subsequent projects in Indonesia, most of them dealing with systemic financial issues in the government health sector. Each time, I found the "thumbscrews" coming down harder on complicated or sensitive subjects. But my Indonesian colleagues were always frank and freely opened all doors necessary to accomplish the tasks at hand.

Consultancies to Strengthen Managerial Capacities in BAPPENAS and MOH

Indonesia's National Planning Board (BAPPENAS) became keen to strengthen the country's organizational infrastructure (often referred to as "brain-ware"), in particular that of the Ministry of Health. Some years after my consultancy with the MOH's Inspector General I was invited to participate as a consultant for other projects in the health sector. This gave me the opportunity to collaborate with well-trained Indonesians in improving the Ministry of Health's 'brain-ware' and managerial systems, with a focus on *'improving governance using greater transparency'* as such things were being described in 2000 by the international development agencies. By in large, our efforts were rewarded with success. It's all well and good to design protocols in the laboratory; fortunately, we had the opportunity to design and develop these managerial tools in realistic working environments, and also trained many staff and senior decision-makers in their application.

Had Nirvana been reached? Not quite. But key steps had been taken to nurture dedicated committed leadership both within the country and amongst the donors of the international development industry. Arrayed against these efforts, however, were the pressures and competition within the domestic and international development agencies to form 'business partnerships' at the central level, to both facilitate personal aggrandizement and maintain the convenient, albeit counterproductive, stranglehold of power at the central level.

Transparency? Protocols? Leaving the jargon and bureau-speak aside, these projects involved designing a health-sector data-base management system for annual planning and budgeting. This was a formidable task because of the extreme complexity of the Indonesian public finance system. At the time, the nation had something close to 26 provinces and 320 districts ('regency' or Kabupaten). [Note: Post-Soeharto in 1999 with an emphasis of decentralization there are over 490 districts.] As discussed above, there were multiple budgets and sources of expenditure, and it was difficult to determine what their relative magnitude was at the provincial and district levels. Without such data it would be virtually impossible to plan and budget effectively, particularly with regard to primary health care.

My task in 1986 (funded under a Government of Indonesia-World Bank project) was to work with BAPPENAS and its team to design the health sector database management system for annual health development (investment) budget and to put this on microcomputer spreadsheets (yes, really using Lotus 1-2-3!). I was also involved in training staff of both the Directorates Generals and the Secretary General offices to prepare their respective annual health development budget projects. In essence this meant carefully reviewing the current budgeting system and designing a categorical system (chart of accounts) to define and record the activities involved within each project.

When the design was finally finished, it was an amazing sight: in the new BAPPENAS computer room, for about two months, staff from all Directorates Generals in the Secretary-General's offices quickly learned the dBase and applied it to their respective annual health budget projects, each containing all the activities with detailed costing.

In the course of this project three things became clear to me and my BAPPENAS colleagues. *First,* virtually everyone involved was terrifically keen to learn about the new computer software and spreadsheets. There were absolutely no inhibitions, no nostalgic attachment to the old laborious typewriter preparation system.

Second, when we did get into the coding of details I was flabbergasted at how many ways there were to describe very similar activities; this allowed near duplicate activities to appear in different categories within the budget. Also, items one might expect to be found as recurring expenditure could have a category in the development budget—for example, as described above, with INPRES Drug Fund being one-third of the development budget.

The rationale was extra personnel costs, transport and disposable items are needed to get the development activities initiated and sustaining. After all, that was the intention of the activities within donor-sponsored projects, wasn't it? That's how things work and Indonesia cannot be unique in this respect. To the extent that these were the conventional 'rules of the road' are understood and consistent the system continues. The major problems include the lack of transparency and in the operations—particularly getting the money to work at field level, as described in this and other chapters.

Third, as I examined in detail the activities and expenditures within each of the hundreds of projects, it soon became apparent to me that the overwhelming majority of these activities in each Directorate General took place at the central level. I was forced to conclude that nothing was really going to change as a result of the new system with regard to the allocation of funds. This new technology would only further solidify Centroid Power in the Ministry of Health.

This dBase system was applied in BAPPENAS Ministry of Finance for the Ministry of Health and with some adaptations, for nearly twenty years (updated in Excel) it served its purpose, and I understood it was extended to education and other social sectors. The dBase for health expenditure was used by the World Bank teams for intensive studies as well as for formulating projects over many years, and I participated in some of these studies.

The data-base system described above did help planners in the health sector select, prioritize, and budget their activities rigorously, specifying inputs and 'unit costs' provided to them and linking the allocations to specific outcomes. It also allowed for intermediate measures for activities such as "number of EPI vaccinations given" and "number of patients seen." Final 'work done' output measures included items such as how many construction health centers, sections of hospitals, and low-cost latrines had been completed. Other important outcomes such as Infant Mortality Rates required more involved epidemiological surveys over longer time frames, which are being pursued even today by the appropriate technical units.

SECOND ASSIGNMENT

My second assignment was to work on a program designed to accelerate implementation of foreign assistance donor loan projects. This was of critical importance because the government of Indonesia was required to pay a 'commitment fee' to the donor on the 'unused' amount of the loan. The faster the implementation, the lower the fee. Delays in implementing foreign-assisted loan projects also resulted in higher program costs, and they caste a negative light on the ministries involved, leading senior decision-makers in BAPPENAS to question whether they were worthy of further donor project funds.

Thus, in 1989 I set to work with Indonesian colleagues to design a database that followed the processes from contracting to payment and produced standardized summary tables. Such monitoring would make it more likely that the required government processes and procedures were followed rigorously and that the budgeted funds were disbursed properly. One case study was a World Bank supported project to build teaching institutions in multiple provinces; an investment to expand qualified staff and upgrade personnel. The project has main components of physical infrastructure (construction), selected equipment and staff training.

Our first step was to familiarizing ourselves with the various forms, procedures and steps involved in disbursement. We could then proceed to align the payments with the planned quarterly disbursements. Due to my involvement in writing the programs used to generate the annual health development budget, much of this terrain was already familiar to me.

The next issue we tackled was 'pre-contracting.' The problems were legion in this area, and I was left wondering what it would take to get civil works projects, which are phased-in over years, completed. Somehow contracts were awarded and we had these records and specifics. *Despite numerous rules and regulations from the Ministry of Finance and the donor agencies, it is in contracting and disbursements that many doors remain open for abuse and corruption.* In the end, I decided that although the result might appear unwieldy, the best move would be to incorporate all the steps in all the forms into an 'operational link database' to track foreign assistance projects in the health sector. This 'link tracking and ledger' data system became known as the 'long form'. Daily working sessions with colleagues provided instant critiques that led to numerous revisions. This 'long form' was used by BAPPENAS and Ministry of Health Directorates Generals to monitor foreign assistance loan projects for years.

Excessive paperwork

Throughout my time in Indonesia I was struck by how redundancy of information retarded the contracting process in foreign-assisted projects. My Indonesian staff colleagues tended to agree, though they were powerless to present these issues to their superiors. As an independent consultant I was not similarly constrained. Trying to be as diplomatic as I could, I spoke directly to senior colleagues in BAPPANAS, Ministry of Health and the World Bank (who financing this consultancy assignment) about the issue, and described in my reports specific ways the number of required formed could be reduced.

As usually happens, many thoughtful senior Indonesian civil servants agreed with me and saw the need even to expand on my recommendations. It seemed doubtful, however, whether anyone in the Ministry of Finance would be swayed by such recommendations. In subsequent visits with my Indonesian colleagues the same issue was raised, though I am uncertain whether any new and truly rational managerial practices have been implemented to this day.

Third Assignment

My third assignment was focused, for the first time, on results rather than planning, budgeting and expenditures. The overwhelming majority of Indonesia's foreign-assisted loan projects were focused on getting the budgeted activities *completed*, and the activities were predominantly assessed on 'work done' measures and money spent quarterly. Now senior government officials and donors were pressing to get more *results-oriented* measures, under the affectionate but frequently misunderstood and abused rubric of 'monitoring and evaluation' (M&E). Accordingly, a Ministry of Health Directorate General's office conducted an Asian Development Bank project between 1985 and 1989 in 39 hospitals in four provinces to improve hospital and family planning services. Donor support of hospital investment was part of the MOH's emphasis to improve the referral system by providing access, skilled staff and services for more intensive care to the 'at risk' patients from their local health center. In reality (as seen in other countries), patients 'by-pass' local health centers to seek care at the nearby district or regional hospital. In the follow-up project, I was invited for a multi-month consultancy in

1991–1992 to work with the project's management team to design a Project Benefit Monitoring and Evaluation system (PBME); and then to apply it to the ongoing project.

This PBME assignment was intended to 'leverage off' the two dBase systems I described earlier. The overall concept was to link input, process, and output/outcome. It's easy to say but extremely hard to do. Everyone recognizes that outcomes with health-related indices need a long timeframe, thorough sampling compares to a control with no intervention, and using serious statistical analysis to be worthwhile. Such thorough studies tend to arrive at the conclusion that very few foreign assistance projects meet with anything approaching success! This is due to both bad design and patchy execution.

I worked in close consultation with the project team and specialists in the technical sub-Directorates, who already knew all the 'holes in the road,' to design programs and forms to track the sub-components of the project and assess the pre-contracting constraints, timeliness, and steps taken to fulfill each contract.

Pragmatic Project management software for decision-makers

The result was a collection of project management software *avant le lettre*, capable of bringing more clarity to the key constraints existing within the project and identify ways to remove them. We designed the reports emanating from this system to help both senior decision-makers and people in the field see what was going on more clearly, in order to accelerate the current year's work and plan better for the years ahead.

While such 'project management software' can conveniently accommodate very sophisticated just-in -time (JIT) synchronization of inputs and processes, I am convinced that the most relevant determinants for project success are the human and institutional underpinnings. Unless the human and institutional factors and constraints are well understood and properly integrated, project management software is mechanistic at best. It leaves savvy practical and 'field oriented' project managers and senior decision-makers pretty much where they were before—using their tried-and-true ways with a heavy dose of intuition to insure the success of their projects.

These are no idle comments. When Indonesia and other countries began to accept more foreign-assisted loan and grant projects, it put a tremendous burden on a very limited cadre of managerial and technical personnel, who felt a pressing need to design solid, practical projects and to monitor them closely, in order to make midcourse corrections whenever necessary. Meanwhile, a 'wrestling-match' often took place among the Centroid Power elite over which ministry or contingent would become the 'winners 'within a donor-funded project. Such 'wrestling' intensifies as the number of foreign assisted projects increase, and it's further heightened by the fact that virtually all incentives in a project, both among donors and within countries, are 'frontloaded.' That is to say, the money is spent during the project-formulation stages and associated with disbursement for activities rather than for achievements or results!

FAST-FORWARD 30 YEARS TO THE POST-SOEHARTO PERIOD

In 2008, while it Indonesia working on a foreign assistance project involving several sectors, I found myself walking down similar corridors in BAPPENAS, Ministry of Finance, and other agencies and ministries, including the Ministry of Health. Thirty years had passed. Though several of the central level buildings and corridors were new, and there had been a decided switch to more openness in the post-Soeharto regime—remarkably similar tones and emphasis echoed within the present administration, with various actors solidifying their expected positions within the tight web of Centroid Power. I was lucky to have a loyal friend who kept me up-to-date on the rationale for the changes of power and various details within the policy formulation, annual planning and budgeting processes. We had kept in touch over the years, and we met many times on this assignment.

I remain grateful for his generous tutelage and keen insights. He also provided me with useful information about recent legislation and the all-important systems flowcharts. He facilitated access to colleagues working at critical points in the systems. Indeed, the impression was repeatedly and vividly confirmed throughout the assignment that a major shift took place after the Soeharto period. BAPPENAS was out, and Ministry of Finance was the supreme Centroid Power.

Several high-profile corruption cases involving the Ministry of Health itself have received media scrutiny in the post-Soeharto period of 'new openness' and democracy. Updates of these cases can be found on-line and in the Jakarta newspapers almost daily! These cases put a spotlight on project management, using both Government of Indonesia money and foreign assistance loans. New laws and regulations have tightened up procedures in project management and put direct responsibility on staff for any corrupt practices carried out under the project. The question is: are these merely 'showcase' trials, or has the management within Indonesia's public sectors improved?

> The fact that provisions for year-to-year budget carry-over have also been scrapped also impedes or abruptly truncates activity, with serious implications for the people in Indonesia's districts, rural communities, and urban slums.

While the Ministry of Finance during the Soeharto period challenged project activities that were already approved, and received development budget allocations from foreign aid projects and domestic resources for clarity on what was going to be done and by whom; it was reported to me in 2008 that the hurdles to be negotiated have been increased to the point where many project managers have stopped trying to get funds altogether. At the very least this sets a worrying tone. Of course, project activities have to be specified, but without the countervailing power of BAPPENAS, the forces of Centroid Power have quite literally stopped projects' activities. The fact that provisions for year-to-year budget carry-over have also been scrapped also impedes or abruptly truncates activity, with serious implications for the people in Indonesia's districts, rural communities, and urban slums, who will see fewer resources than ever 'trickling down' for local services. The underlying issues contributing to 'low absorption' of development (investment) budgets continue as Indonesia seeks to reform its budget system in 2012![1] Yes, I fear we've seen this 'movie' before.

Computer-based information systems are commonplace nowadays. That being said, we need to keep in mind that a productive use of the technology must begin with a clear understanding of how policymakers and program managers can best use it. Well-designed management and performance monitoring systems can provide a more transparent, efficient, and effective use of funds, which will help project managers meet their longer-term goals.

Indeed, I have been thinking about how useful it would be to simplify the systems that I have seen and had a hand in developing, in Indonesia and elsewhere. A more straightforward system would help funnel resources to the district level and bring better services to rural communities and urban slums. It would empower local leaders and bring greater flexibility, accountability and oversight to country's efforts to meet key Millennium Development Goals and stir local economic development. I will be expanding on this idea in subsequent chapters.

Jordan

The powerful people who set policy agendas are often visible—but sometimes not. In fact, they often prefer to stay invisible. Even in democratic countries, it's difficult to determine the extent to which the 'people's voice' is actually reflected in policy decisions. In repressive societies all the more so. But all regimes have solid networks to keep abreast of local perceptions about their policies and intentions. They need to know what's going on in the streets and villages, what people are talking about and what the 'sticking points' of the day are.

Such sources of information allowed politicians in Jordan, during the 1980s, to determine that their overlapping government health systems, run by the army, the university, and the government itself, resulted in costly duplication of resources without doing much to improve the quality of care for their 2.6 million citizens. By 1985 they had concluded that a National Health Insurance System for government employees would be more cost-effective. That year I was invited, along with another American accountant, to spend two months evaluating the feasibility of these new ideas.

We focused our attention on collecting and analyzing information concerning the central economic and finance issues from a political perspective. Though it was well-known that the results of our study might jeopardize one or another aspect of the current system, the Jordanian professionals were uniformly cooperative and frank—first-class in all respects. At the onset, His Excellency the Minister of Health met with our project team and several senior members of his ministry to underscore his concerns: How much would a national health insurance system cost. Would it be sustainable? How could it be financed?

The minister was especially keen to make sure that the capabilities of the private sector were fully utilized, and that general practitioners acted as the point of entry into the system. This was because there were more private doctors and clinics than the population required at the time. It was a common state of affairs, attributable to the fact that the medical profession dictates, through its own education and government licensing, the politics of health care, which invariably is dominated by specialists. He also considered it important that the National Health Insurance System (NHIS) be expanded to include people employed in the private sector, who would be given the opportunity to use and pay for private medical services in line with the cost of the national program.

Clearly, the minister and government felt that the health and medical systems could be expanded affordably to a wider population by using the excess capacity of the private medical system.

At the time, I had already worked for five-and-a-half years as a health economist in a British university, conducting research on the British National Health System (NHS) at field level, largely in the area of maternal and child health care. I was familiar, therefore, with the strategy of using general practitioners as the point of entry into a health service system. Whilst the Jordanian concept was similar to British NHS, an important distinction was that the Jordanian NHIS would use private GPs whereas the British NHS had (and has) GPs contracted to and paid by the NHS, as employees.

> Though they all had strong opinions about the feasibility of a national health insurance system, they made every attempt to attend the meetings and round-up the data we requested.

The minister also emphasized the need to use a system of registration cards, due to widespread abuses under the current fragmented system, whereby patients—children and young adults in particular—used uncles and cousins to obtain access to different systems and services.

Obviously, our hosts and colleagues in the Ministry of Health Management and Planning Unit knew the background to the current health systems far better than we did. Though they all had strong opinions about the feasibility of a National Health Insurance System, they made every attempt to attend the meetings and round-up the data we requested. Some of the data were not in their immediate reach but they did their best to accommodate us, which struck me as unusual, considering that bureaucrats are usually very protective of information that might affect their future budget allocations.

My several visits and discussions with the head of the Army's Health Services were amongst the most cordial and professional I have ever experienced, bar none, in any country. This medical doctor and senior officer dissected all the relevant issues with candor and aplomb. I also met a wide range of other health care professionals at the University hospital and Social Security Institute, along with private general practitioners and MOH officials. While their interests may have differed, each genuinely provided healthy dialogue and information. At no time did anyone try to influence my appreciation of the situation, analysis, conclusions, and or recommendations.

Not infrequently, I would walk to a nearby park and savor the lamb in the original gyro (or *döner* in Turkish) from a stand. I don't speak Arabic, but could make myself understood using simple gestures such as pointing at what had been sold to the last customer. Perhaps I was given a few more slices of lamb and chicken, whatever was on the vertical spit, and certainly never less, by the smiling stall owner. It was pretty obvious by my speech, dress, gait, and overall appearance that I was a foreigner. Yet these simple welcoming experiences were genuine, and all the more to be valued during those weeks after President Reagan had decided to bomb Libya. I found such person-to-person interaction heartwarming.

One day I received an invitation to dinner from a general practitioner who was a friend of the Minister of Health. He wanted to know how the assignment was going and if he could help me with anything. (A few days earlier, my colleague had disappeared, informing neither me nor the American project manager of his intended visit to the archaeological treasures of Petra, followed by a bit of scuba diving in Aqaba. He never came back.)

A couple of days later, as arranged, the GP picked me up in front of my hotel. We drove in his new Mercedes for about twenty minutes, further and further from downtown Amman, until we reached a brightly lit house standing on its own, well away from any other structure. Upon entering, I noted that all the large windows had been thrown open. Large leather chairs with low wood tables filled the sitting area, and I could also see a well-lit dining room in the distance. The place very much resembled a British club, though my comparison was based entirely on what I had seen on the 'telly.' Very nice, and truly a gentlemen's oasis. Fair enough. Let's enjoy, my host said to me. Surely the pleasant ambient set a relaxing tone for a similarly relaxed discussion and a delectable dinner.

My host explained that his association with the club's manager went 'way back,' perhaps to when he worked outside of Jordan. A waiter appeared with a teapot, two glasses, ice and some small snacks with extra plates. He explained this was the way things were done. The GP was an engaging conversationalist, and fully up-to-date on all issues. I explained who I had seen, and described the approach I was taking. The GP inquired if there was anyone he could help me meet or any further data required.

One point he made during our dinner I found especially interesting: the lack of a well-functioning referral system in Jordan. After all, my host was a GP—in the proverbial trenches daily—and also a close friend of the Minister of Health. We had a frank discussion of the feasability of having GPs (particularly private ones) serve as the entry point to the NIHS.

Two weeks later, while I was writing up the project recommendations, the American project manager passed on a request from the Minister of Health, who was curious to hear a summary of my findings and recommendations. Two days later, I found myself in the non-ostentatious Ministry of Health conference room, sitting at a table with my hosts and colleagues from the Ministry of Health Management and Planning Unit, and several other senior MOH officials. There may have been fifteen of us in all. The Minister gave me a brief introduction, and then my two page report was distributed around the room. I spoke for about five minutes, highlighting our findings and conclusions as best I could.

In brief, three scenarios for health systems were considered. The preferred option would be: (i) Streamline to a unified health care system. (ii) Invest mainly in qualitative improvements (largely through manpower development). (iii) Seek to achieve a high compliance with a registration card and referral system focused on entry point being the primary health and/or general practitioners.

The data available suggested that such a scenario for the Jordanian health system would be financially feasible and sustainable, though to insure a solid start to the new system, large amounts of information, particularly related to actuarial analysis, would need to be collected and analyzed. It would be essential to 'flush out' the details of a National Health Insurance System including: how it would function; system cost estimates over time frames; how it would be financed; how it would be monitored; and how appropriate changes would be made over the years. My report contained a series of recommendations along these lines, which I discussed briefly at this meeting.

We discussed various other financial issues briefly that day, such as subscription fees, copayments, mandatory referrals, and user fees designed to limit the common habit of bypassing the less intensive primary health care facilities for more intensive hospital care. We touched on the importance of keeping abreast of utilization patterns among insured and uninsured populations in both the public and private sectors to facilitate planning, and examined cost-containment initiatives. The idea of raising taxes on tobacco to cover revenue shortfalls was kicked around. The feasibility of standardizing 'unit costs' of services and creating incentives for efficient and effective health center managers was also discussed.

At the end of the meeting the Minister said, "Translate and distribute the interim report with the recommendations"! The meeting adjourned, and we went our separate ways. Yet I was troubled by some parts of the process. As a 'field man,' I always try to meet with people in different communities wherever I work. The conversations I have at such times enlarge my perspective on the issues I've been assigned to study. Lack of time and access are poor excuses, when one is trying to present independent professional advice to decision makers on policy or operations, but in the case of Jordan, those are the only ones I can think of. I never did get the opportunity to interact with the public during that assignment. Basically we were adjunct to the Ministry of Health. It seems doubtful that our hosts willfully kept us at a distance from the people who would be using the NHIS, given the openness shown to us on other matters throughout the assignment. Perhaps the fact that the new Jordanian NHIS was to be available only in government circles made such contact seem superfluous, given the impending deadlines.

Following the meeting, it still remained for me to complete the report. Such a task, with an assignment as large in scope as this one, is never straightforward. Office hours are largely devoted to meetings and data digging. The report writing takes place at night and on weekends, though on many assignments, evening and weekend meetings are also common. Many countries have six day work weeks—these are anything but holiday positions and assignments. (I did not bring my scuba tanks to Jordan, nor do I have any.)

The USAID, like most donor agencies, conduct at least one exit/final meeting with those who have been out in the field on a project. At the conclusion of my visit to Jordan, I met with its Population, Health, and Nutrition section at the US Embassy compound. My debriefing session went well; the division head with whom I met knew many of the details of the Jordanian health systems and had discussed the interim report already with the American project manager. Debriefings are only useful, however, if we get to the protracted issues of realities and feasible next steps, which we did discuss. We quickly moved on to some of the sensitive political issues involved in furthering the work, such as the complexities involved in actually reducing redundancies in the health system and limited those costly hospital visits for minor ailments and injuries. We also had a frank discussion on Jordon's economic prospects and its dependence on Iraq for the flow of goods.

Not long afterward, the head of Population Health and Nutrition informed me that at the request of the Jordanian government, USAID was planning to pursue the next phases of feasibility regarding Jordan's health care system. I expressed an interest in continuing my involvement, though in the end nothing came of it.

Jordan's complicated and pivotal position

Obviously Jordan is smack dab in one of the world's politically charged hotspots, with all too frequent 'eruptions' that affect all Jordanians. During the lengthy Iraq–Iran war (1980-1988) which killed an estimated 1 million soldiers, militia, and civilians, Jordan's trade with Iraq increased. My economic growth potential of 5 to 7 percent annually was considered too rosy by some who read the report. And in recent decades Jordan has absorbed an estimated 1.7 million Palestinians, nearly 17 percent of which live in camps under the UN Refuges Works Agency. Clearly these demographics have huge implication for Jordan, the neighboring countries, and the whole world.

In 1997 whilst visiting colleagues in the World Bank, I learned the Jordanian Health Insurance issues and systems had indeed resurfaced. A serious project was being formulated by the World Bank and Jordan. The officer designing the project confirmed, when I spoke with him, that he had only recently read my report of twelve years earlier—after the current project had been formulated. He confirmed that our early analysis had been largely valid and that our recommendations paralleled his own!

A card to King Hussein

Learning of King Hussein's diagnosis of non-Hodgkin's Lymphoma, and that he was being treated at Mayo Clinic, I had the temerity to send him a card, expressing my appreciation for his valiant work for peace and wishing him well with his current battle. In my card I listed my previous assignments including my experience in the Hashemite Kingdom of Jordan. About a week later I received a telegram from The Palace, acknowledging my card and wishing me well too. This telegram remains among my prized possessions, along with the many lessons learned from my generous Jordanian colleagues two decades ago.

In 1998, I saw the famed Jordan River again—this time, from the other side. I was engaged, following the Oslo accord, in what turned out to be a six-month assignment with a project to help the

Palestinian Authority take over several key sectors and services from Israel. I lived in Ramallah, though I traveled often to consult with our team in the Gaza office. Traveling in these historic lands during uniquely peaceful times, on occasion I thought King Hussein would have supported the initiative and especially the efforts of the Palestinians to improve their health system. But such moments of harmony and growth are always fragile and usually temporary, even with demonstrated goodwill from all parties. Breakdowns and reversals are all too common in this part of the world, and many others, with dire consequences for everyone involved.

Lessons Learned

My experience in Jordan reaffirmed the notion that any project will proceed more smoothly when one's counterparts and colleagues are well-prepared, keen on the main issues, and prepared to share what they know. All the same, most of the problems addressed by the aid industry are rooted in complex social, cultural, historic linkages that make viable mid- and longer-term remedies difficult to sustain. There is no guarantee that, once started, a planned trajectory can be adhered to, even with continual monitoring and deft interventions; there are too many bureaucratic vagaries and vested interests working to alter its implementation. In some cases, the problem lies in the fact that the problem to be solved was never clearly defined in the first place. At other times, a client may well present a problem along with the desired "solution." The consultant conducts the work and regurgitates the desired "solution," winning the day among the client's peers.

In the case of Jordan, senior officials in health and presumably ministry of finance, wanted to institute a National Health Insurance System. Their leadership asked the appropriate questions carefully and arrived at a new set of workable policies.

Ghana

I first became aware of Ghana's importance and uniqueness as a country and people while studying at the London School of Economics and Political Science in 1960. I met many African students from the British colonial systems (now the British Commonwealth) there, and found the Ghanaian and Nigerian students especially self-assured and forthright in expressing their respective countries' need for independence. Three years earlier, Ghana had become the first sub-Saharan African country to escape the colonial yoke under Kwame Nkrumah, and Nigeria followed in 1960 under Nnamdi Azikiwe. Clearly these were exciting times, and I'm sure several of the African students I met at LSE became leaders and economists in their newly-independent countries.

Thirty-odd years later, in 1988, I took a six-month assignment in Ghana as a member of a team focusing on health policy. My brief focused on health sector financing. Ghana had been buffeted by years of poor administration, and both the economy and public finance were in a shambles, inflicting great hardships on the social sectors, particularly health and education—hardships felt most deeply by the poorer communities. International donors were eager to work with the government to reverse the slide by initiating a new primary health care policy and also new economic strategies. As is all too frequently the case, however, such an initiative involved conflicting principles and objectives. Specifically, the IMF agreed to provide loans, but only conditional if the government made dramatic budget cuts to the ministries of health and education, while also increasing the fees charged for the services these ministries provided. (Note: a more thorough discussion of Structural Adjustment Policies and these loans as part of the Washington Consensus are found in the next chapter.) I would like to think that some of the very vocal economists I met at the LSE were among those Ghanaians who insisted that the IMF reverse their Draconian mindset, and begin to promote measures to *maintain* social welfare among society's poorest people.

My contribution to the scene was to conduct field research focusing on three areas: (i) How, historically, the Ghanaian recurrent and capital health budgets were allocated and actually used? (ii) What changes could be recommended to make them work better without undermining health care objectives? (iii) How were 'unit costs' determined, and what low-cost changes to the methodology could be sensibly institutionalized? Further, how would such changes affect the programs and financing of primary health care?

Fortunately, two Ghanaians joined me to conduct the field work and analysis. Their insights into local systems, culture, and institutions were invaluable and their diligence in both collecting and analyzing data was a marvel to behold.

Most of the results of our study remained unchanged for more than twenty years and our figures were consistent with those gathered in other developing countries where foreign aid directives were intended to have a positive impact on poor people and their communities. Here are some of the main patterns and results.

Less than $10 per person, and often less than $5, were allocated in most countries from government recurrent budgets, including donor projects. About 60 percent was going to hospitals, (district, provincial and central levels) and 60 percent of that total was devoted to personnel costs. About 20 to 25 percent was going to primary health care initiatives and activities.

Delayed budget releases typically skewed the distribution of funds across time, with only about one-third being spent in the first nine months and a larger amount (but not necessarily all) being spent in the last three months of the fiscal year. Capital budgets (maybe 20 percent) of the total health expenditure invariably favored high-tech curative care at central level hospitals.

Virtually all planning was of the 'top-down' variety, with virtually no 'bottom-up' element derived from village needs or experience.

Another key issue to emerge from our study in Ghana was the 'leakage' of pharmaceutical supplies, which during the five years preceding the study amounted to roughly 50 percent of the total. Both hospitals and health centers suffered these losses due to pilfering and corruption, though in the end it was the poor who suffered most. In September 2010 a leading news magazine reported that in 2000 Ghana lost 80 percent of the money allocated for drugs and supplies due to such leakage.[2]

Some years earlier, a dynamic and very insightful US academic economist had observed to me that our clients should be ministries of finance and not health. He pointed out that ministries of finance were far more concerned about the design and financing of cost-effective programs to reduce poverty, whereas decision-makers at the ministry of health were nearly always clinically trained medical specialists with active private practices who were more concerned with illness than with wellness or prevention. Over the last two decades this has changed somewhat; more genuine public health specialists with appropriate training and managerial savvy are reaching leadership positions in government health systems. Today many ministries of health have specialist clinicians in key decision-making positions.

In any case, while I was in Ghana, our 'home base' was the Ministry of Health. It quickly became apparent that I should be introduced to, and work part of the assignment with, senior members in the Ministry of Finance, specifically the Economic and Planning section, whose responsibility included the Ministry of Health. These contacts were easy enough to make in Ghana through family relations among the two departments.

Data Digging

Our data collection at hospitals and health centers unearthed a wealth of information on the specific kinds and magnitude of pharmaceuticals that were 'leaking' from these institutions—an obvious area where cost-recovery methods might be put in place without denting the patients' resources. I showed the Comptroller and Accountant General our findings. He, too, was perplexed, and with excellent dedication instructed his team to dig out the relevant hospital and clinic records, showing the same zeal that I had seen in other senior officials in various ministries and health centers. There was no mistaking the genuine interest taken by many Ghanaians to improve the welfare of the poor people and families in city slums and throughout the countryside by reforming their programs and institutions. Using our findings the World Bank project manager persuaded the Ministry of Health to adopt a novel low-cost 'cash & carry' system for the health centers and hospital to replenish their drug and supplies from the government pharmaceuticals stocks. Given the above reported situation in 2000, even this 'cash & carry' system must not have had much carry over. (Unfortunately we get used to seeing successful initiatives wither away when the immediate financial incentives controlled and shared among a few are too great to maintain the discipline within subsystems.)

Consensus Building Through a Working Group

Reflecting on what I perceived to be a genuine interest among public officials to run programs effectively, I devised a means to sustain ownership of this six-month project within the Ghanaian power structure once the consultants (including me) had submitted their reports and departed for good. This was to form a committee (as a Working Group) of senior officials from the ministries of Health and Finance that would meet about six times after the fieldwork was done to exchange insights on the key issues and findings. I prepared material for each session and distributed the drafts personally. Each session was well attended and the issues were thoroughly discussed from a variety of perspectives. Many of the participants were unfamiliar with such open dialogue on delicate issues, but everyone supported our final recommendations, particularly on the financing specifics.

Fieldwork in Ghana

Traveling in Ghana with our four-member Ghanaian team prior to these meetings had expanded my horizons considerably. Getting out of the cocoon of the Ministry and facilities, hospitals and health centers, staying and working in the countryside for months, allowed me to better appreciate Ghana's history, values, and difficulties—including those presented by its own institutions. The experience left a deep impression on me, and strengthened my belief in the need for structural change in the development industry. Here are some quick field notes that may convey some sense of what I experienced.

Slave Deportation Center Memorial, Gold Coast: If anyone needs further convincing of the many centuries of depredation and disease experienced by the victims of slavery, they only have to visit Ghana's Ground Zero at the Gold Coast. The dignity of my Ghanaian colleagues was mirrored by the memorial and museum there. The subjugation of poor and illiterate people is hardly a thing of the past, of course. It remains a reprehensible scourge, though such subjugation also serves to shore up the power elite in many corners of the world.

Visit with the village headman: coming from a health center out into the countryside on a good hard surface dirt road, we stopped at a village to discuss local health services and local development initiatives. In the afternoon heat, many villagers were seeking a respite from their work in the fields by exchanging stories under a coconut and other trees. I have frequently seen gatherings of this type among villagers in sub-Saharan Africa, and guess it's more the pattern than the exception. Our stop for courtesy and introduction was to the village headman, most likely appointed by the government and extremely knowledgeable about all aspects of local development, agriculture, water quality, health care and education. The villagers in the shade under the trees seemed reluctant at first, but some minutes later the village headman emerged from his well-built one-floor government house wearing what looked to be a nifty US-made Gant shirt, complete with a button-down collar. As most of the villagers were wearing local tie-dye shirts, this gentleman was prepared for guests.

The men formed themselves into an assembly of sorts, sitting on tree trunks arranged in a circular form. A chair from the house was brought for me. We exchanged a few introductory compliments and then a gourd-like bowl was passed around and everyone present took a swig. The drink resembled the local *pombe* 'homebrew,' a mildly alcoholic concoction the main ingredient of which is millet.

The question arises: How to say no politely in such situations when you do not want to risk illness? The answer is, you do not. There were lots of laughing and joking, but I blew the floating clump on the surface of the drink towards the far side of bowl and took a small sip before it rebounded off the far edge of the vessel. I swallowed, blinked, and agreed it was very tasty! All applauded, even the village head. Indeed, the older gentlemen knew that I had done that before. Then my colleagues translated my brief story of getting hepatitis in Tanzania which allowed me to pass the bowl back to the headman and it skipped me in subsequent rounds.

> We exchanged a few introductory compliments and then a gourd-like bowl was passed around and everyone present took a swig.

In became evident during our conversation that the headman knew his locale. He agreed that the pressures on the central government had curbed even basic essential services in the village which they all would have used. There was a village school, well attended by both boys and girls, but the supply of books and supplies was meager and children had to share. Parents paid a fee to the school and the central government paid the teacher a salary and provided teacher housing. The health services did provide occasional village clinics as well as services for maternal and child health which were popular. Oh yes, malaria was endemic, particularly during and following the rainy season, and shortages in medicines at the government clinic were occasionally alleviated by private sellers. Malaria combined with malnourished under-fives accounts for among the country's highest mortality rates.

One indicator of prospects for empowering people and communities, including bottom-up planning, is how the local people interact with the village leader. Such measures are always imprecise and impressionistic, but in this case I was impressed with the openness of the dialogue around the circle and the consideration and respect given to everyone's input. The village headman asked for and took a wide range of comments. Nobody seemed intimidated by his station or power.

Bumper Tomato Crop

The headman recommended that we drive a few miles to some tomato fields. As I recall it was stimulated by the donor project, maybe USAID. In the midst of a generally arid plateau, water had somehow been secured for a ten-acre plot (about four hectare) overflowing with bright green tomato plants. The tomatoes themselves were bright red and up to baseball (or cricket ball) size. The field was an island of production unparalleled for many miles. We were told that it was farmed cooperatively, and were not surprised to learn there was a reliable source of water nearby for irrigation.

The problem lay in the distance and transport costs associated with getting the tomatoes to market. It must have been obvious to the farmers picking in the field as well as to the village headman and all his neighbors drinking *pombe* in the afternoon that success would depend on transport and marketing. Why were these key elements not integrated into the project? Perhaps that would have made it too expensive and thus not financially viable. But tomatoes rotting on the vine are not financially viable either. One thing seems very likely. Whoever designed the project never asked for input from the villagers themselves. Such unfortunately is the way of many projects.

'Desertification'

Heading north on the tarmac road to a new province which lay inland from the Atlantic Ocean and Gold Coast by a hundred miles, I noticed that the weather was becoming exceedingly hot. I also observed heavy-duty trucks coming from the north carrying huge tree trunks on several occasions. Perhaps forty trucks streamed by us in the course of our several-hour drive, each bearing a single huge tree trunk. I was informed by our team that these were tropical hardwoods—likely teak or mahogany—with diameters up to fifteen feet and the full length of the truck's chassis. Although I had heard of famed tropical hardwood deforestation in the Kalimantan/Borneo forests of Indonesia, I was not aware that the practice was also widespread in Ghana, though colleagues hastened to inform me of the link between such practices and the dramatic rise in temperature already taking place as the vegetative cover vanished. The process of desertification we have heard about! This was as well, a reasonable "early warning" of the "micro-climate change." The corrupt distribution of licenses to local businessman which was destroying Ghana's irreplaceable tropical hardwood forest had reached the attention of the central government, however, and it was already in the process of restricting the indiscriminate logging and requiring a more selective cut. It had also initiated an aggressive re-forestation program. That was in 1988; I wonder what those forests look like today.

Land Rover 'Bone Yard'

Returning south, then going east to a district hospital, I was struck by a sight that later became rather common in African countries recently freed of English colonial rule. (Perhaps the sub-Saharan Francophone countries have an equivalent phenomenon, la Peugeot.) It was a single Land Rover—that majestic, and ubiquitous, symbol of post-war British colonial development efforts—sublimely rusting away in a nearby field under an acacia tree. That vehicle had been a symbol of country life (the new Land Rovers are favored in US suburbia) and the vehicle of choice for colonial regional directors, commanding the immediate attention (no doubt with mixed emotion) of the local population. To postcolonial developers, it represents exceedingly poor judgment due to its required maintenance, although regular checks and a few pennies per thousand miles on lubrication of the 'old war horse' might have kept it going on the rough-surfaced roads throughout the tropical climes.

Virtually all international donor projects have allocations for new vechicle purchase; yet by simple and regular maintenance schedule, vechicles such as the Land Rover (where in most instances ample available spare parts already exist) can run for decades in the hands of the experienced local mechanics. In the happy days of post-independence, new projects had budgeted cost categories for vehicles which the donors and international agencies were more than happy to supply from their own countries, as a form of 'tied aid'. In the immediate postcolonial period the Land Rover and Peugeot were favored, though for twenty years now the Japanese Toyota Land Cruiser has been the vehicle of choice. Basically new vechicles have become just one of the offical personal perks from development agencies. Yet government vehicles for real business such as providing support to villages for MCH sessions can be extremely hard to come by. I have a vision of a circle of rusted Land Rovers circumventing the equator to represent the development industry from post WWII to the present!

The Old Water Hole

On one of our trips to a western province, way off the main road, we saw a group of men working around a water hole. We stopped and introduced ourselves to them and inquired what they were doing. The water hole was about eight feet in diameter and the depth was about the same. The soil was rocky and dry, and the hand digging with rudimentary long-handled shovels and other tools in the tropical sun and humidity made the task extremely laborious. But this was the traditional water source for this village. It was a very dry season and they were trying to renew the supply so the women of the village would not have to travel so far for water—a distance of several miles or more. The water was for domestic use, though there were no barriers to keep the cattle for using it, too, other than a steep incline that would have kept the larger ones away. The water was brackish and deep brown—likely from the current digging. But the villagers told us it was not dissimilar from the normal quality provided from this source. Clearly it was below any WHO standard for potable water use by families for cooking, bathing, and drinking. I asked the villagers if the women boiled the water for a few minutes and set it aside in a separate vessel for drinking. They said that some do, but many do not.

Even today the experience could be repeated throughout Ghana, sub-Saharan Africa, and the Tropics. This explains the persistent call by international agencies, donors, and NGOs to put more cash into water and sanitation projects to combat the multiplicity of harmful health consequences of poor water quality and unreliable supply. To these inexpensive improvements to basic infrastructure, we might also add the basic sanitation facilities (simple latrines costing less than $10 in materials and the family's own labor) and improved garbage collection and disposal, particularly in dense urban areas.

But it seems to me that a second cry ought also to be heard, one which asks what has been the impact of money going to water and sanitation projects for the last 50 years? Where has that money gone? Is it merely population growth and plastic bags that have exacerbated environmental quality? With higher population density, particularly in urban slums and urban areas in the Tropics, with deficient water, sanitation and environmental infrastructure, together with climate change that brings even hotter temperatures and extended rainy seasons—the local populations are at best on a slow downward slide.

BACK IN ACCRA, A FEW MEMORABLE EXPERIENCES

Back to the watering hole. The villagers would like to have been optimistic that the central government would send either money or the physical parts to construct a deep well with a hand pump and adequate cement to surround the site so the water would be reliable in the dry season; then they would consider options to improve water quality at the household level. The villagers agreed they would take care to maintain the well and pump year-round. But they were not holding out much hope about government assistance and did as their custom and social tradition dictated—they were doing the work themselves.

A message from our loyal driver, who kept us accident-free day after day on hundreds of miles of Ghana's roads: One of our close-knit team of four has malaria and won't be coming to the office this week, and possibly next week also.

I know a bit about malaria. I have seen many under-fives suffering from the dreaded cocktail composed of malaria, poor nutrition, and diarrhea, which often leads to death. And I once suffered through a bout of malaria myself, alone in a small room at a bar in Nzega district Tanzania. For a week I was in Nzega writing a report on our findings along with having discussions on how this project linked to development efforts with the district agricultural and water officers. And in these small towns local bars are the usual source of 'hotel rooms.' Fortunately the bar-owner's wife got me some Nivaquine at the local pharmacy and covered me with many blankets for the shivers that come and go throughout the day and night for a few days—if you're lucky. Fortunately the Nivaquine 'kicked-in' and I was back to work at my small table in a few days.

I was surprised when our driver informed us that our healthy and vibrant friend had been so suddenly incapacitated. My Ghanaians friends were not. These residents do not take a malaria prophylactic, and over the years these prophylactics lose effectiveness in any case. Rather, a substantial number of Tropical residents opt to suffer the random onset of malaria perhaps twice annually. At that point, the invalid will begin to take whatever drug and dosage is currently prescribed in the community. Our friend was a healthy, young, and fit: he recovered in about two weeks, for which we all were grateful. Yet this event called to mind the high fatality rates among the very young (mentioned earlier) and the elderly in most developing countries due to malaria, including the resistance to anti-malarial drugs, notwithstanding the large amount of money and resources from foundations and organizations that has been directed toward research for antimalarial vaccines that could be operationalized and provided at field level.

Early Years of HIV/AIDS

Returning from government offices late in the afternoon, we frequently passed a funeral procession en route to or returning from the large central Accra cemetery. I was struck by the prevalence of younger people and couples with the children in these processions. Also quite frequently I heard of government staff that had to attend the funeral 'that day.' Discussing this as discreetly as possible with our team, I received an explanation—many of the funerals were for HIV/AIDS patients. That was in 1988, before knowledge of the disease was wide-spread, and long before high mortality rates worldwide spurred intensive research into possible antiretroviral treatments with readily available long term maintenance regimen—coupled with proactive educational messaging and prevention programs focused on the most vulnerable groups.

Ghana Gets a Reprieve

We now come full circle in Ghana's economic cycles. Off-shore oil has been discovered, to the tune of an estimated 120,000 barrels a day, and drilling will soon begin with earning being estimated to reach $1 billion annually as the potential output targets are reached.[3] That is potentially terrific news for Ghana, though in light of the May 2010 spill in the Gulf of Mexico and the alleged large-scale corruption in other sub-Saharan African countries blessed with a petrochemical industry, the Ghanaian leadership will face some difficult decisions along the way. Are the existing laws and regulatory bodies sufficiently strong to ensure that deep water construction will include the safeguards required to prevent 'blowouts'? Is there any way to stop the graft and Big Fish corruption that other petro-rich countries have experienced, which have siphoned off most of the revenue derived from the oil, leaving a mere trickle for the treasury? Or will the rigor I saw in those LSE students several decades ago manifest itself in current leadership and programs that actually yield direct benefits to the country, reducing poverty and stimulating local economic growth? The pressures will be enormous on Ghanaian political and business leaders.

Yet there are signs of hope. At the UN MDG Summit in September, 2010, it was reported that Ghana's long-term investments in agriculture have cut the poverty rate there in half. Similar investments in education and health care conform to expectations the international community cherishes with regard to Ghana. Let us hope Ghana experiences similar success in handling it offshore petroleum reserves, using that resource to build further upon its human, cultural, institutional, and yes, economic strengths.

Malawi

Two decades after working in Tanzania, I received two assignments with the World Bank that gave me the opportunity to return to the region. I welcomed the opportunity to update my familiarity with developments among the (largely) Banda people, and perhaps add some polish to my by-now very rusty Kiswahili.

The first assignment was as a team leader on World Bank-funded project with a Government of Malawi, which shares a border with Tanzania; the second was as a consultant in a project in the health sector. I spent a total of five months in Malawi on the two projects, during which time I made several field visits and also worked closely with the ministries of finance and health at the central government level.

Things had changed considerably since my first visit twenty years earlier. For one thing, a new airport had been built to serve Dar es Salaam, Kilimanjaro, and other tourist centers in Northern Tanzanian. I was cheered to see that the region had been deemed worthy of such investments in infrastructure, although the Tanzanians I spoke with expressed decidedly mixed feeling about the modernization; in fact, their comments often exposed a degree of stress and even plight. Admittedly the sample I was drawing from was small, yet it seemed to me that in a nut-shell, the older Tanzanians were pleased with the development spinoffs that had come their way over the last twenty years, while younger Tanzanians did not consider themselves so fortunate.

On the day I arrived in Kilimanjaro the sky was crystal clear, and as I stepped out the door of the plane onto the runway, the famous mountain seemed to be only yards away. Though I couldn't help noticing that she had lost most of her sparkling glacier in the interval since my last visit, the sight of The Special K gave me a sense of stability as I vividly recalled the lovely five-day trek I had made in 1971 to reach the summit.

Malawi is known as" the warm heart of Africa" and the Malawians are certainly as cordial and genuinely personable as any people I have been privileged to work with. This pleasing temperament stands in stark contrast to the blows the landlocked nation has received from outsiders time and again. It was freed from its colonial past under a domineering United Kingdom only to find itself down-trodden once again by the harsh rule of Dr. Hastings Banda and his entourage—President for Life, as he was always referred to publicly and in print. Such unrelenting Centroid Power eventually undermines the spirit of a people and becomes a near indigenous part of the culture.

This combination of factors has given Malawi the dubious distinction of remaining among the lowest-ranking 10 countries worldwide in per capita income. Such endemic poverty, coupled with endemic malaria, diarrheal diseases, HIV/AIDs, and meager accesses to health services, results in persistent high infant mortality, and maternal mortality rates, make it clear that Malawians are stuck in the *country and family poverty trap* with seemingly few options at their disposal to improve their condition.

Recent improvements in income have been noted statistically, yet tobacco still accounts 70 percent of total exports revenue, crowding land out of corn/maize production and hurting small producers. Improvements have also been made in education, but the fact remains that nearly all families in the agricultural community are landless peasants with few alternatives, while day laborers typically earn less than subsistence wages.

Prominent among Dr. Banda's passions was an elite Latin grammar secondary school and Kazumu Academy located in Kasungu District. It was modeled after Eaton in the UK and attended by the very highest achieving students, who almost invariably came from the wealthy families whose members also filled most senior civil servant and business positions. The exceedingly high standards and elitist mindset engrained in students and their families by this well-greased system guaranteed that Malawi life would remain firmly in the control of the 'gentleman's' hand, with Hastings Banda at the top of the heap.

A typical graduate of Kazumu Academy could scarcely imagine the life challenges that 99.9 percent of Malawians faced daily, though most Malawians were fully aware of the role played by graduates of Kazumu Academy in controlling *their* lives. As were those of us who visited the country in an effort to improve the nation's prospects.

My first assignment in Malawi was to work with two other international consultants, a Dutch medical OB/GYN and a Ghanaian economist, on a project to strengthen maternal and child health under the primary health care rubric. The overall Ministry of Health policy at the time was to raise the level of health of all Malawians through a sound services delivery system, while simultaneously increasing productivity. Among the strategies to be pursued were early prenatal visits, delivery by trained staff, child immunization, baby weighing, nutritional consulting, micronutrient supplementation, and family planning.

Our efforts were a small part of a much-larger $50 million World Bank project to strengthen Malawi's health system while simultaneously incorporating key reforms, one of which was a *cost-sharing* program. It was clear that many patients were by-passing the local health centers and clinics which the Malawi government had invested heavily in because they couldn't afford them. Similarly, the high cost of medicines put them out of the reach of many poor Malawians. The plan we were investigating was to expand the health center/clinic network to selective district and central level hospitals. One unfortunate part of the plan was that the patients themselves would be required to absorb more of the cost of treatment.

On the face of it, many parts of the plan seemed eminently logical and reasonable. Yet it was surprising that both the graduates of Malawi's elite Kazumu Academy and the representatives from the World Bank failed to notice striking resemblances to a cost-recovery plan instituted by the Banda government twenty years earlier. That plan had been crushed beneath the sheer force of public pressure from both urban and rural families. The Banda government had simply dropped it. Not having the benefit of that history, our small team moved ahead undaunted, first formulating the principles that seemed required to operationalize such a scheme, and then making some trips into the field.

The World Bank and officials from the government spent a good deal of time conducting discussions within the health sector, and gave themselves a lengthy two-years-plus preparation time to study the relevant demographics, epidemiology, personnel capacities, management and delivery systems and financing issues. It soon became clear that sufficient funds would never become available for the required investments in physical infrastructure (mainly health centers) and manpower training.

Furthermore, the population was well aware of the difficulty of getting care and drugs at the chronically underfunded government health facilities, and often sought free attention from hospitals. The thought behind the cost-sharing idea was that if patients were required to pay a fee depending on the service, they'd be far less likely to leap-frog the clinics in their rush to visit intensive care facilities.

Once the local population had renewed their faith in local clinics—a process facilitated by greater government investment in that area—programs could also extend from health centers outward to the villages. Meanwhile, after the undue burden on hospitals was lifted, it would be possible for a referral system to function as intended. For example, a pregnant woman identified as 'at risk' at her village clinics would be transported to the obstetrics departments of the district or central hospital. The fees collected through the cost-sharing program would be returned to the treasury to support recurrent costs of medicines and disposable items.

The clinics at the central Hospital in Lilongwe were the busiest I'd seen—even more crowded than the district hospitals in Java where population density rose above 950 persons per square kilometer. I found it hard to believe that any positive health or medical care could be delivered in such a pressurized environment. At the out-patient department a long queue of people kept pressing forward, though they remained orderly, to the long table where several Malawian doctors were writing prescriptions hour after hour, while (from what I could discern) seldom asking the patients a single question. The doctors' heads were down, though they were undoubtedly listening to their patients' names and perhaps to their maladies. For the most part they were furiously writing prescriptions, then ripping off the forms and handing them over, only occasionally looking up to greet the patient. A similar scene would have met a visitor to the hospital pharmacy, where patients were arriving in a continual flow to get their prescriptions filled. Among the throng were mothers and grandmothers with their babies wrapped to their backs in colorful traditional African katanges, often with a toddler or two in hand as well.

We also visited district hospitals in Lilongwe and a few 'up-country' district and provincial hospitals. In the busy courtyards patients were milling around in the queue at the pharmacy waiting to have their prescriptions filled. We learned that some visitors were there for antenatal clinics, though the main business of these district hospitals was to provide inpatient bed care. The head doctors were typically foreigners. Evidently the Dutch had an exchange program under which Malawian doctors trained in the Netherlands while their Dutch counterparts put in two or three years in Malawi. These Dutch hospital directors worked with the district doctors, expanding services, especially maternal and child health in the district and at the health centers. The district hospital located near the presidential retreat had an American hospital director.

The American who was serving as the hospital director at the time seemed clueless as to the public health issues facing the country, in stark contrast to the Dutch district hospital directors we'd visited a few weeks earlier in districts south of Illowenge. Having worked with many Dutch consultants in Indonesia, I can assure you the Dutch are very independent thinkers, and professional in their judgment of a nation's doctors. To me the suave American had every earmark of a CIA plant. But then the CIA would understandably want to be as close as possible to the President for Life, should any ill fortune pass his way.

The hospital staff remarked on the meager quantities of equipment and disposables and the difficulty involved in replenishing supplies. The patient's wards were running at more than 100 percent occupancy, with patients on cots, under beds, and on mats placed on the floor. Closer observation showed numerous very gaunt patients with what our Dutch doctor said was HIV/AIDS. These HIV/AIDS patients obviously did not have any antiretroviral or other medicines and were quite nobly hanging on to their shred of life with the help of a relative, or more often a fellow patient. HIV/AIDS was on the rise by that time, though no effective antiretroviral treatments had been developed yet.

The second large class of patients was young children, many of them suffering from a cruel combination of malnutrition and malaria that was then (and still is) the scourge of low-income families throughout much of sub-Saharan Africa. Mothers and grandmothers were all too familiar with the condition, though they held hope that the few available feedings with rehydration and some medicines might yet revive their failing children. Many of these valiant Malawian women had exhausted themselves on the treadmill of poor education and back-breaking farm labor under the feudal conditions, and all too often their husbands had succumbed to HIV/AIDS or simply abandoned them. Yet their dignity and courage radiated across the quiet wards. Given the vagaries of the power system they faced daily, was there any way to empower them, or their daughters?

Rural Health Clinics

The government health centers in rural areas were often solid, surprisingly new structures, most with easy access to water but few staff and meager supplies of even basic drugs. This may account for the fact that most of them were nearly devoid of patients. Malawi apparently had begun to invest in a network of such rural health centers with World Bank financial support, though the generally bucolic atmosphere of these facilities made us question the government's commitment to providing primary health care in rural areas. More to the point for our assignment, until a fully functioning health center with adequate supplies, basic medicines, and well-trained personnel could be established, patients would continue to bypass local facilities on their way to district hospitals. This was the pattern we had been told about and had seen ourselves.

Villagers are usually adept at letting one another know what services and supplies are available locally, how much they cost, and how good (or bad) they are. They have a seemingly innate knowledge of what will benefit them and their families. They've been tricked repeatedly, yet they remain receptive to things that will improve their lives. Indeed, we stopped at the village/community-based MCH/antenatal clinic which was being conducted by the nurse midwife from one of the empty health centers about a half hour away by car. On a crystal clear afternoon, this beaming woman and her assistant had traveled to the village on their bicycles.

(We were told that some of the health centers provided motorbikes for outreach clinics, but only for longer distances.) About thirty women, all in their colorful garb, were in a semicircle along with their children, who were helping them to harness babies one after another into a traditional market scale for weighing. All this was taking place on the grounds of a small house equipped with a chair, a desk, and few supplies for the nurse/midwife. Everyone was cheery during their visit, which they perhaps made regularly on a quarterly basis. It was unclear to me what, if any, nutritional supplements would be offered if an underweight child was seen. Being aware that sometimes parents are reluctant to bring a sick or undernourished child to the session, I did ask if all the children of the village were present. I was assured that they were. We were told that this house and community outpost was also used for the immunization program, though the district-level immunization teams weren't available on that day. During the discussion we learned that all of the village women were happy to attend these outreach clinics and eager to pitch-in and help when asked. It was a sign of willing community participation that might possibly, or so it seemed to me, become the thin edge of a wider program for community empowerment. On the other hand, the fact that this village was relatively close to the new health center might have given that facility greater acceptance in the community. More remote communities would be less eager to make use of them.

HIV-AIDS: THE SKIPPED GENERATION

Driving through villages and farm communities, we also saw hard-working men and women toiling to eke out a small production for their family needs, and perhaps even a sufficient surplus cash crop to pay for school fees and simple medicines, and clothes. In Malawi maize/corn was generally both the cash crop and the staple food. This situation often presented problems, since in time of emergency the staple food crop would be sold, usually at the low prices which had been rigged by those who controlled the markets. In those parts of sub-Saharan Africa where cassava is the staple food, that root crop remains underground in 'storage' until needed by the family.

As we continued our progress across the largely level terrain of the midlands and the more traditional tropical land south of Lake Malawi, one fact dominated the landscape. Time and again we saw the grandmother digging and weeding with the traditional hoe or shovel in the hot tropical midday sun with the grandchild strapped to her back in the traditional manner. The HIV/AIDS that was devastating the urban areas was also clearly crippling these farm communities. Rather than being taken care of in old age by their daughters and daughter-in-laws, the situation for these elderly women had been reversed. As the 2010 MDG data reveals, even if HIV/AIDS situation is stabilized through education and treatment, a generation has been lost to the scourge, and it will have a brutal impact on the remaining population for years to come, and indeed on the whole fabric of society.

Developing Rapport with Senior Officials

When my fellow team consultants had finished their assignments, I gathered the notes of our discussions and began drafting the report. In the garden café of the hotel I stayed I met with a senior member of the Ministries of Finance several times to clarify such things as the operational mechanisms of returning fees to the treasury. I never doubted that these meetings were being monitored by Banda security systems. That is the way regimes operate and at that time I knew my guests were very brave.

In formulating the report I suggested the working group approach I used in Ghana, and was delighted when the senior officials from the ministries of finance, home affairs, local government and health agreed and fully participated in six lengthy and highly productive sessions. The technique I had developed in Ghana was to circulate each chapter I had completed around the ministries of health, finance, and local government for a few days before each meeting, eliciting their advice, and also, not incidentally, garnering their respect and giving the senior Malawian civil servants a heightened sense of ownership in the project.

During the meeting we thrashed around the various issues involved in the program. The discussions were lively and full of insight. It must be understood and emphasized that I was working directly with senior officials, most of whom had been through President Banda's approval process before arriving at their present lofty status. As a test of 'mirroring' I used the technique of taking off my suit-jacket, which was the staple of daily ministry attire. To my surprise, the 'old boys' of Kazumu Academy also took their jackets off when we sat in the conference table. Of course I did not unbutton my color, loosen my tie, or roll up my sleeves—that would have been going too far! Note: often civil servants wear their suits and ties in the field. Surely this let the villagers know who was in control!

By the second session around the large Ministry of Health conference table, the members of the working group seemed comfortable working in their shirtsleeves for the two-hour sessions. By the end of our sixth and final session we had arrived at a solid consensus on the main strategy and tactics to be presented in the report. It was a highly sensitive subject—but the report faithfully focused on pragmatic approaches to initiating a cost-sharing program to strengthen a new and fledgling primary health care program being adopted in Malawi. This draft was further distilled by the gynecologist and me before I finally submitted it to the World Bank.

And What Became Of It All?

My understanding is that the World Bank appreciated the cost-sharing strategy with the appendices of details for implementation. I was invited with the World Bank team to present the report. I thought it would have greater likelihood of acceptance within Malawi's Centroid Power structure if only the World Bank team (without the consultant) present the volumes of the report and discuss these with Malawian officials. Later, I asked a Malawian with whom I had worked what the upshot of it all had been.

"So how is the implementation?" I asked. "Were there many changes to our plan? Is it going on course?" The reply was a classic: "It was not adapted—it was too sensitive."

Even in a very repressive country like Malawi, with a President for Life firmly ensconced, village voices matter.

Yet a few changes were made in health investment to nurture a primary health care program with local health centers and community-based maternal child health and family planning support. Numerous international and national NGOs continue to provide basic health care, education services and support to Malawian living on the 'absolute edge.' And Malawi is marginally better off than it was twenty-five years ago. President Banda passed away (reputedly ninety-nine years old) in November 1997, and I have not followed Malawi governance or health system for several years, though it seems that Malawi's Centroid Power operating system has not changed much. Unfortunately this impression was recently confirmed by the current president, Joyce Banda (no relation to the first Pres. Hastings Banda). She told the *Financial Times* (November 19, 2013) – "the looting of government money has been going on for the last fifteen years and this is a president that has decided it has to stop." Western donors, who provide about 40 percent of the government's budget, have stopped payments worth $150 million and are ratcheting up pressure on Ms. Banda to tackle graft.[4]

What will it take to energize Malawi's political and economic operating system? Who will make the changes, and when? These are the core questions for the international development community, and for Malawi. At this stage all indications are that the international development community is impotent, preferring conferences and summits to action-oriented programs.

4
A Brief History of the Development Industry

As I described in Chapter 2, the phrase Centroid Power refers to the complex web of international and domestic institutions that collaborate with one another, and with various interests in the private sector, to manage the wealth that flows through the development industry. Anyone familiar with the workings of this vast machine is likely to arrive at the conclusion, soon enough, that the policies it establishes and pursues, with regard to allocating funds and managing resources, are designed primarily to insure the continued life and health of the elites within the halls of the system itself, and only secondarily, if at all, with the task for which those funds and resources have been generated, raised or donated—to address the social and economic ills of the developing world. It would not be much of an exaggeration to say that the main barrier to reducing poverty in many places is the bureaucratic power structure of the development industry itself!

Such remarks may sound far-fetched, conspiratorial, and also a little abstract. On the other hand, it's well-known that vast sums have been directed toward achieving Millennium Development Goals (MDG) in recent years—to take an obvious example—but the results have not been commensurate with swollen budgets. Why? In this section, I'd like to 'drill down' within that web of Centroid Power, focusing on a pattern of linked components (we can call them the 'main and sub-gears') within the development industry that serve to operationalize its wasteful and self-serving practices. Having described quite a few specific personal experiences with projects in the previous chapter during the course of which these 'gears' and 'linkages' can be distinctly heard, grinding away, I now propose to move to a level of *generalizations*. Whilst the specific components I'm going to describe are not exhaustive, and vary in intensity among institutions and countries, I'm confident that as you follow my chain of inferences, it will become clear how the Centroid Power Elites have cleverly and deceitfully *"built the development industry to fail"!*

Background Periods

Before we get to where Centroid Power truly 'ran off the rails,' the interested readers and students of the development industry may wish to have some highlights of the background periods of Official Development Assistance (ODA). Those interested in these background elements of development as well as a full range of topical issues will easily find many detailed references, including learned and professional articles, on the Internet and in libraries. I also commend Roger Riddell's *Does Foreign Aid Really Work?* (2007) as a highly useful and thorough (if not a bit ponderous) text covering many development issues and adding many explanatory notes and references. Additionally, Ravi Kapur's 2003 short handbook, "The Economics of International Aid," is filled with solid background and insights.[1]

In the last half-century many sterling contributions have been made by academicians and administrators to buttress the principles and operations of ODA. Human nature being what it is, other academicians and administrators have used their theories and bureaucratic skills to undermine ODA. I describe the legacy of such efforts in this book using the shorthand term Central Power Elites. Permit me then to use a broad brush to describe several phases in the history of ODA, focusing on the main background issues, policy sets, strategic frames, and overarching trends.

In the 1950s and 1960s—an era during which many colonized countries became independent—the overriding goal of developmental assistance programs was to accelerate a country's economic growth, with the associated issues of poverty and inequality invariably in mind, though not always clearly stated. It was felt at the time that the major constraints to such growth were a lack of savings and capital for investments. The more shrewd observers recognized that beyond the issue of capital scarcity lurked others of equal or greater significance: lack of skills, and inadequate and corrupt institutions, for example. At the time, many in the development industry also recognized the importance of being sensitive to differing socio-cultural mores and actively involving a program's beneficiaries in growth initiatives. [2]

To augment the savings and investment gaps was the easy part. Foreign aid, delivered through the soon-to-be-burgeoning institutions in the 1970s, would in effect "jump start" a nation's economy, leading inevitably to growth, savings, and sustainable institutions. Of course, each country would have to be considered uniquely, but the generalized pattern set from the expanding international development institutions could easily be modified to fit individual cases. This generalized pattern resembled a cascade of ever-more specific operations: "policies" were followed by "strategies," which in turn were used to define, plan, fund, implement and manage "programs" in a specific country, with donor funded "projects" filling the gaps. Attention could be focused variously on training the workforce; strengthening institutions such as banks, agricultural production and marketing services, community based health under the rubric of primary health care, hospitals, and primary education; and bolstering and expanding the physical infrastructure—roads, markets, electricity, sanitation—required to keep the population healthy and also to keep goods and services circulating from the projects' "multiplier effect" and creating households' demand in respective locales. If and when this cascading sequence of initiative was successfully completed, it was reasonable to assume that domestic surpluses would arise, trade would expand, and the economy would grow.

But things didn't turn out that way.

During the 1970s, the challenge of reducing extreme poverty gradually drifted from its mooring on the pillar of broadly-based economic development. Specialists in various disciplines—health, education and agriculture—with funding from aid agencies, began to administer a myriad of projects that addressed critical issues in their specific fields. Many of these projects were oriented toward strengthening the capacities of government infrastructure and services, usually with a central-level focus. In terms of the political continuum the 1960's and 1970's, the projects were generally state oriented, and might be described as "leftist", "socialist" or "statist" in aspect. In addition to new UN development agencies, traditional volunteer support through churches continued in poor provinces throughout the developing world. In the 1980s the NGO movement also began to build a head of steam, and subsequently expanded dramatically, providing services (many in the health services) at local levels in many countries; with increasing amounts contracted by donors and government.

The mood among academics and aid administrators shifted during the 1980s toward a 'marketing and sales' strategy, as the 'pro-leftish' ethos gave way to a 'pro-rightist' stance, and a new set of cascading policies were developed not only in the West but also in China and India. Regardless of their proven worth, many countries and agencies fell under the thrall of the 'neoliberal' economic policies exemplified by President Reagan and Prime Minister Thatcher and commonly referred to as Reaganomics or supply-side economics. Strange as it may seem, a key element of this body of doctrines was disdain for government services, particularly for disadvantaged members of society. Nevertheless, during the Reagan era senior decision-makers (and villagers) in developing countries received dramatically different policy packages and strategies than they had hitherto. These directives, in turn, were distilled into guidelines and then into fundable projects.

THE WASHINGTON CONSENSUS

In 1989 these guidelines were given a name by John Williamson, an economist from the Institute for International Economics. In an influential paper[3] he distilled the neo-liberal principles of the era into 10 policy prescriptions which, taken together, made a standard reform package for any nation troubled by economic crisis. He called this package of reforms the Washington Consensus.[4] In brief, the ten points were:

1. Fiscal policy discipline;
2. Redirection of public spending from subsidies toward broad-based provision of key pro-growth, pro-poor services like primary education, primary health care and infrastructure investment;
3. Broaden the tax base and adopt moderate marginal tax rates;
4. Interest rates that are market determined and positive (but moderate) in real terms;
5. Competitive exchange rates;
6. Liberalize imports, with any trade protection to be provided by low and relatively uniform tariffs;
7. Liberalize of inward foreign direct investment;
8. Privatize state enterprises;
9. Abolish regulations that impede market entry or restrict competition, except for those justified on safety, environmental and consumer protection grounds, and prudent oversight of financial institutions;
10. Legal security for property rights.

Williamson almost immediately regretted coining the term Washington Consensus, and once remarked that "it is difficult to think of a less diplomatic label."[5] Observers pointed out that many of these "Washington" principles had already been kicked around and then implemented in several Latin American countries. Williamson insisted in later years that many of the neoliberal initiatives undertaken at the time had nothing to do with the principles he had codified in any case.

As with any 'thumbnail' listing of policy reforms, many who paid lip service to them stuck to the main points and disregarded the nuances of the text. Here are three examples Williamson clarified in 2003.

(i) On 'Reordering Public Expenditure Priorities' he emphasized switching expenditure away from 'nonmerit' subsidies to pro-growth endeavors such as basic health care education an infrastructure.

(ii) In 'Privatization', he warned against having it done in highly corrupt processes and stressed the importance of guarding against the transfer of assets to privileged elites at a fraction of their value.

(iii) On 'Deregulation' to ease barriers to entry and exit, Williamson made an exception for safely and environmental regulations, which, he felt, ought to be strengthen rather than eliminated.

Certainly few of the sins committed under the mantel of the Washington Consensus can be attributed to Williamson's neat formulation. On the other hand, there was serious naïveté to be found among those who implemented the policies during the years of the "Consensus" and the consequences are still being suffered by the middle and poor classes in many parts of the world. We can only imagine how much better off the world would be today if these principles had been applied with the subtlety and intelligence possessed by some of the pioneers of the aid industry back in the 1970s.

As it turned out, the Washington Consensus became the first on the list of "gears" inhibiting effective administration of development programs. It was adopted by a variety of multi-national institutions including the Two Sisters (IMF and The World Bank), bilateral development agencies (especially USAID), selected transnational corporations (TNCs), think tanks, and academicians. It's overarching theories and pronouncements became policy-guidelines which after further formulations and 'sleights of hands' were (and continue to be) distilled into particular policies and programs.

Drawing on this unassailable consensus, development agencies, usually with the World Bank's lead, devise 'themes' and strategies (usually for sectors) as 'bridges' to design donor projects which, in turn, are directed and 'hustled' to this or that national government. Once specific sector strategies and policies of the multinational banks are secured, they become 'sold to' and 'mirrored' by national governments through whichever of their internal ministries would logically be involved. [6]

Once such a project becomes operational, the World Bank policies serve as de facto guidelines for the regional development banks—for example, the Asian Development Bank (ADB), African Development Bank (AfDB), a host of specialized UN agencies, bilateral development agencies like USAID and EU, and the larger international NGOs. Over the decades, a veritable merry-go-round of different policies for projects have become fashionable, only to be shown the door a decade later when results fail to materialize and another "pet" theory arises. It might be Free Trade one year, Privatization the next, then Structural Adjustment (discussed below), the 'big daddy on steroids,' Globalization, primary health care; and in 2000 the Millennium Development Goals.

A most egregious set of policies emanating from the Washington Consensus was given the name 'structural adjustment program' (SAP). It began in the 1980's and has continued up to the present day to have a colossal negative impact, particularly on the 'very' and 'moderately' poor.

Structural Adjustment Policies are often required to qualify for loans from the World Bank or the International Monetary Fund (IMF) loans. Though the specifics may vary from country to country, in general these policies and conditions include requiring a given country devalue its currency against the dollar; lift import and export restrictions; desist from deficit spending, and remove price controls and state subsidies on foodstuffs and others essential commodities such as fertilizer. All of this has the effect of making the goods produced in that country cheaper for foreigners to buy, while making foreign imports more expensive (due to the local currency devaluation). All well and good. In theory.

Unfortunately, a nation will usually reduce its budget deficit by cutting aid to programs like education, health and social care, while simultaneously increasing fees that fall disproportionately on poor families. The result is lower participation rates by the very people who need the services most. The removal of subsidies on basic foodstuffs such as rice and milk obviously compound the problem. Why would a nation do this? Because it was only on such terms that it would be able to receive the technical assistance and loans it needs to "develop."

During my half-year assignment in Ghana the harsh impacts of structural adjustments on plans and budgets, particularly in health and education, caused senior Ghanaian officials and colleagues to mount one of the early 'push-backs' on SAPs to the World Bank and IMF. The negative impact of 'structural adjustment programs' was eventually recognized by notable personalities, NGOs and eventually some Northern politicians and G7 and G8 members. As a result, a considerable chunk of third-world debt was simply cancelled, though not with an extended song-and-dance regarding terms, conditions, and amounts to be written off. [7]

Although surely mismanagement and corruption existed (and exist) in ODA related projects, which add further to a country's debts, the basic argument for debt relief is as follows. That paying of interest on debt, coupled with the direct negative effects of the 'structural adjustment program', deprives the country of the funds necessary to implement proactive pro-poor programs, particularly in health and education. This keeps the most vulnerable people in society mired in a 'poverty trap.' On the other hand, investment directed toward implementing solid pro-poor programs would begin to provide poor people and their communities with investing in the 'building blocks' to earn more and help "grow" the economy.

Most interesting was that the negative fallout from SAPs directly lead to a major new element being added to the development industry's evaluation tool-kit: *human development.* This concept was placed front and center, and the efforts of UNICEF, ILO, UNDP and the World Bank produced the annual Human Development Reports Human Development Index, comprising life expectancy, education, and standards of living, including poverty levels, for all countries. [8]

The 1990s saw major changes throughout the world again, in part stimulated by the policies of the Washington Consensus. The Soviet Union collapsed in 1991 sending huge ripples throughout Russia and Eastern European countries, and the twin mantras of 'economic shock therapy' and 'privatization' were on everyone's lips, with concomitant policies and 'packaged solutions' to bring 'free market liberalization' with economic growth destine to benefit all segments of society. Simultaneously on the Washington Consensus's agenda and 'drawing board' were the institutions and effects directly linked to trade liberalization and to the creation of the World Trade Organization in 1995. A year earlier NAFTA went into effect, liberalizing trade between Canada, Mexico, and the United States. Since 1998 there were dramatic increases in direct foreign investment, shifting a hefty portion of the world's manufacturing to China. China's inward Foreign Direct Investment (FDI) between 2000 and 2009 totaled US$ 679 billion and the percentage in manufacturing went from 30% (2001) to 49% (2009). [9] The Washington Consensus felt the heat of criticism from Dani Rodrick who emphasized the importance of *improved governance and greater access to information.* Some departments within the World Bank later tried to adopt some of his policy recommendations in an attempt to crack down on corruption in World Bank financed projects. [10]

What we know is that development is a dynamic process, even when it operates within the grip of overriding theoretical assumptions. There are differing factions within the halls of Centroid Power, and some of them have proven responsive to pressure from both the public and the countries with whom they deal, creating a momentum to ameliorate and in some cases reverse the excesses (as in the case of debt relief) that have resulted from implementing Washington Consensus policies.

Shaping the 21st Century: Development Cooperation

Preparing for the new century, some factions within Centroid Power studied the situation with an eye to change. The results of this self-examination appeared in 1996 in the OECD report: 'Report Shaping the 21st Century Contribution of Development Cooperation,' which signaled a major shift in emphasis within the ODA.[11] The report suggested, in a nut-shell, that focus be placed on *the recipient countries*, including policy formulation with the cooperation of local civil societies. This *explicit partnership* between donors and recipient's was actually something new. It was based on numerous assessments in the field documenting that great hardships and poverty remained untouched, if not compounded, by Washington Consensus policies. Another main reason: it was strongly advocated by a movement of recipient countries' Centroid Power elite, who argued that as member governments to the international development banks, they were paying the loans and wanted to have more say in the whole developmental process.

The increase in HIV prevalence and the HIV/AIDS epidemics in most sub-Saharan African countries was one obvious example of problems that the Washington Consensus had no good theory to address or control. Additionally, reducing hunger and malnutrition became more prominent in the 1990s and in 1996 FAO convened the World Food Summit (WFS) which, with representatives from 185 governments, heightened public awareness to the seriousness associated with the multifaceted issues and problems.[12] WHO and its member countries recognized series of poor health related indices; obviously the major primary health care initiatives were not meeting expectations and numerous reasons particularly in the poor countries. The 2000 UN Summit led to the formulation of Millennium Development Goals (MDG) which remains today the standard measure for all foreign aid among all donors and recipient countries.

The MDG were at the top of the agenda at several subsequent G8 forums. As a result, the developmental programs favored by Centroid Power met criticism from several factions within the industry. Undoubtedly some bureaucrats and decision-makers clung to traditional policies and conditionality, while others, perhaps for their own security, sought to limit the damage done by the Washington Consensus so as to lessen the carnage of peoples and communities. Foremost among the critiques, perhaps, was the book *Globalization and Its Discontents* (2002), by Nobel laureate Prof. Joseph Stiglitz. [13]

Each G8 forum contained substantive background reports on specific subjects, for example: (i) debt relief on loans by qualifying countries (Cologne: 1999)[14]; (ii) expanding trade, making foreign aid more effective, with less corruption and greater accountability (Monterey: 2002)[15]; (iii) further emphasis on debt relief and maternal and child health for highly indebted poor countries (Gleneagles: 2005)[16]; and (iv) food security (L'Aquila:2009)[17].

Furthermore, and notwithstanding the apparent sincerity of the North, the US and Europe continue to maintain their huge and expensive agricultural subsidies to farmers and the agribusiness industry. Such policies have led to extended stalemate in the Qatar Rounds of the World Trade Organizations efforts to stimulate trade and reduce protectionism. The negotiations got underway in 2001 and remain deadlocked.[18] If an accord could be reached, it would greatly increase the incomes of even smallholder farmers in Central

Millennium Development Goals (Between 1990 and 2015) with Key Quantifiable Targets

Goal 1: Eradicate extreme poverty and hunger
– Halve the proportion of people living on less than a dollar a day.
(In 2008 the World Bank raised the level of 'extreme poverty' to $1.25 per person per day at 2005 purchasing-poverty parity (PPP). Current reporting on MDG1 is at the $1.25 level.)
– Halve the proportion of people suffering from hunger.

Goal 2: Achieve universal primary education
– Ensure by 2015 that all children complete a full course of primary schooling.

Goal 3: promote gender equality and empower women
– Eliminate gender disparity in primary and secondary education at all levels by 2015

Goal 4: reduce child mortality
– Reduce by two-thirds the mortality rate among children under five

Goal 5: improve maternal health
– Reduce maternal mortality by three-quarters
– Achieve universal access to reproductive health

Goal 6: combat HIV/AIDS, malaria and other diseases
– Halt and begin to reverse the spread of HIV/AIDS
– Provide universal access to treatment for HIV/AIDS for those who need it
– Halt and begin to reverse the incidence of malaria and other major diseases (esp. tuberculosis)

Goal 7: ensure environmental sustainability
– Reduce by half the proportion of people without sustainable access to safe drinking water and basic sanitation
– Achieve significant improvement in the lives of at least 100 million slum dwellers by 2020

Goal 8: develop a global partnership for development
– Adapted from the United Nations Development Program, Millennium Development Goals, see http://www.undp.org/mdg/goal1.shtml

and Latin America, sub-Saharan Africa and parts of Asia. As it stands, Centroid Power protectionism increases poverty and reduces the nutritional intake of millions of people in developing countries.

Regardless of the increases in ODA for the Millennium Development Goals, reports delivered at the September 2010 UN Summit revealed that some progress had been made in most countries toward reaching the specified targets, with only five years to go.[19]

In preparation for the post-2015 Development Agenda, the UN Economic and Social Council, all UN agencies including the World Bank and its member countries have devoted considerable resources and efforts to provide updates on the MDG indices, some to 2012.[20] These reports show substantial gains in providing access to drinking water, and in reducing extreme poverty, undernourishment, and deaths from malaria and tuberculosis.[21] While these gains are encouraging, deeper reading reveals significant variations among countries and regions. The reports also reveal large gaps in data due to inadequate collection and highlights, for each MGD, the number of countries who are moderately or seriously off target.[22]

Some recent findings on key MDG indices for Goal 1, 4, 5, 6 and 7 are available in the appendix.

Many critiques on the MDGs are available online. This set of independent assessments in discussion papers and blogs review how the original MDGs were establish and provides insightful analysis on moving forward post-2015. In this series, the 2010 paper "MDGs 2.0: What Goals, Targets, and Timeframe?" by Karver, Kenny and Summer, with multiple background sources provides an exceptional review of the MDGs and a nuanced, realistic approach to accommodate wide variation among countries in setting post-2105 MDGs.[23]

COMMISSION ON GROWTH AND DEVELOPMENT'S POSSIBLE ACCEPTANCE

The development processes will never remain static, and the continual review of evidence makes a far better basis for altering programs and policies than visceral value judgments. Yet as the preponderance of poor result from programs based on the Washington Consensus grew ever larger, a new independent group entitled Commission on Growth and Development emerged to review and formulate a new approach to the developing world's economies and people. The Growth Commission is comprised of a worldwide group of 22 senior economists, finance ministers, and at least one former head of a major transnational banking corporation. After several rounds of deliberation they issued their report in 2008.[24] Salient aspects of the report are distilled in the Kanbur (2008) – and consist of overview statements and a list of 'bad ideas'. (I discuss them at greater length myself in chapter 10.)

In summary, the Commission on Growth and Development retains the pro-market orientation of the previous Consensus, but rejects dogmatism or institutional fundamentalism on this point; the 'one-size-fits-all' approach has failed. In fact, the Growth Commission no longer considers growth to be the object, but merely the vehicle whereby focused effort through the MDG's are seriously addressed, together with broader development enabling people to be productive and creative. Another major feature of the Growth Commission's report is the realistic acknowledgement that countries can, and should be encouraged to; find their own path and agenda to development.

Indeed, I joined Kanbur (2008), Rondick (2008) and others on welcoming the Commission on Growth and Development's formation of a flexible policy orientation for growth. And whilst the Growth Commission does not have a continuing institutional presence to promote its worthy advices, there is reason to hope that the reputation of the various commission members will give the report a lingering impact at the World Bank and the UN, so that the advice it contains will continue to influence strategies and projects in the future. Many of the *tactical facets* presented in the pages of this book dovetail nicely with the Growth Commissions rationale and recommendations.

Though I remain positive regarding the future, we must also be realistic. The worldwide financial and economic meltdown of the fourth quarter in 2008 reflects the principles of the Washington Consensus *writ large*. By removing all serious institutional safeguards and oversight of the financial industry, and allowing the financial elite in Washington and London to 'self-regulate', the door was opened to various 'equity bubbles' that in the long run hurt the poorest members of societies most.

Further, we must consider the that the healthy changes in strategy advocated by the Growth Commission's overview will require a relatively long time frame to bear fruit. It's more than likely that such changes will be difficult to sustain in the fact of Centroid Power's entrenched system of linkages among the political and technical elite, not to mention the vested commercial interests among both donors and recipient countries. *It will take a 180-degree shift in focus to ensure that a significant portion of aid and local growth from developing domestic resources (such as energy-related) is dedicated to local infrastructure and reliably functioning systems at the field level.*

5

The Barriers to Change

That, in brief, is a history of how the aid industry got where it is today. Let me return, then, to an analysis in more general terms of the various barriers that stand in the way of reducing levels of poverty in the developing world.

A Lack of Sustained Commitment

One barrier that is often mentioned when considering the failure of any particular plan of attack to improve village life is that the management and implementation of the program were poor. The not-so-subtle implication is that the weaknesses lie at the 'lower levels' of bureaucracy and in the field, notwithstanding the fact that only a small percentage of project money ever makes it to that level. In such situations, it is usually the case that projects were ill-conceived in the first place and could *never* have succeeded. It is most likely the elites had no idea what would or would not work, but they got the 'money-out-the-door'—a point we'll examine more fully later. Hence, Centroid Power's arrogant *modus operandi* is to deny any responsibility or culpability in failures, but take all the credit when a project succeeds.

Once the shelf-life of a development-theory is reached, a new one is inevitably concocted within the 'bowels and wisdom' of the Washington Consensus. At that point the hype begins to build again, projects are funded and hustled to the compliant elites of a given country, who also have a lot to benefit from keeping the projects and money flowing. Time after time, the development industry 'bobs and weaves' to new policies and themes.

As bureaucrats, academicians and consultants move from one

infatuation to the next, one fundamental (but inconvenient) truth escapes their notice: *unless a program commits itself to setting up the infrastructure capable of genuinely empowering local communities, and succeeds in sustaining that infrastructure over a long period of time, it will fail.*

This idea will never be fashionable.

Perverse Incentive Systems

Among the donors, particularly the multinational development banks, the staff members who have direct decision-making in preparing and managing projects are promoted and remunerated on the basis by getting projects approved. These incentives are quite literally linked to 'push-money-out-the-door' of the banks to the recipient countries. The project managers willingly comply with the 'fall and winter fashions' of theory and strategies that senior management is currently promoting, and hustle them, in turn, to their national counterparts. For example, there may be a push for large civil works—say roads and bridges in the country's large conurbations. A few years later, everyone is keen on sequential five-year projects to decentralize in health systems and building district hospitals, with added funds for training the staff. Such abrupt changes in focus offer an illusion of innovation and development, but they undermine interest in the complex long-range programs that are far more likely to be effective and needed to demonstrate impact. Depending on the intervention(s) impact will not be measurable in ten or even fifteen years; a five-year project will leave the country bearing the burden of recurring costs without producing measurable positive results.* It's a prescription for failure, though a five-year project cycle remains the modus operandi for most developing agencies.

Meanwhile, most monitoring of projects boils down to simple quantifiable assessments of 'work done measures' such as "schools

---

* See Chapter 8 for a discussion of the 'rigorous impact evaluation' methodology of the Millennium Village Project.

and health centers built," "training sessions attended" during the life of the project. This has some validity, but it would be more revealing to assess long-term changes in health, literacy, and income, which become relevant only when a program has a continuing flow of annual operational costs. (Donors prefer to have such costs carried by the host nation, which may be reasonable but also *de facto* undermines efforts to keep long-term programs active.)

To be sure, some projects initiated by development agencies cost hundreds of millions of dollars and appear to include all the elements required for success, such as training personnel, building infrastructural capacity, improving management and delivery systems, and increased reporting. But such programs are the exception, rather than the rule; and in any case, getting agreement 'on paper' and in meetings with senior host country officials is one thing: keeping it going is quite another. The ministry in charge typically faces many hurdles and wrestles with many logistical and financial issues, including annually adding the project activities to the budget, getting the funds released from the finance ministry in a timely manner; and implementing and managing the various activities within each component of the project. Is it any wonder that the results seldom come anywhere near expectations?

CIVIL SERVANT REMUNERATION

One added element I ought to mention is that remuneration packages for employees in international and bilateral organizations are more than generous—and invariably far higher than the salaries of those within a given country who are involved in a project. These highly paid civil servants, academics, and consultants, who carry no real responsibility for a project's sustained success, are anathema to economic and social development, and often create resentment amid the ranks of a nation's civil servants.

Similarly, most national (recipient/host countries) civil service remuneration schedules and packages (i.e. cars with the petrol allowance, free or highly subsidized housing) are quite low when compared to international counterparts. Patriotism and good will can take a program only so far, however. *Money* is also required for the civil servants of a given nation and their families to live and educate their children. One reason that projects seldom earmark funds to be spent at the district and field levels is that such funds are likely to be directed toward activities (some phantom) and expenditures other than the ones for which they were intended, creating sizeable leaks in the Green River of cash that nourishes any lengthy project. Over the past decade, some countries have begun to address this problem by simply paying their civil servants more, though with no sustained success.

Rising Debt among "borrower" Nations

One further effect of this perverse incentive system is that it fosters indebtedness among host nations, even when the loans involved are concessional. Project managers from international agencies have repeated contact with the elites of the countries that are borrowing money from them. This feeds different avenues and kinds of corruption by the well-placed elite, as the projects are tailored to specific activities of benefit to those involved. Over time, a close relationship develops between an international agency's project task manager (mentioned above) and his or her counterpart within the government ministry handling the project.

Once the project is included in the annual budget and the budget is released, the processes to get the project's annual activities flowing begin. This usually provides the project manager from the agency near-immediate access to the 'task manager' who is responsible for authorizing the all-important ('non-objection') approval of contracts and selection of consultants for budgeted activities. This, in turn, sets in motion the procurements apparatus, which in most countries will involve visits from the project management unit (PMU) to the appointed official at the minister of finance who has the signature that unlocks the real money.

The process of "non-objection" is perhaps worth an extended note. It allows the project manager (PM) to move a project ahead without taking responsibility for actually approving it. The PM does not want to be responsible for the selection, contract, and work performed but does want the money to be spent to keep the project's activities moving ahead. Hence, having easy access to the PM to give the 'non-objection' virtually opens the approval mechanism for the PMU to get to the ministry of finance as described above.

In order to receive the coveted 'non-objection,' the PMU sends all the documents to the PM, who may hold up a contract, request different terms, work done, etc. Often civil works require interaction between engineering, technical, and procurement specialists in the line ministry and the World Bank's (WB) specialists, to make sure the documents meet specified details. Any questions raised by the WB will take time for the government specialists to answer. Thus, decisions for the 'non-objections' to conduct most of the expensive activities within projects often take many months. Meanwhile, the WB's lawyers are scrupulously sniffing through the contact details for signs of corruption. Hence, the entire procurement process is an enormous can of worms. Many simpler project activities are more straightforward. Often the key activities that will need the WB's 'non-objectives' are planned in advance; yet flexibility exists to modify this list as project progresses. When the PM and DG/Directorate-Project Director have been working together for an extended period, they develop a degree of rapport that allows activities to go forward, but all the same, there can be many non-objectives in each year for a single project.

This way of doing business is not well-suited to the kinds of long-range programs that reduce poverty. Unfortunately, though the ends toward which the loans are directed never quite materialize, the loans still have to be repaid. Thus the international development community exerts a stranglehold on peoples living at the lowest levels of human sustenance, and the endless cycle of debt and poverty continue. Nevertheless, the policies established by the multinational banks become a model for other multi-national (UN) and bilateral agencies, with similar harmful effects.

Competition among Agencies

The World Bank is the premier multinational organization for designing and funding projects. It employs about 10,000 staff, two-thirds are based in Washington, DC, while the remaining third are at work in more than a hundred country offices in the developing world.[1] In the course of the last fifty years the multiplicity of UN agencies, other multinational, bilateral development assistance organizations, international NGOs, and Funds (i.e. Gates Foundation in 1994) has proliferated, populating the 'development' landscape with hordes of management and staff personal in offices at regional headquarters and within host countries around the world. † [2]

The World Bank itself also maintains a top-notch knowledge and research center and an impressive network among academics and other development agencies.

Yet the sheer number of such agencies, in the end, has a deleterious effect on reaching the goals ostensibly shared by all of them. This plethora of agencies and NGOs creates systemic competition rather than coordination within the field, often accompanied by an unhealthy 'self- protection' mentality and a 'we know best' attitude. The effect is to redirect resources away from local initiatives toward organizational self-promotion and defense. The will to endure and

---

† Not surprisingly it is extremely difficult to get relevant estimates of the number and levels of staff and consultants in the UN and particularly its specialized agencies focused on the type of developmental work we're examining. One reference point is that the UN figures employs about 75,000 people in different agencies; but it will take persistent research to extract the details of the UN's employment. Riddell, whilst acknowledging the huge growth of NGOs over the last 20 years, presents aggregate estimates of numbers of NGOs and people employed; but understandably convey the difficulties knowing much about this gargantuan and amorphous sub-industry of atomistic entities. Hence, it's virtually impossible to conduct cohesive analyses in assessing the effectiveness of tens of thousands of NGOs. In Chapters 9 -12 I will be discussing recommendations on 'rationalizing' UN personnel and NGOs.

prosper may come as naturally to organizations as to individuals, but it does nothing to reduce poverty or stimulate economic development. And such a situation also has a negative impact on the bureaucracy of host nations, who must adapt to a wide array of protocols that differ not in their purpose, but only in the details. Mountains of paperwork, and more recently electronic media and endless e-mails, overwhelm the ministries offices, trained technical personnel and managers who might better have devoted their energy to strengthening systems at the district level and extending services to communities. This trend can be seen most dramatically in projects calling for heavy infrastructure development, notably the sectors of agriculture, water and irrigation, forestry, transportation, population-nutrition-health and education, all of which can have a profound impact on Millennium Development Goals and local economic growth.

AFFINITIES AMONG AGENCY PERSONNEL ACROSS THE INDUSTRY

Every organization has a distinct culture that shapes the way it does business. By the same token, every industry has an unspoken system of acceptable practices that guide its behavior. And the development industry is no different.

This is in some ways remarkable, when you consider the diversity of nations and organizations involved, but it's true. We might call the 'rules of the road' that have been adopted by international agencies the 'UN type' approach. This approach affects not only how a given agency views itself, but also how it views its role with respect to the district administration and to people living in real rural communities and urban slums. In a word, a significantly stronger bond exists between officials in international agencies and their counterparts in national agencies, than between either of these groups and the staff and residents at district level or people in villages and urban slums whose lives are the object of interest.

This neocolonial mindset is widely shared by policy-makers and bureaucrats from international and domestic organizations, agencies, NGOs, consultants, and academics. They entered the field with a desire to improve the lives of underprivileged people, presumably, but have great difficulty absorbing the fact that these people, who mostly live in rural communities and urban slums, actually possess the necessary skills and experiences to pursue their own interests effectively, given half a chance. Along similar lines, some apparently clever people I have met from outside the development industry still hold the cheery view that individuals living 'on the edge', poor and malnourished, in squalid conditions, scrambling to find some cash for their children's school fees or medicines, are actually content and may not even welcome improvements in their standards of living.

> ...a significantly stronger bond exists between officials in international agencies and their counterparts in national agencies, than between either of these groups and the staff and residents at district level or people in villages and urban slums whose lives are the object of interest.

The reality is entirely different. Women farmers (both smallholder owners and laborers) and mothers as heads of families in urban slums, daily demonstrate at least as deep an understanding of allocating very scarce resources for their children as international and national bureaucrats on their secure incomes and perquisites command. They show similar savvy in making use of the latest low-cost telecommunications that are now available in remote communities in Asia and expanding throughout African countries. Real people can and do learn and innovate with meager resources. Most unfortunately, this neocolonial mentality remains deeply ingrained and is pervasive throughout and particularly among the elite of the development industry.

Let me give you some examples of how this neocolonial mindset affects policy decisions and project design. As I mentioned earlier, when the harmful effects of the 'structural adjustment program' of the 1990s became widely known, the IFI's (International Financial Institutions) promoted Poverty Reduction Strategy Papers (PRSPs) in which each recipient country was to formulate its country's own recommended development strategy, focusing on the specific background and a proposed long-term approach to reduce poverty. Yet there was great similarity among the PRSPs offered. Why? Because regardless of a county's specific problems, its senior officials in planning were in the habit of relying on the strategic formulation favored by the World Bank and other chief donors. As a result, many of the problems associated with the SAP's continued to plague the projects emanating from the strategy papers.[3]

Second, the MDG processes spawned a burgeoning group of NGO-type advocates, many of them with specific targets, in maternal and child health or education, for example. These groups have been classed as Civil Society and communicate through various platforms in the UN and World Bank. NGOs may participate as advocates through a consultative status with the UN Economic and Social Council (ECOSOC) or the UN Department of Public Information (DPI).[4] Rather than remaining independent and performing the role as civil society advocates for those who have no political voice, NGOs have been co-opted and contracted by international and domestic development agencies to perform functions and deliver services to poor people in their communities. Unfortunately, this does nothing to strengthen district and local level infrastructure and delivery systems. As we have learned in the 'development game', few things happened by accident, and Centroid Power has orchestrated the growth of NGOs to take the 'sting' out of local grievances and undermines local empowerment. In fact, it remains a brilliant strategy for controlling civil society, maintaining a "sincere veneer," and retaining wealth and power at the wrong end of the social pyramid.

Third, regardless of how many meetings are held, in the end the design and handling of projects falls within the purview of a country's line ministry, and particularly the finance ministry, which delivers the cash to get things done. In this sphere the neocolonial-type linkages between the donors' managers and the respective ministries continue to be of critical importance, and these linkages leave little room for local input into needs assessment, project design, or implementation. (In Chapters 9 - 11, I discuss how we can change that state of affairs.)

Patronage and Nepotism among the "Country Elite"

As if the neocolonial mindset were not difficult enough to penetrate and unravel, in most countries, political influence is controlled by wealthy individuals who have little or no contact with 'moderately poor' or 'extremely poor' people. They do, however, have close ties to the private businesses that are given the contracts, particularly the larger ones, associated with development. Indeed, in some countries, the tycoons become government ministers themselves, whose responsibilities include awarding important contracts for civil works and natural resource development.

These nested relationships between senior government officials, other members of their immediate and extended family, and their close business colleagues are further strengthened by international and national suppliers who also stand to benefit by the arrangement. This closely held power directly impacts a multi-year project's design, and guarantees 'locking' into an ensuing process that is includes many kinds of procurement activities. Needless to say, within this welter of ever-shifting money and paperwork, opportunities for "contract rigging" are rife, and few leave a recognizable paper trail. An official in a regional development bank once mentioned to me in passing: "When the door closes in the tender committee, all bets are off, even though we vet each submission very carefully and usually know which one should win and do the work." Others would say, "They're local, and they know how to do the job."

No one can deny that corrupt practices associated with awarding contracts have plagued many countries and will continue to do so without serious challenges by international donor or national authorities, regardless of the well-developed procurement procedures, auditing procedures, and legal penalties in place in most government ministries and agencies.

Brahmin Project Cycles

The World Bank has a formal ubiquitous seven-stage 'project cycle' [5] which has been refined over several decades. It includes: identification – preparation – appraisal – approval – implementation – completion – evaluation. Each of these phases is to be conducted and completed according to prescribe standards. The regional development bank and other large donors like USAID have similar project cycles. In the hands of dedicated senior decision-makers, sufficiently trained national counterparts, and adequate information, the cycle serves a useful function. It also provides useful 'internal checks' to allow professionals to assess the 'soundness and viability' of a project from different perspectives and resolve issues prior to final approval.

Yet as we saw in the case of Indonesia, in most countries the design phases of a project are of special importance, because they establish what should be done by which offices, the decision-making framework, and the time-frame. The respective directorates' generals and head of directorates who design a project tend to emphasize a central orientation and formulate their objectives without much input from the field level. Hence, these important projects stages have come to resemble Kabuki theater, with various international and domestic development teams focusing on specific elements and interventions and projecting their approach and suitable deference address the constraints on the ground.

This is true of both specialized projects within a sector and projects that draw on multiple funding sources and seek to incorporate multiple initiatives within a single ministry like health or education.[6] Most multi-year projects take two plus years to prepare, with substantive background review, including trips with national counterparts to different parts of the country to collect data and discuss with regional and local officials the perceived constraints in implementation and managing the project. As you would imagine, these preparatory stages vary greatly from one country to the next, and you are as likely to hear, 'Oh yes, we will have ample operational/recurrent costs' as 'You had better ask at the central level.' This often means that projects are justified to, and then approved by, senior management on the basis of invalid assumptions, which are only fully recognized during implementation, and become more evident with each advancing year. Also, invariably front and center in the early perception of a project are the mix and initial 'back of the envelope amounts' of the 'categories of expenditure', such as civil works, equipment, goods and materials, consultant services, in-country training and overseas fellowships, seminars, project management and sometimes operations costs.

The respective teams begin focusing on specialized subject areas and identifying sets of activities which become project components with detailed activities that, in turn, are 'costed' and budgeted. Hence, if health is identified, within health comes a safe motherhood project or one focused predominately on nutrition or sanitation (not even necessarily linked to a water supply). The string of ever changing (like the seasons) policies described above and then since 2000 with the MDG give justification or 'cover' for such projects. Depending on the sources and kinds of external funds (loan or grant), the international organization is appointed (but determined in preliminary informal discussions) and a national agency is chosen to be the lead 'host' ministry and Executing Agency.

The way the initial 'ground rules' of 'ownership' are set determines most of the subsequent decisions made during the multi-year life of a project. Directorates Generals and their lead Directorates who 'host' projects, most often determine how much of the project's technical inputs and money will be controlled by the central level relative to field level. De facto this central level domination negates the oft promulgated development lingo of 'needs assessment' with 'bottom-up' planning and real 'local empowered' people and their communities. These 'vertical' programs are sometimes 'mixed' with more horizontal efforts as the local skill base develops and begins to take on greater responsibility. For example, in education programs, constructing schools and hiring teachers can be dealt with locally. Similarly, civil works for district level water and sanitation projects and health centers can be localized. On the other hand, running a mix of maternal, child health prevention, and basic health services, even at field level, will likely be dominated by the central level, since the central level possesses both the overall technical expertise and responsibility, though support might also come though the regional, district and local health center 'health teams' and mothers in the community.

As a result, in many countries the way projects are designed and budgeted at the central level means that a portfolio of projects has emerged that are designed to fragment efforts in the field, rather than coordinating them. We might call it the 'hyper-silo' mentality, which protects a given professional or Ministerial, DGs' and Directorates' empires but does little for the people in need of the aid. [7,8]

Furthermore, based on the project design, the international agency stipulates their *categories of expenditure*, such as civil works, equipment, supplies, training and seminars and consultancies, together with the modes of contracting and payment methods (domestic and international) for the activities. (See Chapter 3 for specifics.)

Knowing these 'cards in the deck' is only a small step toward contracting and procurement. Over the decades, international agencies have put tremendous effort into refining tools so as to facilitate and 'guarantee' wider tendering and unbiased selecting the 'winner of tenders,' including many safeguards from the funding agency. Unfortunately, the tight oversight that would be required to make such tools work is seldom adequately applied, and corruption is still prevalent.

One thing Centroid Power is very good at is jumping through

the many hoops set in front of it by donor agencies and national ministries, thus insuring a steady stream of projects flowing through its coffers.

The Problem of Staff Selection & 'UnCivil' Servants

In many countries, civil service appointments are political or nepotistic, based on cronyism and patronage rather than merit. This includes senior advisory and managerial positions. The same methods extend to the international agencies. After holding a sinecure as Director General in country 'X' for a series of donor projects, an individual might be appointed to a lofty position in a UN agency from which those projects were derived. Why? There is a woeful lack of transparency in hiring practices at every level of the industry and particularly in the impenetrable and chief foils for Centroid Power, the Human Resources departments.

A complementary feature of this system is that in many countries, all positions and staff are screened repeatedly for loyalty to the administration and their senior colleagues. Independent, critical or creative thought is frowned upon, and those who question the current group-think are quickly shelved and dispatched, maybe to a remote part of the country. When civil servants are promoted from the provinces, they find it professionally expedient to fall in line with the Centroid Foci, abandoning any enthusiasm they may have previously espoused for development efforts at the district and village or urban slum levels. In a very real sense, the ambient throughout the development industry guarantees that people with certain characteristics become virtually 'self-selected' at their position irrespective of where in an organization or agency they gravitate to. On the other hand, those who buck the organizational culture are 'sniffed' out early and seldom prosper.

It's worth pointing out that most of these professionals have had very limited experience living and working in rural communities or urban slums. Hearing about the rigors of life there, they certainly have little desire to be part of it on an extended basis. Meanwhile, bureaucrats coming from a disadvantaged background 'don't ever want to be poor again'—and will do everything they can to make sure their families never have to return to that environment.(Note: This motivation is also detectable among professionals and support staffs in multinational and bilateral aid agencies and consultants.) Thus few reminders are required to keep them in line with the Centroid Foci. And if any are required, they're likely to take the form of bullying on the part of senior colleagues who are already more deeply entrenched in the chain of Centroid Power.

Another reason for the virtual dismissal of local area development in central level decision-making is simple math. The proportion of 'the project pie' would be dramatically reduced at the central level if more were invested with the necessary recurrent budgets following on for many years at the district level. Such a shift in focus would also entail far more travel and time spent in difficult and perhaps insalubrious local conditions.

'Slow-walking' the process

There is a tremendous amount of 'paper passing' and e-mailing exchanging going on. This includes the selection of candidates for various committees, trainings, and associated activities. Were an independent observer to review how much of this kind of work goes on, he or she would be shocked at the series of endless meetings and training sessions (with the participants frequently getting paid to attend) and reports completed without any managerial oversight or any genuine action being taken.

A second set of delays arise due to the donor agency's need for further clarification on numerous project activities that require the donor's 'no objection' (discussed above) prior to funds being released. Dealing with multiple agencies, each having their own administrative processes, merely compounds the problem. Additional delays are involved when the project management team within the directorate requests money for activities which have been approved in the annual budget. Generally the project management team within the directorate prepares all documentations and then proceeds to the ministry of finance for approval, which is required before the money can be dispersed. The regulations established by the ministry of finance can be complex—particularly when the money and activities are conducted at the provincial and district levels.

All of these time-consuming, foot-dragging activities make it necessary for agencies handing out loans to charge a 'commitment fee' (frequently 1.5% of the remainder of the total amount of the loan which has been reserved by the donor) to expedite the process. Such fees increase the burden on the next generations, and extract monies that might otherwise be used for future projects.

Not infrequently, the numerous delays I've described above lead the donors to suggest that the project should be extended by a year or two or morphed into another project, which will then go through the 'merry-go-round' to be formulated, researched and approved.

Meanwhile, over the decades the number of consultants and NGOs involved in the development industry has expanded dramatically. Many of them come from academia and private sector companies. They each have an area of expertise, and their input into the process invariably compounds the silo-effect that I described a few minutes ago. Since there is no universally accepted accreditation process for such consultants and NGOs, their skills and contributions vary wildly, but one thing many of them are adept at is 'playing the development game' with clients and patrons. Among the cardinal rules of that game is to be a 'tame' consultant; willing to acquiesce to the clients demand without questioning. After all, the client is picking up the tab. Mountains of reports get written, usually under tight time constraints and with very little oversight or independent review or critique. And who knows to what extent these reports and seminars are used? Nobody. It's part of the development industry's mystery pie.

Certainly upgrading skills at all levels helps to build a cadre of capable professionals and staff. However, tremendous amounts of money go for training sessions, though it's seldom ascertained whether those who received the training will ever be put in a position to use it. Projects payments for output of consultants' reports and trainings (with all costs) are based on where, when, and if the training took place. But who really knows if this information is correct? And on what basis were the 'favored' attendees from central-level departments chosen? It is difficult to find adequate answers to these apparently straightforward questions.

> For most observers, it has become increasingly difficult to locate an 'ethical spine' within the development industry, particularly among those in leadership roles.

Very few independent-minded consultants and NGOs care (or perhaps dare) to question the clients and/or the strategic and tactical issues involved. Even when *invited* to give independent advice, those consultants and NGOs who 'challenge the boss' or 'rock the boat' by questioning policies and tactics with polite professionalism are frowned upon (and long-remembered) in many cultures.

Can we really be surprised, considering all these counter-productive forces at play, that inadequate progress has been made toward meeting the Millennium Development Goals in the last decade?

Conclusions

The *Collusion of Corruption* among major donors and recipient/host countries remains powerful, despite years of effort given to refining laws, procedures, policing, and auditing techniques. Why? I have presented a few of the underlying reason here. Some might fall into the category of structural reasons. The culture of poor nations tends to be based on hierarchies, family ties, clans and patronage. Under such conditions, the money flowing from the developed world toward the problems of a huge underclass is likely to vanish into the bank accounts of those who have never known that slice of life (and their relatives), or who have escaped from it. Other reasons might be gathered under categories such as "specialization," "human nature," and "turf-control."

For most observers, it has become increasingly difficult to locate an ethical spine within the development industry, particularly among those in leadership roles. But that is not to say that change isn't possible. International and national institutions and organizations are the product of humans and can be changed by humans, in order that this developmental aid is redirected toward improving the lives of all humans, not only for the Centroid Elite.

In the next chapter, I'm going to show you how.

6
The Challenges of Decentralization

My years in the field and behind the scenes in the development industry have led me to the conclusion that both aid programs and national development initiatives, to be effective, must be carried out largely at the district level. The elites in the development industry have, time and again, underscored the importance of strong central government to the effective administering of aid. That may well be. But strong central governments are also very much prone to corruption, inefficiency, and misdirected effort, however anodyne their stated intentions may be. At its best, developmental aid can reduce poverty and spur economic growth, and especially local economic growth (as opposed to national balance sheets)—the kind of growth that benefits people and communities in rural areas and urban slums. My contention is that such goals can only be met through a decentralized approach to aid administration. And the same is true of administering national development efforts involving the extraction and sale of natural resources. A decentralized focus is likely to be more successful at reducing poverty, raising living standards, and all the rest.

The centralized method of aid distribution in widespread use today in the industry, on the other hand, might fairly be described as premeditated, legalized, grand larceny among the power elites of the development community, working in collusion with authoritarian regimes who also benefit from the associated prestige and cash-flow involved. As you know, I have termed this multilayered labyrinth as Centroid Power.

Such forms of government will probably never go away among the nations who are most in need of aid, and any realistic plan or reform will have to take that fact into account. Yet I am convinced of the necessity to develop methods to decentralize aid programs and national development efforts to the district level. Why? In most governments, the district is linked to providing support to villages, urban slums and communities, and also to receiving support (financial, technical, managerial, and administrative) from the provincial and central levels. As such, the district is uniquely positioned to deal efficiently with investments on a sustained basis, and to empower and galvanize support from the communities it serves.

This being the case, it seems to me I ought to be more explicit about how decentralized aid management works.

Decentralization's core idea is that the central level of authority should have a subsidiary function, shouldering only the tasks that can't be carried out at a more immediate or local level. In the development industry, both the international and domestic development agencies spend a good deal of time justifying their role by convincing each other (which is not difficult) that the region/provincial level, and more especially the district level, is unable to perform any but the most minor duties without the 'enlightenment' assistance only they can provide. As a result, all too often funds are dispersed cautiously, thus starving the district of resources and creating an obvious neocolonial dependency. No one would question that it takes time, money, training of specialists and staff to develop district-level infrastructure, capacities, and systems. But that's what aid and national development money is for. It is precisely these activities (and recurrent expenditures) that enable the local areas to perform tasks effectively. To those skeptics and naysayers who detect an inherent weakness in local personnel that renders them unable to learn techniques and handle responsibilities, I say, it isn't so. (Perhaps these critics have not been to the field and seen innovations in recent decades.)

The question then becomes: How can the distribution methods

used by the development industry be re-oriented to insure that a greater proportion of aid is actually put to use productively at the district and village levels. That's the point I propose to elaborate here, offering a general framework of the functions that a decentralized system must perform. (I'll provide further specifics in subsequent chapters.)

Under a more decentralized scheme, the role of the *central government* would remain critical. However, it would be refocused toward the functions it is best suited to fulfill.

(a) It would serve as a "knowledge center" dedicated to storing, analyzing, and making available to others the data and information gathered throughout the provinces and districts.

(b) It would remain in touch with various regional legislatures and districts to establish consistent policies, and monitor the failure or success of ongoing programs, making use of inputs from district administrators and locally empowered groups.

(c) The central agencies entrusted with a foreign-assisted project or national development efforts would have fiduciary responsibility for it.

(d) Consistent with all functions, the central government finance responsibility would include budgeting, and set budget ceilings in its various regions appropriate to the region's issues and resources. It would establish low-cost planning and budgeting protocols and work with regions, districts and empowered local groups to determine mid-term and annual budgets.

(e) It would establish technical guidelines within and among sectors, departments and agencies, and pass on relevant information as new techniques and technologies prove their worth.

(f) It would supply the overarching perspective necessary to determine where and when it would be beneficial to integrate sectors or technical specialties.

(g) It would conduct oversight and monitor technical guidelines and performance; and give explanation and guidance on how to improve performance.

(h) It would audit programs, evaluate performance, and present findings for taking action. This auditing function will inevitably raise interesting questions, such as: What percentage of income generated in a resource-rich region should remain there, as opposed to being 'sucked up' by the central government or more equitably distributed to its neighbors?

In essence, these functions would involve collection and management of information, coordination of resources, evaluation of results, and distribution of technical support to the districts. The Central government would retain its fiduciary responsibilities but would be less deeply involved in planning annual and mid-term (five-year) budgets.

The Regional government, meanwhile, as part of the same reorganization effort, would curtail its ceremonial and perfunctory administrative functions, concentrating its attention on providing strategic and technical planning, budgeting, and financial support to strengthen infrastructure and manage operations at district and field levels. It would co-ordinate annual and mid-term (usually five-year) budgeting for districts and also become a 'training hub,' working with central level ministries to provide technical support and field level training to the districts. It would also sponsor and coordinate initiatives for local economic growth with small and midsize businesses in the private sector.

The team of administrators, managers, and technical specialists based at the district level would focus on strengthening essential infrastructure—both the civil works (roads, water supply, health centers, schools and training centers, warehouses and where applicable electric power) and managerial infrastructure, including delivery systems related to agriculture, health care, and education. Some countries already have this kind of district infrastructure; however, in many poor and very poor countries and districts, developing this essential infrastructure will take time and money, as well as a full complement of technical and managerial professionals in the fields of agriculture, health, education, water supply and quality, management, and local economic development. (We will leave for a later chapter the obvious question: If such basic infrastructure is still lacking in many poor countries, where has all the project money been spent over a half-century?)

Meanwhile, data will be collected on an ongoing basis at this level to update needs assessment, and to plan new projects.

Those working at the village/urban slum level will find themselves involved in the nitty-gritty of getting things done, and of dispersing knowledge to all households in the communities involved, with the end in mind of establishing and reinforcing local self-reliance and self-sufficiency. Part of this work will involve nurturing a cadre of local leaders that can support the ongoing work of local empowerment.

> If such basic infrastructure is still lacking in many poor countries, where has all the project money been spent over a half-century?

The main *principles and strategic elements* in decentralization are fairly easy to specify in general terms. I am well aware that some of them stand at odds to the ones that help elites sustain their positions of authority, even at the local level.

In districts and countries that have not developed the local systems I referred to above, NGOs are often the most active agents at work at the district level, and one strategic element of any decentralization program would be to make the most of these groups. In many countries, some NGOs act independently from any government department whilst others provide services on government contracts—for example, to provide basic healthcare services in particular locales. Their programs and budgets often escape close scrutiny and their activities are seldom coordinated with other programs in the field. Yet these groups often perform yeoman service to villages and urban slums. In such situations, it would be important that the initial phase of a decentralized project be focused on district functional infrastructure, systems, and particularly *services* *delivered to villages and urban slums.*[*]

Beyond that, it might be feasible to fund specific NGOs with impressive performance records to continue the same work, paying special attention to training district staff and villagers. The end result would be that the NGO might work itself out of a job. In some activities, such as immunization programs, the NGO could continue to work in conjunction with technical staffs from the central and provincial levels. In some countries the NGO might contract staff to fill district positions and train government candidates for, say, up to three years. The incentive to completing such projects successfully, aside from the obvious one of helping people in need, would be the promise of additional district contracts.

In the initial phase of a pilot project,[†] at least one Regional Integrated Training Center would be required, where professional staff and specialists from the central ministries and province could upgrade the skills of administrators, managers, and specialists at district level. Individuals selected to represent their communities in planning and supporting implementation of the projects would also be involved. The Provincial Integrated Training Center would also offer sessions and network opportunities for small and midsize businesses to learn about new technologies and initiatives and to improve their skills in preparing bids for government contracts, thus encouraging local economic growth in the private sector.

After these 'selected and nurtured' districts are 'renewed' and function with a full complement of personnel, two new elements might be added during a second five-year phase. First, these 'nurtured and renewed' districts will become trainers for adjacent districts.

---

[*] The reader, whether experienced in field level work or not, would have an appreciation for the complexities involved in getting district and local systems to function on a reliable basis, providing services, and creating the environment for local economic growth in villages and urban slums.

[†] In Chapters 9 through 11, I present a framework to address the systemic issues plaguing the development industry and offer details of a multi-phased pilot project which incorporates several of the specifics discussed in this (and other) chapters.

Second, money saved from paying NGOs will be used for basic direct payments for 'community volunteers' to support sectoral and multi-sector initiatives among the families involved. There would be infrastructure investments for a network of District Level Integrated Training Centers (some countries would have multiple districts use one integrated training center). These centers would schedule a wide range of classes for local staff, community leaders, and businessmen.

The planning, budgeting and financing for district level functional infrastructure would be integrated among sectors of local economic development, agriculture and water, health, and education. For example, a district agricultural project designed to combat malnutrition would be linked to local health and economic development initiatives.

It will be essential to build district level infrastructure with *straightforward planning and budgeting, administration, managerial processes, and procedures*. Technical support teams from the specific central and provincial technical units will derive and update appropriate 'best practices' and technologies from ongoing research (that are compared with control trials) into program results, and then work directly with the piloted districts and local levels to implement those practices. Once these 'best practices' are functional and have been tested and monitored, they can be replicated and adapted among the districts. The designed 'packet' inputs are envisioned to be both integrated and uniquely separate interventions in villages and urban slums, with costs linked to performance. On a broader scale, the parameters and results of such programs can be coordinated among donors and adapted to 'scale up' to other districts within the piloted country and also to other parts of the world where similar conditions prevail.

Alongside efforts to strengthen district infrastructure, another essential goal of such programs will be *local economic development*, including small-scale agricultural support and marketing businesses. An obvious differentiation for such development will be physical resources—particularly land and water quality and availability—and the size and accessibility of local markets.

It will cost money, of course, to start the 'engines of progress,' but surplus funds are likely to become available as a result of efficiencies in infrastructure development sufficient for small and even midsize local economic initiatives.

One source of such surplus funds would be through an open and transparent bidding system for local private contractors to hire local personnel to build or improve local civil works, schools, health centers, and hospitals. Such physical infrastructural investments would contribute to a 'local multiplier effect' keeping wages and payments in the community, spawning small-business growth, and improving the market for specialized maintenance services, home-improvement ventures, and so on.

Another initiative to stimulate capital formulation among poor families might be to establish reliable, low-cost systems to legally register property rights in farming and livestock ownership. Along similar lines, it would be helpful to establish and monetize property rights for families living in rural communities and urban slums, perhaps using systems designed by Hernando De Soto and replicated by his teams in several countries.[1] Institutionalizing property rights and passing laws to enable local banks to develop criteria and procedures to loan money on property would, among others, catalyze the home improvement industry and other small businesses. Approaches may be piloted, with strong 'built-in' transparency, that create a 'success' incentive for local banks to participate with the property owners. And giving women and men access to viable and well-managed *low-cost* micro-credit schemes would also energize the local economy and foster *capital accumulation* for these poor families. Unfortunately all microcredit schemes are not designed to benefit poor villagers and scams must be ferreted out early by the various agencies involved, the media, and local populations.[2]

Foreign-assisted projects can also include economic development funds for local entrepreneurs, though the World Bank has concluded from multi-country research that bureaucratic constraints dramatically impede business startups and foster corruption with regard to getting the required licenses, etc. Hence, little progress is likely in this area until laws and institutions are overhauled.[3]

There is no way to know what tax revenues might result from such local economic initiatives, but whatever the case may be, those revenues should be directed to financing *local operating systems* that directly impact business improvements such as public works and communication, and local social services and education. (Small-scale, family-based businesses, some based on *low-cost* microcredit schemes, have thrived in some countries, while in others, very tight control of land resources by rural elites has created a large class of basically landless peasants who work for daily subsistence wages.)

Meanwhile, potential performance maps should be worked up at the district level, highlighting the physical parameters of a given area, including soil type, water sources, elevation, micro-nutrient deficiency, land ownership (tenure, rent, and possibly retaining a share of the production), housing, and health and primary education facilities. Other geographic mapping of populations, demographic characteristics, and needs can be added as the project unfolds. The purpose of such maps is to estimate the performance potential of various localized parts of a district as well as the level and location of investments such as health centers, primary schools, water supply for domestic usage, markets, and local irrigation systems. Such information will be invaluable in determining how successful a given project has been or might be. Electronic information (GIS) can be very useful in some cases, when available, though there is really no substitute for field level research. In any case, the process of accumulating and distilling data for planning and budgeting should not be 'held hostage' to out-of-date and expensive electronic information.

One key requirement for a successful program would be to establish *legal and procedural protocols for transferring money to the districts*. Trials might be conducted to ascertain that these financial subsystems operate efficiently. The use of electronic technology, including electric transfer of funds and information, may be useful here.

In short, decentralization at district level is a dynamic process, rife with potential, but also fraught with challenges in both design and implementation. To make such schemes functional will require professionals who can capitalize on the latest technological developments and are also well-versed in field-work. The flexibility to be found at district level makes it easier to solve problems creatively there.

Professionals in the development industry have been working on various aspects of decentralization for at least fifty years. For example, the World Bank site offers a link, "East Asia Decentralize–Making Local Government Work in East Asia," which I commend to interested readers.[4] In Chapter 1 the authors, Roland White and Paul Smoke, signal three main challenges of decentralization in Asian countries, regardless of the country's political persuasion. (i) To design sound intergovernmental organizational arrangements. (ii) To establish robust financial mechanisms for channeling money to sub-national governments, so as to avoid delays like the one I myself often ran into in Ghana and Indonesia. (iii) To hold local governments accountable for the effectiveness of their management systems.

One also finds in the literature a useful sub-classification of administrative and fiscal decentralization which might help us to deal with the pragmatics faced in the development industry. This classifies administrative decentralization as *deconcentration*, *delegation* and *devolution*. (See box on next page.)

For many countries, deconcentration would be the best option because local institutions remain underdeveloped and require the oversight of central administration. As we will learn in the next chapter, there have not been many successful examples of decentralization in developing and emerging countries. However, with robust infrastructure and delivery systems, continued development of human resource skills, and functioning management and monitoring during the pilot and extended project, a solid foundation could be created

Administrative Classes of Decentralization

Deconcentration consists of transferring some of the central government's responsibilities for specific functions to smaller (sub-national) units of government. Such transfers of authority can involve varying degrees of increased autonomy and local input into decision making.

The term *delegation* refers to a transfer of functions, including health, education and water, for example, in which the central level sets the service standards, designs intergovernmental transfers, controls the degree of monitoring, and sets the balance of decision-making between the central and local levels.

Devolution is the most complete form of decentralization. While there is variation in application, the central government devolves certain functions and sets of services, transfers decision-making and finance aspects (including intergovernmental transfers), responsibility and management to subnational units of government that elect officials and raise revenue from defined sources, such as cost recovery and user charges of services, land and building taxes, and from natural resources. Devolution enables the autonomous local government greater flexibility in determining priorities and hence, public expenditure patterns. Determinates for well-functioning devolution includes (i) the central and local government to keep commitments in devolving functions and providing services, (ii) transparent local government with (iii) empowered local participation.

upon which further devolution could take place. It's likely that central government will retain control, or technical management, of some aspects of health, education and agriculture. And effective anti-corruption measures, as always, need to be taken before devolution can take place effectively. Also, focus on MGD and LED must be sustained, regardless of what form decentralization takes.

Reflecting on the analytic and classificatory efforts of White and Smoke, which are largely lacking in concrete examples, confirms my hypothesis that real decentralization is anathema to Centroid Power.

A host of questions present themselves at this point:

"Did the resources and project initiative get to the villages and people under the coconut trees? If not, why not?"

"What does Centroid Power have to gain by promoting decentralization while simultaneously implementing financial processes that undermine the likelihood of success?"

"What were the goals of the process and how well did the results measure up?"

"What is the likelihood that adequate resources will be available over the espoused lifetime of the project?"

"What must be changed, and by who, to make decentralization really happen?"

7
Six Practical Lessons for Decentralization

I am pragmatic and not a bureaucratic 'process freak.' I seek streamlined and effective institutional structures and governance, laws, regulations, and administrative, financial and managerial processes. It comes as no surprise that I view decentralized functionality from the perspective of all people living and working in districts, their cities, villages, and urban slums. Following that path, I have identified six decentralization projects that provide lessons—positive and negative—for future adaptation and expansion. My choices were influenced by the project's scope (within one or more sectors), size, duration, a likely adaptability to other regions.

THE WORLD BANK

There are few substantive examples of decentralization projects that provides necessary insights on how to tackle the many issues involved. It is our good fortune that the World Bank Independent Evaluation Group (IEG) in 2008 produced a lengthy report entitled: "Decentralization in Client Countries – An Evaluation of World Bank Support, 1990 – 2007."[1] This report gathers seventeen years of experience in such matters into one set of findings and recommendations. It includes results of 222 projects in 20 countries (including two each in Europe and the Middle East – North Africa) of the 89 in which the bank supported decentralization activities. The total amount of lending involved was $22 million—certainly not an excessive amount for the number of projects involved.

One of the main Millennium Development Goals is primary

education, particularly for girls. This is considered especially important because basic education for girls in tied to generational support to their mothers as well as family nutrition and health-related issues, together with economic opportunities for higher income and capital accumulation for themselves and their family. Though we might expect that the decentralization efforts included in the study would be evaluated in terms of such outcome indicators as "proportion of children completing basic education," such data was unavailable.

Based on measurements the study *did* generate, it was determined that the countries that benefited most from the programs already *had* some sort of institutional focus on the functions and responsibilities of elected local governments.

The report presents results from a dazzling array of single-sector strategies directed toward issues such as water resources, forests, sustainable environment, education, and the development of public institutions in rural areas. The Bank was clearly aware that local elites did not often direct resources and provision of services towards the poorest and most peripheral populations. In most of the countries evaluated, the Bank did little to factor in the influence of special interest groups working either to enhance or undermine the efforts toward reforms. Nor did it spend much time assaying which reforms would have the greatest likelihood of sustaining political 'equilibrium,' or what would be appropriate levels of oversight from central or regional levels to the district.

In any case, measuring the impact of decentralization will *never* be easy. It will require consistent long-term monitoring and evaluation at local levels by individuals capable of discriminating between the myriad of factors involved.

The Bank's espoused objective in supporting government efforts in decentralization is to develop sub-national administrative capacities in sector-specific fields. Of course, these objectives are more likely to be met when client states show genuine commitment to the decentralization program. Generally speaking, and occasionally reading between the lines, this report corroborates several of the points I am stressing within these pages. It underscores the necessity of establishing country-specific preconditions for implementation, a long time-frame for development, sustained investment in infrastructure, and an emphasis on strengthening institutions and systems at the district level.

Indonesia

Indonesia's recent history, some aspects of which I described in Chapter 3, provides us with several illuminating examples of programs aimed at decentralization. Despite a drift toward decentralization during the post-Soeharto period, Indonesia's long-standing deconcentration mode took a major change to devolution in 2011 with the Big Bang (discussed later in this chapter). All the same, its Posyandu project (Integrated MCH Service Post) has some valuable lessons to teach us.

In the late 1970s, the leadership was able to corral the various technical specialists in family planning, nutrition, obstetrics, general medicine, pediatrics and child care, immunization, and other specialties, to collaborate in planning modules that were then incorporated in annual budgets at the central and provincial level. These projects were funded through donors and also had substantial government support. They entailed the training of large numbers of staff and volunteers, and complex logistics by health centers teams supported by women volunteers in the villages involved. To mention keeping vaccines to specific levels in the tropics through managing 'cold chains' to tens of thousands of villages throughout the archipelago gives you some appreciation and admiration of the complexities that were overcome through full central, regional, district, and local village coordination. The initiative was popular and continued throughout the heyday of the Washington Consensus, though it was dropped when the Soeharto regime made its exit in May 1989; the democratically elected leadership that followed chose not to sustain a vibrant program. Even with the good will of the public and all concerned, these kinds of programs and initiatives need technical services, coordination, local participation and operational costs, which do not happen by accident. In June 2005 it was confirmed by the Minister of Health that 60 percent of some 200,000 Posyandus nationally were not functioning.[2] Thus Indonesia follows the long-standing pattern by which an incoming regime discards even the most popular and successful of its predecessor's programs. Yet public support health systems for communities have not vanished in Indonesia, so it's not quite appropriate to say that the 'baby was thrown out with the bathwater' when Soeharto left.

Agriculture – Increased Rice Production

Rice was the staple food of the Indonesian diet in the 1970s, as it is today. For decades the government fine-tuned a policy to stabilize rice prices for urban consumers, reducing malnutrition and expanding domestic output. In 1970 Indonesia was a major rice importer but by 1985 it had achieved self-sufficiency and more, producing two-and-a-half times more rice than it needed.[3] Indonesia had succeeded in linking strategic goals with tactical implementation by adopting high-yield rice varieties, expanding the reach of irrigation, and subsidizing fertilizers and pesticides. As a result, between 1976 and 1996 to percentage of 'poor people' in Indonesia fell from 40 percent to 11 percent of the population—an amazing achievement by any standards. The average annual GDP growth rate for that period was 7 percent. Although the rice economy was rife with corruption by many accounts, during this phase of Indonesia's development the strong central government control appears to have used all the levers and finances to improve the rice economy which obviously takes place at quite literally the field level.

> What had taken nearly 30 years to accomplish was wiped out in less than two! Development certainly is serious business, especially when you're a landless peasant in Java…

Community-Driven Development through Block Grants[4]

The aftermath the 1997 Asian economic crisis left cruel legacies. In Indonesia, the pre-crisis poverty rate of 17.6 percent rose to 23.4 percent. *What had taken nearly 30 years to accomplish was wiped out in less than two!* Development certainly is serious business, especially when you're a landless peasant in Java or the Indonesian 'outer islands.'

In the mid-1980s the World Bank began to initiate projects in collaboration with the Indonesian Ministry of Health and the National Family Planning Board focused on decentralization. The focus was on developing the methods and tools to train teams at the district level, allowing them to have greater control of bottom-up planning and detailed annual budgeting for part of their total budget. These projects were mainly in provinces outside of Java and Bali since the 'outer islands' were less powerful politically, with smaller populations and a more rudimentary infrastructure and service pipe-line. In the main, these pioneering projects were not successful, due to excessive meddling by Centroid interests, but they served the important purpose of showing that decentralization programs operating at the district level would be possible to implement under more favorable conditions.

In the late 1990s the World Bank made another thrust based on similar principles, employing a model of community–based development to increase local empowerment and strengthen administrative autonomy and civic capacity at the local level. The model became the flagship of the Community-Driven Development program in Indonesia and elsewhere. One key feature was the use of *block grants* to districts, sub-districts, and villages. The money was used for small-scale infrastructure projects and social or economic activities chosen by the community through a participatory planning process. This program, called KDP in Indonesia, has run from 1998 to the present, with the aid of funding from many sources. By 2008 KDP covered 90 percent of the provinces, about 60 percent of the districts, close to 40 percent of the sub-districts and 50 percent of the almost villages 70,000!

Infrastructure built through these projects cost 30 percent less, on average, than those built through more traditional approaches. More than 70 percent of the beneficiaries of the projects were the poorer members of the communities, with millions of them receiving wages. Part of the funds were distributed as loans to individuals and businesses at market interest, with the interest plowed back to the village's priorities. Overall there has been genuine local empowerment and transparency with these block grants. As of 2006 close to $2 billion has been used for KDP projects. That amount may sound large, but it's perhaps less than 15 percent of the total aid budget over 20 years (in 2006 prices), when all donor projects with government investments and recurrent costs for medical care and the public and preventive services are factored in. Much more needs to be allocated in this way if we are to fully reap the benefits that decentralized aid programs can generate.

An assessment of the KDP in 2002[5]

Andrea Woodhouse, a consultant to the World Bank, conducted field interviews in 2002 to judge the effectiveness of the KDP program. She had the support and cooperation of the Bank, government officials at the Ministry of Home Affairs in charge of the KDP, and various ministries in the provinces, districts and sub-districts where the program had been implemented. Ms. Woodhouse focused on corruption in the KDP, and her report presents graphic illustrations of how powerful local officials used 'tried-and-true' methods to reap personal gain from a subservient population with impunity.

Ms. Woodhouse identifies *three loci of corruption* risks in KDP, in addition to that of the village elites receiving kickbacks. One is nepotism in appointing technical personnel. Another is the habit of implementation teams who buy inferior inputs and pocket the difference. Ms. Woodhouse observes that there are mechanisms built into KDP program to counter such efforts by maintaining transparency during the steps of selection, budgeting, getting bids from local suppliers, checking and verification payments, and reviewing completed projects. And KDP facilitators work directly with villagers to prepare and then implement the grants, and later act as arbitrators if disputes arise related to corruption or misdirected initiatives. Selected NGOs and local media publicize such incidents and throw an unwelcome spotlight on the officials involved. It's significant that in the post-Soeharto period of openness, villagers (often in groups) have shown the courage to protest against corrupt activities in their village, and been rewarded for their efforts.

In KDP, the villagers play a role in planning for their block grant and in every step of procurement, fund management, and implementation. Ms. Woodhouse distills the various features into a chart that touches on many of the virtues of decentralized aid projects:

Community control & simplicity	• Direct transfer of funds into village bank accounts. • No local government control • Villagers control budgets • Financial formats are simplified so villagers can understand them.
Socialization	• Villagers learn how the project is supposed to work, what their rights are and what to do if they are unhappy.
Transparency	• All financial information is made public and publicly displayed in villages. • Simplifying financial formats so that they can be understood easily by villagers. • Complaints database will be published in newspapers.
Limited monopoly	• All goods to be procured require at least three quotations collective village bank accounts.
Limited discretion	• All financial transactions require at least three signatures collective village bank accounts.

Accountability mechanisms	• Regular village meetings to account for funds. Disbursals can be suspended if misuse of funds is suspected.
Monitoring & follow-up	• Regular project monitoring, complaints tracking & follow-up. • Independent monitoring by civil society groups & journalists.

Ms. Woodhouse pinpoints the third locus of corruption as most common—a ubiquitous managerial-type positions appointed by the central government. These employees were naturally prone to developing networks of patronage, making nepotistic appointments, rigging contracts to their own benefit, and so on. She points out that the village representative board (BPD) was elected by popular vote, and has the power to ask for the removal of the village head. On the other hand, board members need money to campaign for their office, which is itself a temptation to further corruption.

But such issues aside, the KDP program stands as a rare but illuminating example of the *long-term block grant program with significant local participation at many levels.* (I will further examine the lessons learned from the KDP project along with Ms. Woodlouse's analysis of them in Chapter 11)

Post-Soeharto 'Big Bang' Decentralization Realities

Alongside these KDP initiatives, in 2001 Indonesia began a radical and rapid decentralization program referred to as 'Big Bang' Decentralization. It passed two laws (Law No. 22/1999 Regional governance, prepared in the Ministry of Home Affairs, and Law No. 25/1999 Fiscal arrangements, prepared in the Ministry of Finance) that gave broad autonomy to districts that otherwise were restricted to obvious national priorities such as defense, security, justice, foreign affairs, and monetary and fiscal affairs. The initiative authorized the local governments, predominately the *kabupatan* (Indonesian districts) retain almost all revenue from land and property tax, the acquisition of land and building rights, and natural resources (including forestry, public mining and fishery sector). In Indonesia's important industries of oil and gas, the central government would retain 85 percent of the revenues from oil mining and 70 percent from gas. Also, the central government would retain 80 percent of revenue from income tax.

In turn, the local governments were assigned a greater burden of obligatory functions in health, education, public work, environment agriculture, infrastructure services and other areas. A prescient article (2002) by Seymour and Turner, with ample references from Indonesian scholars and experts, offered insights into the background to the laws, described the long-term regional and ethnic distrust associated with it, and projected likely abuses in implementation.[6] These include: "the level of autonomy is inappropriate; there is no improvement to fiscal autonomy; there is a lack of overall finance; resource rich provinces are favoured; there are a number of 'grey areas'; and the implementation is being attempted on an inappropriate time scale, concerns being raised regarding human resource capabilities."

The post-Soeharto period has given Indonesian scholars unprecedented openness. An insightful, well-referenced analysis a decade after the 'Big Bang' by Tri Widodo Wahyu Utomo, (Head, Public Administration Research Center for Public Management (PKMK)), corroborated key points of Seymour and Turner's 2002 work, and identified further challenges to the successful implementiation of Indonesia's 'good governance' in decentralization.[7] Among other issues, the author explored the impact of kinship systems involving the families of members of Parliament and wealthy individuals who contined to control the profits associated with natural resourse exploitation, thus undermining services for poor families and eroding trust all around.

Of course, Indonesia is not unique in this regard. Mr. Utomo argues that, in principle, strengthened bureaucratic reform act as an effective counterweight to the power of local dynasties. A 2006 report by the Social Monitoring and Early Response Unit of the health sector found that only 53 percent of districts in the sample met the minimum standards of service set by the central government, and only a few *puskesmas* (health center at sub-district level) had the resources required to meet the minimum standards of service. The modes of corruption, particularly at village level, were similar to those Ms. Woodhouse described.

Mr. Utomo recommended that bureaucracy be reformed by refreshing the leadership and increasing local capacities. He further argued that business regulations be made less onerous and the balance between central and regional agencies be tipped away from the capitol.

Fast forward to 2011, and we find that devolution as 'regional autonomy' (*otonomi daerah* in Indonesian) without adequate preparation in districts and villages/slums has created a 'pincer movement' whereby Centroid Power and local (often wealthy) elites control all central funds, while the local elite in provinces endowed with natural resources also control the revenue from that source. Since central funds are predominately used on personnel with insufficient amounts devoted to the operations, the effect is to further exacerbate distress in the poor regions and district, while leaving health, agriculture and education programs stranded on the runway.

Two reports of note provide an incisive critique of this 'Big Bang' decentralization effort. The two questions are: After all of the pronouncements associated with the 'Big Bang' – How much money and resources actually have been delivered to provincial and district levels? And what was that money used for?

Heywood and Harahap (2008) collected and analyzed financial data for FY 2006 at fifteen districts in three populous Java provinces (each population over twenty million people) the district office and district hospital. They found that public funding to districts for health services more than doubled between 2001 and 2006; and that the districts took on greater responsibility in delivering the services.[8]

The budgeting system in Indonesia is highly fragmented. For example, our work in the late 1970s revealed that a health center could be financed from up to fourteen different sources and the doctor in charge of the health center had little or no discretion on the expenditure pattern or income to be generated. Therefore, Heywood and Harahap found it expedient to focus on actual salaries and remuneration. This understates the amount directly spent through central ministry of health budgets for investments and recurrent costs, which are not inconsequential. To my surprise, the authors found that the central government contributed about 90 percent of the district government's health budget, with about 40 percent of the expenditure for personnel, most of whom were permanent civil servants. Hence, less than one-third of the districts health budgets were discretionary, with implications for what district-level decision-makers might actually be able to fund as second-order priorities. Furthermore, the split between district hospitals and health offices/health centers was 43:57 respectively; and this includes central ministry of health budget support. The authors conclude that irrespective of the hoopla (my imagery) associated with the Big Bang decentralization, *the central level remained in the driver seat for prioritizing programs, projects, and budgets in the Indonesian government health sector.* These patterns and results parallel those which a colleague and I found with an array of provinces including the non-Java 'outer islands' about thirty years earlier! (See Chapter 3.)

The second paper, by Rinaldi, Purnomo, and Damayanti (2007), on fighting corruption in decentralized Indonesia, is more troubling, though not unusual or unexpected.[9] These Indonesian authors were part of a World Bank team that had good access and studied cases of corruption in five provinces including East Java. Their focus was local. The authors interviewed 200 informants and had 13 focal group discussions with 150 participants, including community members, law enforcers, corruption suspects and their legal advisors, 'local anti-corruption actors' and media representatives. They documented the dynamics of how corruption cases are reported and resolved, and also how the corrupt practices were conducted in the first place. They identified 'success factors' and continued weaknesses of local anti-corruption agents. The findings were disseminated through a series of regional seminars in each research location through May and June 2007.

Five years after the 'Big Bang' decentralization program, the authors found similarities among the 'local anti-corruption actors' who collected and analyzed the relevant information, and carried out a few successful prosecutions. The upshot of the study was that *decentralization actually increased opportunities for corruption* at provincial and district levels, since there were inconsistent regulations among the local budgets and generally low levels of public participation in governance. Perhaps we could chalk it all up to the fact that the expedited 'Big Bang' program failed to prepare the concomitant regulations, procedures, and managerial processes required to supervise budget transfers, tenders and contracts, and disbursement. The study also sheds light on how difficult it is to train professionals at the local level to follow up on these administrative and managerial processes.

The report recommends substantive additional support to local civil groups to enhance anticorruption initiatives. It suggests that law enforcement institutions and anti-corruption organizations step up efforts to education the public about the hazards of corruption and also the remedies available. It recommends that benchmarks be established for the duration of each phase of legal proceedings to prevent bribery aimed at stretching out the legal process. And it supports the notion that a letter from the Attorney General's Office be circulated requiring District Prosecutors' Offices to hold case presentations for anti-corruption organizations and facilitate community organizations to conduct public examination of court verdicts.

Some Lessons Learned

Indeed the 2007 report offered prescient advice, to judge from the sobering impressions to be found in a more recent (2013) newspaper account in which the Deputy Finance Ministry alleges that the decentralization of districts and provinces is being driven by local politicians for their own financial gain. One-third (Rp. 586 trillion or $50 billion) of the 2014 state budget has been allocated to regions, and the Deputy Finance Minister expresses great concern regarding who will receive them and how they will be managed. A recent Home Ministry study concludes that only 22 percent of regional governments in Indonesia are performing well.[10]

Indonesia presents us with an especially interesting example of a complex and heavily-populated society (237 million in 2011, the world's fourth most populous country) that has endured the grip of Centroid Power for decades, and yet has seen the need to engage in decentralization efforts—with some success! The Suharto regime provides us with far-reaching programs under which essential technical support from the central level was merged with village-level community participation, yielding decades of improved health status and MCH care. It also exhibits in full measure the continuing challenge of corruption under such operating procedures. Certainly the Indonesian decentralization experiences provide useful points of comparison with other developing countries with smaller populations, both village- and urban-based, who face the same challenging issues.

8
Millennium Villages Project (MVP)

We turn now to the village level and discuss a major project for the UN emanating from and focused on the Millennium Development Goals. As you will recall, there are eight principal MDG's. Albeit a simplification, some of the key goals are to reduce levels of 'extreme poverty,' malnutrition, childhood mortality and maternal mortality, and to increase the availability of potable water, basic sanitation, and basic education, particularly for girls. The target date was 2015, but two years after the UN and other major development agencies adopted the MDG's, it was already obvious that many developing countries would struggle mightily to meet even some of them, and the UN eventually initiated a second program, the Millennium Villages Project (MVP) under the Earth Institute at Columbia University.

Since the MVP was (and remains) a high-profile project with lofty goals and objectives, it deservedly receives close scrutiny from professionals within the development industry. It bears our attention here because it offers compelling evidence of what aspects of a well-funded, highly articulated program might work, and why. At the same time, it exposes places where results fail to meet expectations, regardless of the talent and funding involved.

Overview

The MVP began in 2004, focusing on ten sub-Saharan African countries. But the project's focus (as the name implies) was actually more tightly circumscribed than that. It involves eighty villages clustered into fourteen different sites that encompassed approximately six hundred thousand people. The clustered sites are located in widely dispersed agro-ecological zones representing farm systems used by 90 percent of the population in agricultural and 93 percent of the agricultural land in sub-Saharan Africa.[*][1] The Overall Goals of the MVP, put in its simplest terms, is to spark local economic development in these fourteen population clusters, all of which lie in the poorest regions of rural Africa.

The methods employed are not terribly innovative. They include supplying provision of high-yield seeds, fertilizer, and basic medicines; digging drinking wells and building sanitation facilities, erecting schools and clinics; distributing insecticide-treated bednets and antiviral drugs; and trainings local staffs and members of the community.

What makes this project different? Perhaps it's the high-profile intensity of the approach, the ambitious breadth of the interventions, and the focus on demonstrable results within a circumscribed area and period of time. As two professional observers remarked: "The trait that defines the genre is the simultaneous introduction of a broad package of intense and expensive intervention in a limited area of poor, rural regions over a few years in order to spark lasting economic development once the intervention ends." (Clemens and Demombynes: see page 159.)

The MVP intervention costs approximately $150 per resident per year in each MV cluster (in 2009 dollars) which is about the average income per capita for each residence, or about as large as the entire local economy of the intervention site. This level of support was based on international targets of 0.07% of gross national income in ODA (though only the Netherlands and the Nordic countries currently contribute at that rate).

Many private corporations have collaborated in the MVP project, including Ericsson (mobile telephony and wireless internet coverage), General Electric (healthcare equipment), JMEagle

---

[*] I encourage readers who wish to understand the background, current features and longer-term direction/aspirations of the MVP to go to the website http://millenniumvillages.org/the-villages/ ; which also has a full set of past and updated reports.

(large-scale water piping), Swiss Re (new weather-based insurance), Becton Dickson (diagnostics and pharmaceutical supplies), Novartis (malaria medicines), Pepsi (village-based irrigation), Lenova and Sony (supply computers) and Sumitomo Chemical (long-lasting insecticide-treated bed-nets). Other companies are looking for opportunities for socially-responsible giving, as well selling their products and services to the MVPs. Certainly private-sector collaboration can supplement support for MVPs.

Meanwhile, developing countries in many parts of the world have been pursuing the same Millennium Development Goals without benefit of the MVP. Yet the 2010 UN Summit did not produce many examples of substantial progress toward those goals. Unfortunately, neither did the Millennium Village Project. The project's website emphasizes the importance of *local ownership* in the Millennium Villages. It describes the need to include community participation and training for both men and women. Local committees are supposed to identify village-specific project initiatives that are deemed most appropriate and cost-effective. Other reports mention input from local government but less explicitly. Indeed, the framework for 'local ownership' of MVs is progressive.

> …beneath the veneer, it is a 'top down' program (despite a few meetings with local people in villages) with a pre-set template of distinct sectoral interventions that dovetail with the Millennium Development Goals.

Is this really taking place? Several seasoned commentators think not.[2] Edward Carr's assessed the MVP and came to the conclusion that beneath the veneer, it is a 'top down' program (despite a few meetings with local people in villages) with a pre-set template of distinct sectoral interventions that dovetail with the Millennium Development Goals. He seems to think that it will reinforce local power interests without yielding the anticipated MDG results.

Carr has solid appreciation for the heterogeneity of localized and village development in sub-Saharan Africa. He advocates a low-cost 'critical grassroots approach' that doesn't accept solutions *per se* beforehand, but begins in a process by investigating 'who gains and who loses' from any prescribed solutions. It is only after identifying the local power interests and vulnerable members of society, and determining which local problems affect the most vulnerable people, can an appropriate course of action be decided upon. He points out that using indigenous systems often reduces costs and hence aid dependency, and this, in turn, yields solid local participation and sustained results including MDG indices.

Carr presents an interesting hypothetical on inequities within households which he suggests is quite widespread in sub-Saharan Africa. In an era of rapid climate change, households divide farm production by gender: men raise crops for sale and women farm for household subsistence. In years of shortage the men's "market" crops command a premium surplus, which puts the women in a position of greater inequality in the household. This state of affairs works directly against several Millennium Development Goals. Carr's 'critical grassroots approach' seeks to develop a 'livelihood strategy' to counter this fluctuating inequity before blithely adopting packaged intervention. His pragmatic and flexible approach is refreshing, to say the least.

Commentary by Clemens and Demombynes (2010) [3]

Analysts and statisticians Michael Clemens, of the Center for Global Development, and Gabriel Demombynes of the World Bank, recently offered independent, insightful remarks on the Millennium Village Project. In their view, the design of the project will render it impossible to determine convincingly whether or not it has been effective. They suggest that selective changes in the design would allow for a 'rigorous impact evaluation' over a longer term, preferably fifteen years but also within shorter preview frames of five and ten years.

Beyond its relevance to the MVP, Clemens and Demombynes's paper describes a number of concepts and low-cost analytic tools that could be highly useful for evaluating a wide range of development initiatives. Here are a few examples:

The MVP follows a pattern. The authors show that the MVP is only the latest in a long line of village-level development packages undertaken in recent decades in several parts of the world, all of which sought to show that intensifying combinations of interventions would have long-lasting improvements in the living standards of rural residents. Such experiments were undertaken in rural China from the 1930s through 1970s, in India in the 1960s under the intensive agriculture district and community development, and by the World Bank during the 1970s (a program combining agriculture, infrastructure, health, finance, and communication), in Tanzania from the 1960s to the 1980s, and once again in Southwest China in the 1990s. Evidence briefly summarized from the references suggests that *all the efforts were eventually abandoned without producing sustained improvements in rural people's living standards.*

Clemens and Demombynes were keen to compare *input and output indices* from the village clusters receiving the MVP interventions to similar villages that had not been included in the program. What would've happened at the MVP site *without* the MVP interventions? The comparisons would include: (i) similar villages in the same country, (ii) rural region of the same country and (iii) the rural area or province/region where the millennium villages located.

Three of the fourteen village clusters were used with two criteria: (i) the MVP midterm evaluation (June 2010) which had before-and-after data and (ii) publicly available Demographic and Health Survey (DHS, funded through USAID) data that establishing broad trends in the timeframe of the MVP and on most development indicators. Three main village clusters in the analysis were in Kenya, Ghana and Nigeria and some data requirements added two other clusters, one in Uganda and another in Malawi. Among the indices they considered were (i) access to improve drinking water sources, (ii) measles immunization, (iii) birth delivered by skilled personnel, (iv) HIV testing, and (v) insecticide-treated bed net usage. The outputs indices included (a) chronic malnutrition, (b) gross primary school attendance,

(c) mobile phone ownership,(d) malaria prevalence, (e) maize/corn yields. As with many *post hoc* studies and evaluations complete data is unavailable; but the authors provide sets of tables and graphs of the results; and I direct you to the report for the details.

The overall results are striking in a number of ways; let me mention some of the patterns here. First, for many of the indicators, MV sites *did* perform better than the surrounding areas. But Clemens and Demombynes went on to compare that improvement to how neighboring villages that were not in the program had fared during the same period. In Kenya and Ghana, the other villages had also improved, but at only half the rate of the MV sites. They also observed that some indicators suggested the country's rural areas as a whole showed improvements comparable to those highlighted in the MV study. These last two results show that the MV's evaluation technique overstates the effect of the program for most indicators, *because far-less-costly investments in other parts of the regions involved also netted good results.*

Clemens and Demombynes go on to list five main weaknesses with the MVP evaluation protocol, and then suggest modifications that can be brought forward in the next five years of the MVP to make its results more meaningful.

Here briefly are the weaknesses. First, the MV intervention sites selected often had greater political buy-in and community ownership than the comparison villages. For example, the Kenyan village, Sauri, had already been working with international aid groups for fifteen years when it was chosen for the MV project; its local government officials and the villagers could hardly be considered a typical Kenyan village, drawn from random. (I have seen 'favored' villages and districts selected repeatedly for 'trials,' each time becoming more adept at management and better endowed with personnel, so that the results were far more positive that anything a village selected at random would have been likely to produce.)

Second, the *comparison* villages need to be selected more

randomly. Third, the broad baseline data needs to be better. Fourth, the sample *size* needs to be bigger. This becomes highly relevant in detecting changes in child mortality, for example. In the MV project, the size of the plan sample used for measuring child mortality would have required a drop of 40% to be noticed—more than twice as great as the MDG's specified as a worthy target.

Fifth, the time horizon for the evaluation is too short. The MVP is scheduled for two five-year phases, which is insufficient to arrive at definitive conclusions regarding its effectiveness. Though the point is simple enough, it is central to any proper understanding of the challenges facing those who design aid projects: it takes not only sophisticated measurement techniques, but also a long time and a good deal of recurring operational expenses, to determine if a given program actually works.

What's going on here? Why is it that well-financed programs created by very clever people and organizations in the development industry have not delivered reliable positive results? Might it be, as I have been suggesting, that such top-down approaches will never clear a 'pathway' for sustained poverty reduction among the extreme and moderately poor people and families? I'm well aware this generalization is a broad one to throw across the diverse cultures of developing countries on several continents. Yet as all of us who have walked the halls of Centroid Power know, results just don't happen without years (really decades) of investment and recurring expenditures devoted to building the district and local infrastructure, improving people's skill capacities, and strengthening delivery systems. It is also of the utmost importance to cultivate the participation of the people who are to be beneficiaries of these development initiatives, not only because their contributions and perspectives are valuable, but also because as they develop a real stake in meeting their own needs and improving their local delivery systems, the effects will be felt in the morale and sense of empowerment throughout the community.

As I have noted elsewhere, essentially this is very much an *accreationary method of capital formation*. I have also been suggesting that it is not even vaguely within the interests of Centroid Power to see any successful result from decentralization efforts. After all, the essence of decentralization, whether with the *deconcentration* or *devolution* models, extracts money and power from the central level. Don't wait to see if Centroid Power will enable and facilitate sustained success from decentralizing their interests, power and money. They won't.

Agronomic – economic issues

Substantive agronomic research and experience in low income tropical agriculture has identified uses of diverse legume crops to improve soil fertility, thereby improving the quality and yield of food for households at very low costs. One example, in Ekwendeni village (in northern Malawi) using legume crops and non-hybrid seeds, food and health communities project (SFHC) demonstrated similar achievements the Millennium Villages though at substantial lower costs.[4] Comments: Since unexpected escalating fertilizer costs negatively impacted MVP villagers (and the MVP budgets) alternatives such as 'Legume Best Bet' projects sponsored by Collaborative Crop Research Program[5] should be available into small-holder, village based agricultural schemes. The impressive crop research done by the Collaborative Crop Research Program to find ways to increase food security for resource-poor people in seventeen countries (Africa and Latin America), together with the linkages between agriculture and health exemplified by SFHC initiatives, should be tapped. Indeed, it's essential to incorporate field level results from numerous national-based applied agriculture, water, health, energy-related research and "knowledge center' organizations into small-scale schemes and those deemed viable provided by the private sector. I'll be elaborating these points in the proposals put forth in Chapters 9 through 11.

Extended phase of MVP 2011 – 2014

Following analysis of its successes and failures, the program's project managers issued a report (The Millennium Villages Project: The Next Five Years 2011 – 2014) distilling the results from 2006 – 2010 and outlining the path head.[6] To summarize, the main strategies for the next five years include: (i) financing, where the project-type funding 'scales back' from the current 50 percent total estimated costs to zero by 2014 and (ii) 'scale up' new villages in East, Central and West sub-Saharan African countries. Over the next five years the MVP will focus on four main activities: (1) support business development (focused on agribusiness), (2) design real-time information systems, (3) create open-source tools and technologies and (4) transition to full local ownership.

The MVP is building skills and capacities within the countries among villagers and the MVP network; together with predominant MDG modules to improve farming yields and households' nutrition, water and sanitation, local health and educational systems for villagers. These improvements, include advances in information systems and other technologies, shared solar energy systems in remote areas and solar powered lanterns, improved cooking stoves, long-lasting insecticide-treated mosquito nets, integrated soil fertility management, better tools for infrastructure planning, and enhanced community health worker (CHW) systems. They have applicability in villages throughout sub-Saharan Africa and indeed with modification to benefit poor people in other parts of the world.

Despite the optimism within the MVP and United Nations on the positive contributions of the MVP, it is incumbent to address the core issues.

- In the area of financing several questions arise. The report lists approximately 250, individuals, foundations, governments, institutions, corporate partners who generously supported the MVP. While that's a staggering amount of goodwill and resources, it's largely concentrated in the initial five-year MVP phase.

Where are the funds going to come from to finance the remaining five-year period of the MVP, and beginning 2012, the 'scaling up' the MVP concept in the thirteen sub-Saharan African countries selected to participate? The projects goal of providing incentives for small-holders and midsize agribusinesses to adopt innovations will require support from the government, external partners (several UN agencies) and communities. Alas, we are all too familiar with the platitudes of government officials saying *'why certainly, yes we can pay for that.'* All too often, they can't—or won't. *In many countries the pro-poor agenda does not have many forceful advocate within Centroid Power.* Despite negotiations and all the genuine goodwill and relationships developed within the MVP, government funding to expand and sustain MVP projects, *especially the important 'public goods' components* is likely to fall far short of expectation.

- In the area of monitoring and evaluating MDG's, the report describes a two-part process.[7] It first assesses Project performance against a fixed set of goals. The Millennium Development Goals make an obvious choice, though the report also makes use of a few of its own, which may perhaps highlight successes that might have gone unnoticed by more conventional measures. It then works to determine if the observed changes are the result of the Project itself or of more general economic forces such as dramatic weather or other external shocks that would also have a noticeable impact on production in regions not involved in the program.

Will the approach for impact assessment and 'scale up' new villages in East, Central and West sub-Saharan African countries (beginning from early 2012) meet the criteria set by Clemens and Demombynes in relation to rigorous impact evaluation? Two points. First, since the current MVP intentionally did not add 'control villages,' and the MVP villages had greater 'political buy-in and community ownership,' it's difficult to see that the (unspecified) 'reference data' will provide a valid comparison over the ten years, which is a more appropriate time frame to evaluate. Indeed the report (on page 33) emphasizes the MVP is a demonstration project and acknowledged that… "many interventions being assessed are already being scaled-up continent wide, making it nearly impossible to find nearby control groups that are entirely unexposed to their effects." Indeed that is what Clemens and Demombynes analyses concluded—and at far less cost than the MVP!

After MVP second phase, why would we expect any different results when using the Clemens and Demombynes analytic approach? Second, the MVP's ambitious 'scaling up' will be conducted under the aegis of MDG Centers for (i) West and Central Africa (ii) East and Southern Africa, in conjunction with a bevy of UN agencies and thirteen countries covering diverse agriculture, together with a campaign for one million community health workers (a point further discussed below) is more than impressive. Leveraging with the two MDG Centers, the respective countries, most with donor support, will apply the MVP in different contexts, consistent with their strategies of poverty reduction and growth. Examples of 'scaling up' in the MVP phase 2011 – 2014 are distilled from the report (pages 27 and 29) and are being applied in a mix of approaches and new settings.[8] Apparently the MVP did not incorporate Clemens and Demombynes's basic advices for the rigorous impact evaluation (including village selection, control villages and longer time frames). Hence, the results from the 'scaled up' examples and original eighty villages clustered into fourteen different sites by 2014 could lead to misinterpretation. Furthermore, the report does not appear to indicate what, if any, risk analyses has been part of MVP's scaling-up approaches and initiatives. I hope in the race to 'scale-up' the MVP has not 'jumped the fences'; and naturally we all wish the MVP and all the villagers well and full success.

Clemens and Demombrynes's impact evaluation work on the MVP stimulated controversy from numerous commentaries, including the MVP, diverse professional and interested groups; using a wide range of communication from academic journals (including The Lancet), noted symposia (including Oxford University) to blogs in creating democratic critiques with new transparency in development economics.[9] Essentially Clemens and Demombrynes's impact evaluation work (discussed above) was assessed to be a valid cost-effective approach; with the analyses giving correct results. In formulating the set of recommendations to reorient the development industry (Chapter 9) and then specifically for a pilot project (Chapter 10) – I include the rigorous impact evaluation as an essential element. (See page 203).

A read of the Millennium Promise 2012 Annual Report [10] indicates that the controversy surrounding the MVP seems to have had a salutatory effect within the project as it focuses on 2015 and beyond. For example, extra effort will be directed to villages with sharp disparity in water, sanitation and hygiene, and girls schooling. The section on monitoring and evaluation includes household surveys, 'real time' outcome monitoring, process evaluation, and economic costing. The initiatives are broader than a single MDG target, involving one million community health workers (CHWs), community education workers (CEWs), living classrooms, and programs for school meals and girls' empowerment. They also prepare communities for local ownership of infrastructure improvements (a key aspect to the pilot project in Chapter 10). Future updated information on the extent that these initiatives have been implemented will be closely followed. Issues of sustainability and scaling-up to other villages will challenge the MVP due to the high costs of the MVP. Essentially, the MVP is not going away. The appropriateness of using the MVP will be to carefully study and selectively adapt some of the lessons learned and best practices, including the organizational and financial aspects.

A special point on the community health worker (CHW) has been a support to rural communities in the form of China's Barefoot Doctors and, acknowledged since early primary health care initiatives.

Successful CHW schemes only function in support of district and local systems that are financed, functioning and continually being upgraded. Furthermore, in earlier chapters we saw that it is indeed the lack of investing and continued supporting district level system and services that creates the gap (gaping schism) to reach villages and people with MDG and LED initiatives. In the chapters ahead I proffer a multipronged approach to remedy this protracted situation.

Global Alliance for Vaccines and Immunizations

Let me describe the following situation, which emphasizes a decentralized focus on the district and field levels. Periodically there are numerous well-publicized donor meetings to elicit funds pledged for MDG initiatives. On 14 June, 2011, such a donor conference for GAVI (Global Alliance for Vaccines and Immunizations) was held in London. During the conference $4.3 billion was pledged for additional worldwide coverage for pneumonia and antidiarrheal (for specific rotavirus) vaccines; this exceeded the conference's expectation by $600 million.[11] There was a great acclaim from attendees that the vaccine manufacturers involved have offered to lower their prices significantly, though one prestigious international NGO (Oxfam) objected that equally effective vaccines might actually be purchased at even *lower* cost from countries such as India. Mr. Bill Gates, a major donor, justified focus on these vaccines on the grounds that: "For the first time we can say poor children will not be refused the vaccines the children in the richer world would get because there is not enough money."[12] In any case, we all know that vaccines are not delivered to the villages and urban slums' children's from thin air. They are delivered to mothers and children through a wide variety of immunization clinics at disparate far-flung locations. Indeed, all vaccine management requires the linkages of trained personnel with complicated logistics, (including the temperature-controlled

> ...And why should these MCH services be provided by a contracted NGO who, however well-meaning and attentive, will add nothing to the 'cement' of district and local infrastructure?

'cold chain' supply-line required for some vaccines), transportation, and local community involvement. Billions for vaccines is wonderful, but...district-level infrastructure and systems, working in conjunction with organized village mothers' groups, are also a critical factor in the equation of developmental aid.

Furthermore, childhood vaccination is only a part of maternal and child health care. If every child is 'entitled' to the pneumonia and rotavirus vaccines, should they not also be entitled to receive the rest of the MCH services provided by the local clinics on a regular basis? And why should these MCH services be provided by a contracted NGO who, however well-meaning and attentive, will add nothing to the 'cement' of district and local infrastructure?

In most societies, there are built-in cultural mores for community participation amongst the poor and less privileged people and families. This generosity takes many forms and is seldom coerced. In many societies, local business people also contribute regularly to the well-being of the community, often making small, incidental payments to support the delivery systems in health, education, agriculture, and related local economic activities. This type of community participation is considered part of a 'social contract' with the government-funded and provided services, fostering genuine local empowerment while improving transparency and thus inhibiting corruption.

You might ask whether such concepts aren't merely a 'retrograde' to the expanding statism of the 1960s and 1970s? After all, aren't even many of the poor countries on the growth pathway? I would argue that, on the contrary, the recent decade, focused on Millennium Development Goals, policies, and strategies, have not produced impressive results. On the other hand, the policies implemented before the Washington Consensus became fashionable in the mid-1980s did, in some cases, score some sustained successes even in complicated systems and countries. The statistical growth experienced recently in some emerging countries were associated with 'land and resource-based' development which concentrates ever-greater wealth in the hands of Centroid Power and leaves in its wake even greater inequity on the local level.

Concluding Remarks

Independent observers and people from all ranks working in the development industry have come to the same conclusion I have outlined in the previous remarks: that poverty reduction initiatives, including the Millennium Development Goals, will not be met using existing systems in most countries. Nor is the long-tern solution adequately addressed by contracting with NGOs (however, well-meaning and professional) or thinking that the private sector can deliver what are essentially 'public goods.'

In short, it's time to get real! It is not a retrograde step to make a long-term commitment to invest and continue to fund significantly strengthened decentralized systems and services at the district level in most countries. We are fully aware that the development industry's traditional Centroid Power are likely to 'throw sand in the machinery' at every step of the way. National differences will determine the specific forms and processes for successful decentralization at district level. The challenge, therefore, is to provide a pragmatic framework to transform the development industry, investing in physical and 'non-physical' infrastructure and the allied support for the recurring costs that program development requires. In the next few chapters I present such a framework, and go on to elaborate a few details about how a pilot project could be implemented and sustained. I trust you will welcome 'getting on board' the transformation train.

9

The Five Levers of the Development Industry
(and what we can do to make them work better)

Well, how have you liked the journey so far? I've shared a bit of my background, described some experiences in the field and in the halls of Centroid Power, and tried to give an inkling of some of the structural barriers and negative incentives that make it possible for so much aid to have so little impact.

I have also said a few words in Chapter 6 about the central role that decentralization will be likely to play in any meaningful reform or transformation, and introduced some constructs of the pilot project. The time has come to make some specific suggestions for changing the sclerotic development industry. Given the generally dysfunctional nature of the situation I've described, it should be no surprise to learn that I'm going to propose some changes in the very architecture of the industry. Anything less dramatic is unlikely to have much of an effect. In Chapter 6, I indicated, in general terms, how important it will be to return the pyramid to its proper base, with a foundation in the field, for people living in the villages and urban slums. A second radical change in emphasis will also be required—namely, that activities of various types will need to be closely coordinated to maximize the effect of any given project. Today, projects are too often pursued in blithe isolation from one another.

Alongside these shifts in emphasis, my proposals also offer a concrete response to the ever-present issue of corruption. They're designed to insure greater accountability and oversight among those managing a given program or project, and also more sophisticated enforcement mechanisms. They direct efforts toward both saving money and expanded sources of revenue. They deal with the methods used to plan, manage and monitor projects, which currently often leave a great deal to be desired.

In light of the challenges faced by the high-profile Millennium Village Project (MVP) which we reviewed in Chapter 8, and the fundamental elements that will need to be altered in existing institutions, it seems to me that any pilot program is likely to require an initial three-year preparatory period to lay the groundwork for success. This preparatory period would cost money, of course, but the innumerable failed programs of the past have also siphoned the funds of well-meaning donors into the coffers of Centroid Power at a steady pace to no real purpose. Following this start-up phase, the programs I'm suggesting could conceivably be inaugurated during a five-year pilot in ten carefully selected countries, with the thought that these projects could be extended once the results of the initial effort have been analyzed and the program modified accordingly

My proposal rests on the notion that there are five key levers of power within the multi-dimensional labyrinth of institutions and systems that make up the aid industry, and how all of them need to be fixed. Some lie within the jurisdiction of the country receiving aid, others are under the control of those dispensing it.

There is no easy way to overhaul such a system from the bottom up. After all, it's been more than fifty years in the making! But the pilot projects I'll be describing make an effort to implement the new architecture and operating system on a small scale, from one end of the process to the other, within a specific country together with selected systemic changes in international institutions. A large number of "moving parts" need to be coordinated in order for these projects to become effective, and I fully realize that each country will differ in the degree to which it can be brought up to speed. Yet I am thoroughly convinced that all five Levers must be functioning in order for the pilot projects to work. This is not a 'Chinese menu' from which each participating nation can choose what's palatable; rather, it's like an engine, with rods and cams and valves that work in a coordinated fashion—or don't work at all.

Though the task may seem daunting, the good news is that most of the required parts are already in place. It's just that they're seldom adjusted correctly or brought into play at the appropriate phase of a program. What I'm advocating here is a major reorientation in several existing international and domestic institutions and agencies. I call it the New Dynamic Approach.

I'm also proposing that incentive systems be modified, and also the criteria by which personnel are chosen to carry on the work. The result of these changes will be, in a nutshell, that the pilot projects will reorient the focus of activity away from the halls of power and toward the district level systems that administer and manage services to people in rural communities and urban slums. These projects will also seek to empower men and women at that level who are directly involved in local economic development. I am certainly under no illusion that the 'dinosaurs' in the development industry will be eager to promote such programs or find them attractive. They know which side their bread is buttered on, after all. But the first step toward change is to make the case for change convincingly. Bear with me now, because the complexities involved are considerable.

The New Dynamic Approach

I'd like to begin by giving an overview of the Levers whose reorientation would be the work of the proposed pilot projects. (In the next two chapters I'll address the issue of how this new approach could be initiated and sustained.) The five Levers to which I referred briefly above are as follows:

Lever One consists of those international agencies who provide donor funds and technical support for the Development Industry. Under the New Dynamic Approach I'll be proposing, a more distinct divide would be maintained between the financial and the technical aspects of program development. This would entail the creation of technical agencies on the international, national, and regional levels that would cooperate with one another. This will also include independent 'high level' assessment among and within the development industry to reduce overlaps of functions, personnel, systems (including information) and services.

Lever Two consists of a given nation's Ministry of Finance or treasury. Under the New Dynamic Approach, mechanisms would be developed to move funds more swiftly through the halls of power and out into the field.

The third Lever in any nation program *is largely absent at present. I'm proposing a new National Integration and Coordination Board, operating at the Central Government Level.* Under the New Dynamic Approach, this board would coordinate various programs active within its purview to reduce waste and duplicate services and expenses.

Lever Four consists of those international organizations whose function it is to curb corruption. These include the International Criminal Court, International Environment Court, International Bank for Settlement, UN Office on Drugs and Crime, The Basel Institute on Governance (International Center for Asset Recovery, ICAR), The World Bank (Stolen Asset Recovery Initiative, SARI) and the new International Corruption Hunters Alliance. Under the New Dynamic Approach, these agencies and institutions would turn their gaze more steadily toward the working of the international development community.

The fifth Lever exits today only as a scattershot collection of independent initiatives undertaken by NGOs and some businesses, mostly transnational corporations. I'm proposing that another new feature be added to the aid landscape—an institution dedicated to fostering, supporting, and monitoring innovative aid activities—in short, a development *avant-garde*.

These Levers are 'located' at different parts of the system and perform different functions; the restructuring I'm suggesting will require changes at every point along the line. Such changes cannot be affected overnight or across the board, of course. I'm proposing that a pilot project be initiated to establish protocols, work the bugs out, and lay down a track-record of success.

Lever One:
International Organizations

A host of international organizations now exist to manage the funds dedicated to elevate living standards for people in the developing world, the World Bank and the United Nations and it's agencies being only the most prominent. The growing number and size of international donors has led to a duplication of uncoordinated efforts which burdens any host country with severe and undue bureaucratic responsibilities. This needs to be changed. I am proposing that two radical changes would be especially beneficial. The financial and technical aspects of donor agencies ought to be split, and the many overlaps among the international donor organizations and NGOs ought to be identified and eliminated as much as possible.

As for the first point, I'm suggesting that things would work a lot better if the technical support for any given project were supplied to a host country independently of financial decisions regarding the loans themselves. That way, a host country could sustain a wide spectrum of effective personnel without so much counterproductive overlap. The result would be a more sustained (and therefore more productive) effort. At the same time, the administrative and technical services of the donor agencies would be streamlined, reducing overlaps and duplicate personnel.

The UN system would make a good first target, and some UN agencies within the pilot project could probably be streamlined almost immediately. A number of studies have begun to assess where 'rationalizing' UN agencies could take place.[1] This assessment for action is urgently needed, and can be done without the vested Centroid

Power's interest beginning in the first two years preparing the pilot project discussed below.

Following a critique of the UN agencies, similar reviews in bilateral and grouped donor development agencies and NGOs might follow more easily. Assessments of the respective development organizations' chief points of focus, linked to available resources, would lead to savings in the international and national agencies that could be plowed back into the work of reducing poverty.

Perhaps the big question is, how can the financial and technical aspects of a program be separated? During the pilot I'm proposing, which would involve the World Bank, the Bank would create a Project Funding and Financing Division. As the name implies, this division would have two main functions. It would work with the Technical Assistance division (discussed below), and other sections in the World Bank that focus on the macroeconomics issues within the country where the proposed project will take place. And it would also work with the finance department of the recipient country, along with various 'line' departments under which the project will be carried out—for example, agriculture, and health, education.

Depending on the scope of the project, such funding coordination might take two or three years.

The Second function of this Project Funding and Financing Division would begin once the project is underway. It would deal with the 'nuts and bolts' of keeping the project on track, and assess the selection, bidding, and contracting procedures and processes for work to be done. Beyond that, it would oversee disbursement and accounting for payments.

Beyond mere accounting, this division would also be concerned to identify which offices and positions serve a genuine function along the decision-making trail; it would also have the authority to hold the designated offices and persons responsible for their decisions.

An important part of this Division's tasks would be to review existing project regulation, procedures and processes for selections and awarding bids, procurement, contracting, financing, disbursements, and expenditure verification for any given finance and legal department. Since many of these regulations and procedures may have changed over the years, the pilot's three-year preparatory period would provide the opportunity for this Division to streamline and reduce the overlaps and work with some of the piloted countries to synchronize and clarify numerous details. This will improve the efficiency of the entire contracting and disbursement process.

Technical Services

Alongside the new Funding and Financing Division I'm describing, a second division would also be created under the auspices of the World Bank: the International Technical Advisory Center. This bureau (ITAC) would have two main functions. It would act, first of all, as the prime unit working with the country's departments to design the project being funded. It would also facilitate the exchange of information as results begin to accrue.[2] Over the last decade the World Bank has been promoting itself as a 'knowledge center,' and the ITAC will formalize and expand the scope of the construct.

The ITAC would provide consultancy services to member governments involved in MDGs and local economic growth (LEG) projects. It would also provide outreach support on technical and managerial aspects of a given project at every level from the central government to individual districts and communities, in conjunction with counterparts, specialists, universities and relevant resources in the host countries. It's important to note that this agency would provide technical support without dictating what a given project's composition or activities entail.

The ITAC would have two main levels of aggregation. The macro section would be composed of a core group of economists to assess trends, information, and analyses used for policy and project design at international agencies as well as for member countries. The World Bank already has skilled personnel and resources to conduct this kind of analysis and dispense recommendations. The macro section would also allocate technical personnel to coordinate with the 'local' sections, whose prime focus (as mentioned above) would be to work with the project contracting/financing staff in the Project Funding and Financing Division. The macro section would also allocate technical specialists to work with the staffs preparing the country projects as well as those in the Project Funding and Financing Division. An essential feature would be for the technical sector specialists in ITAC to work with country counterparts (which we'll meet later in this chapter) to design and formulate projects. This would include improvements in all the functional managerial features; which over the years have been the major predictable bottlenecks in projects' implementation. The ITAC will have several functions and groups of specialists which would be fielded and contracted from UN agencies, other donors, private consultant companies and academia. In order to select candidates, companies, university departments and NGOs an International Quality Assurance Board (IQAB) would be established and set criteria and procedures for section and review performance. The details of ITAC functions, including the IQAB will be elaborated in the next chapter in conjunction with preliminary work for the pilot and aspects during the pilot.

How are new projects created?

Chapters 4 and 5 present the central role of projects in the aid industry. When we drill down and ask how new projects are created at least two modalities become evident. One model is seen in countries with a well-developed central-level strategic and planning apparatus, processes with experienced teams. Another arises in countries that, at best, have such an apparatus in place only 'on paper,' but lack the experienced personnel to fully engage with the donors.

Prominent donors such as the World Bank and USAID have their own infrastructure, including personnel and networks, access to information, analytics, and money. As new policies and themes (usually on a sector basis) emerge, such donors can draw upon this reservoir or resources. A designated project manager will visit the recipient country and discuss the nascent project with officers in and the ministries of planning and finance, and also with the line ministry who will be 'hosting' it. Depending on the size of the project, such discussions might begin two years before the real money begins to flow, though expenditures for planning and preparatory field work begin immediately.

Countries with experienced personnel and solid institutions (like Indonesia, Ghana, Uganda and India) will have developed a solid framework and methodology for their midterm (five-year) development plan.* The priorities: (i) national, (ii) regional (geographic), and (iii) main subject areas for donor projects, for example social-cultural, economic, science and technology, infrastructure, natural resources and environment. Since formulating the countries midterm development plan can take two-year plus, there is plenty of opportunity for the donors project managers to interact with senior officials including those within ministries' directorates' generals who are likely targets for donor projects. Such preliminary discussions would have constructive give-and-take and may well result in 'back of the envelope type' assessments between the government officials and the donors on specific projects which enter the 'green book'— the list of projects the government proffers to donors during the midterm development plan.

For countries lacking such personnel and institutions, despite the development industry's parlance of 'partnership,' the donors' project managers usually initiate the ideas and many of the details regarding multi-year projects. As mentioned in Chapter 5, most countries prepared their Poverty Reduction Strategy Papers (PRSPs)—a

---

* Ministry of National Development Planning/National Development Planning Agency (BAPPENAS), Regulation of The President of the Republic of Indonesia Number 5 of 2010 Regarding the National Medium-Term Development Plan (RPJMN) 2010 – 2014, Appendices, Book 1 National Priorities, (2010) Jakarta, Indonesia.

proposed long-term approach to reduce poverty, which parallel strategic formulation favored by the World Bank and other chief donors. These strategy papers provide an umbrella for discussion as projects are being formulated. All the same, in countries struggling with poor administrative and managerial infrastructure, the project manager supplied by the donor can make positive, and often invaluable contributions to any particular scheme.

After the lead donors 'break the ice' with an innovative project, other agencies and donors often follow suit, putting similar projects into their portfolios. The most serious difficulties emerge in the implementation phases due to inept management, which often leads to mediocre results. It strikes me that better results could be achieved if there was less emphasis on sophisticated planning and more on a project's operations and "follow through."

Lever Two:

Strengthen and bring greater transparency to National Ministries of Finance

There is a great deal of variability in the practices of donor agencies and the countries they work with. In many cases such practices could easily be improved. Historically, ministries of finance have exerted their power through (i) revenue projections (with other government departments); (ii) multi-year and annual budget planning, including specific support to donor projects (loans and/or grants) and line ministries; (iii) disbursement and accountability. All finance ministries are governed by regulations and highly-complex procedures, and when they are the funding signatory to international donor projects (e.g. international development banks) they're also obligated to comply with the donor's regulations and processes. Countries usually allow the designated executing agency of donor projects (e.g. Ministry of Health, Department of Education, Department of Agriculture) to comply with the contracting provisions after annual budgets are approved, while the Ministry of Finance retains fiduciary contractual obligations to the international development banks and most other main bilateral donors' projects.

Several problems typically beset a ministry of finance dealing with these issues. There are many ways that project money can be 'shorted' for a specific budgeted activity, leaving the project under-funded. Then again, a nation's financial position can change after budgets are approved, thus reducing the funds available. Finally, the mechanics of releasing and disbursing funds are typically complex and time-consuming, which makes it challenging to manage a project dependent on those funds, even with all the good will in the world. For example, if Quarter I funds are not released until Quarter IV and there is no 'carry over' authorization provision, 'work done' performance measures will simply not be reached. Unfortunately, such delays are the norm in some MDG-deficit countries!

> **It strikes me that better results could be achieved if there was less emphasis on sophisticated planning and more on a project's operations and "follow through."**

It is sometimes the case that donor funds "by-pass" the ministry of finance entirely and are channeled directly to the specific line ministry (e.g. Health, Education, Agriculture) with whom the donor has developed the project. The theory is: 'less bureaucracy and less corruption.' An unfortunate result of this practice is that the ministry of finance does not have a proper account of money and resources devoted to specific projects. Herein lies a challenge—to improve financial accountability when some prestigious international development agencies and county's bilateral agencies arranges projects and activities directly with one or more departments this undermines the very credibility of the government by circumventing the ministry of finance's 'books.' While this 'off-line practice' may create a 'surplus' for certain activities and in specific locales, other more genuinely underprivileged districts further spiral 'downhill' into greater poverty.

Meanwhile, the issue of corruption remains widespread in ministries of finance. Yet it is of prime importance for a country's reputation to have the public sector and particularly the Ministry of

Finance exhibit high ethical standards, extending both to personnel management and training, and also to the way it carries out its fiduciary responsibilities. Is this possible? What would it take to create the 'clean environment' in ministries of finance and in all agencies?

One method of reducing corruption in the finance ministry has been to substantially increase the level of remuneration, particularly for decision-makers, including those with responsibility to approve the release of approved project budget allocations. Indonesia conducted some trails along these lines during the 1990s in the economic sectors, increasing pay in both finance and planning ministries as well as to Members of Parliament and high level officials in ministries… without much success, I'm afraid. The end result was one large corruption case involving a mid-level Department of Finance official and a notable case involving senior officials in the Ministry of Health. And the Jakarta media continues to report on similar type events and cases. In short, there is no 'magic answer' to this endemic problem, though it ought to be faced as squarely and openly as possible.

Timely disbursement to those who will use the funds

Yet experience suggests that to develop infrastructure, strengthen systems at district level, and deliver key services at the village and urban slum level, two procedural norms need to be maintained. Money needs to be disbursed in a *timely* way throughout the year, and if possible, it ought to be *disbursed from the donor agency directly to the local government offices* to be used by the designated unit's work program (usually under the direction of the local unit's head and/or project manager), rather than indirectly by way of the ministry of finance. Controls and safeguards will need to be maintained, of course, but such *officially approved* 'by-pass' funds can be transferred for specific activities to a project's bank account in a given region, district, and locale, where the funds will be used and quickly accounted for, and entering the books *ex post facto* at the district, regional, and central offices of the finance ministry within a quarter of their expenditure. Most countries have instituted secure electronic transfers to local areas, some using post office as well as commercial bank networks, which conveniently and safely operationalize 'by-pass' procedures.

Another advantage of this abbreviated chain of disbursement is this: since government finances are invariably stretched among competing needs, the new *officially approved* 'by-passing' procedures will ensure that funds get to where they're intended.

Other incidental measures that might help ease corruption include: (i) adopting 'early warning' systems for suspicious disappearance of funds, etc, (ii) tightening 'loop-holes' in approval and disbursement mechanisms; and (iii) tracking information on paper and electronic trails. Such methods will further enhance the finance ministry's credibility with the public and act as a deterrent to contractors and the power elite. Prosecution would also be an important element in any effective anti-corruption campaign. Stiff financial penalties would be enforced, including stripping individual and family assets from corrupt individuals and companies.

The regulations established to govern fund transfers will need to distinguish between classes of project funds, for example projects originating and with prime responsibility through ministries and the Integration and Coordination (I&C) Board (discussed below, in Lever Three) and 'block grants' intentionally distributed to local governments or villages for physical infrastructure and/or microcredit loans. Such funds are entitled to 'by-pass' the finance ministry to be deposited, used, and accounted for at the district, and village/urban slum levels. Members from the communities receiving the aid and conducting the projects would be responsible for following the procedures for procurement and financial accountability. Training local staff to this purpose would be an ongoing part of the project. Community leaders and local NGOs can be instrumental in whistle-blowing campaigns. All of these 'new by-pass features' would be incorporated into all donor (as discussed in Lever Two) and 'solely government financed' projects. (It would also have a part to play in distributing money and resources coming from the "Avant-Guard" groups, as I discuss in Lever Five.)

LEVER THREE:
INTEGRATION AND COORDINATION BOARDS

Historically, aid projects have been developed and administered within the context and under the purview of ministries or departments, more specifically, within respective directorate's general and their technical directorates, which all boast increasingly minute specialties and sub-specialties. I have been trying to suggest that this approach may make sense from the point of view of power politics and corruption, but it doesn't do a very good job of addressing the issues for which funds have been allocated.

Why not? Because funds tend to be spent, to an inordinate degree, at the central level of administration. No one would deny, I think, that central administration, with its technical capacity and expertise, has an important part to play in any development program, formulating and administering policy, selecting the respective technical interventions and activities, training, finance, auditing, and exposing and prosecuting corruption. Indeed, I advocated for these central functions in Chapter 6. But as a project gets underway, and increasing percentage of funds ought to be devoted to operations and training on the district and local levels.

It's usually the case that the specialties units of the donor work in close co-ordination with their counterparts in the specific Directorate General. Examples of specialty and sub-specialties units are Maternal and Child Health (MCH), immunization, nutrition for MCH, rural water supply and sanitation, urban water supply and sanitation, basic education, specific crops and irrigation. It's often the case with foreign/donor assisted projects that Directorates General game the activities so that they receive the preponderance of the expenditures, with relatively little being spent in the field.

In contrast to the increasing compartmentalization of ministry bureaucracies (as I have discussed in other chapters), community life, almost by definition, consists of a wide variety of integrated activities. It would seem logical that programs and projects designed to improve well-being within a community use a similarly integrated approach, though the specific issues needing attention might fall under the diverse category of agriculture, health, or education. As the preceding remarks may help to clarify, the current structure of aid administration to a given region or locale makes that very difficult to do. The integration and coordination boards I'm proposing will make such coordinated efforts far easier to sustain.

My own experience in Indonesian provided me with a case in point. For almost 30 years, starting in the mid-70s, President Soeharto clearly understood the important linkages between family planning and improved health services; he was also aware of linkages between improvements in rice farming and economic development. He was acutely aware of the 'silo mentality' of government bureaucracy, though he couldn't fully control or eradicate it. Accordingly, he and his government established the National Family Planning Board (BKKBN) which had direct operational linkages with all ministries and encompassed both foreign aid projects and solely government projects. Through a wide portfolio of mixed sector projects, the full range of family planning services were provided to families in villages. The result was a decline in the birth rate, improved standards of living, and less poverty.[3]

Soeharto's success may be considered a prototype of sorts for the national integration and coordination boards I'm proposing here. Though the specifics would vary from country to country, a national integration & coordination board (I&C Board) would consist of representatives from ministries of finance, planning, agriculture and irrigation, culture, health, education, local government, local (rural and urban) economic development, water and sanitation, and the national audit board. Whilst many details would have to be worked out at country level, I can give you a rough idea of how such a board would function.†

The board would hold meetings to define policies, managerial regulations, and processes for integration and cooperation. It would also serve as a *Joint Lead Executing Agency* for all donor projects. Donors would formulate and manage projects in cooperation with the Board. Such coordination among Ministries would make it easier for the Ministry of Finance and the international donor agencies to inspect contracting procedures, monies being transferred, disbursement and accountability.

Perhaps most controversial is that the I&C Board, as a Joint Lead Executing Agency in projects with respective Ministries/Departments, *would have signature power* over financing of the projects (as an executing agency). This means that the I&C Board would mitigate the interest of individual Ministries and their Directorates Generals. This, in turn, should act as a countervailing force whilst simultaneously establishing greater transparency, thus curtailing Centroid Power, and funneling a greater proportion of MDG and LED project funds to district levels.

The I&C Board would include a National Technical Assistance Center (NTAC) that would work in concert with the international version of the same agency that I described above (the ITAC). The NTAC would mirror the international center in including both technical and finance specialists. Its purpose would be to provide advice and liaise among the donors, ministries, region, districts, and field levels in genuine 'bottom-up' project formulation, then with the

---

† As described in Chapter 8, the Millennium Villages Project integrates selected interventions packages and agriculture, health, and education. Also, we learned that the MV effects of the program were overstated for most indicators, compared to other parts of the region at far lower costs. The New Dynamic Approach by focusing on decentralization, the Integration and Coordination Board (Lever 3) together with International Organizations (Lever 1) and the ministry of finance (Lever 2) would provide technical and financial support to operationally strengthen districts that deliver services and initiatives to empowered people living in villages and urban slums.

operations and management.

In addition, a National Quality Assurance Board (NQAB) would be established to provide support in screening and hiring national consultants from the pool of academia, UN agencies, and NGOs. The NQAB would have direct coordination with the International Quality Assurance Board (IQAB) being able to adopt standards, criteria, procedures and share data bases of organizations, universities, NGOs, consultant firms and individuals that could provide specialized services in countries; and assess performance of services provided which would be used for further rehiring and engagements.

Among other things, the NTAC would lend support to regional technical agencies (let's call these RTAC). The RTAC will have access to current 'best practices', and new technology available with support through the ITAC and NTAC network. As a result, no village or urban slum will remain unfamiliar with the wider world of innovation, while the experiences of local villages and slums can be shared in the worldwide network. Such information-sharing will be a significant breakthrough, contrasting markedly with the myopic self-protection mechanisms encrusted in the development industry's current operating systems.

Community Participation

The difference between the regional technical centers and current regional units lies in the RTAC's ability to strengthen district-level capacities and nurture local empowerment. Today, the regional administration in many countries serves merely as a glorified arithmetic and post office, receiving and sending predetermined perfunctory allocations to the ministries and directors' generals. This one-way relationship is exemplified by the oft-repeated pattern whereby the central administration, early in the annual planning and budgeting process, says: 'Please give us your needs estimates.' Then, after the requests have been received, the central level totes the sums and says, 'No. It's way too much. Here is what we will 'give the regions.' This pattern keeps the common people in their 'preordained' position of servitude, and makes the local population aware they are extremely lucky even to get the crumbs released from their local representative of Centroid Power, the esteemed Regional Governor.

Consistent with a policy of local empowerment, the planning methodology must primarily be 'bottom-up,' with direct local involvement in determining community needs. The projects' operations, management, and monitoring will also have community involvement.

One specific set of issues dealing with 'costing' deserves an added note here. First, the relative ratios of costs for specific project, such as personnel, supplies, and civil construction, have typically been prescribed at central level, most often by the line ministry planning the program in consultation with the ministry of finance and/or planning. Though the ratios seem somewhat arbitrary, they became conventions within many government agencies.

Meanwhile, the challenge of estimating the costs of a specific service provided—a 'fully vaccinated child' or the full package of basic MCH care, for example—in a given region can now be checked *de facto* with periodic monitoring. It will therefore become possible to refine the current planning and budgeting methods and adopt conventions that take into account the real differences in costs among regions and locales. Since these 'costing' issues are essential components to solid planning and budgeting, I would suggest the necessary analysis become a part of the three year preparatory phase of the pilot study I mentioned earlier. Further refinement of the tools and techniques will likely emerge as the program develops.

The RTAC will also conduct trainings for local businesses in an array of 'best practices.' The focus will be on sustaining local economic growth. In this way the investment of the RTAC will have an expansive role, fostering personal and business networks within the district and communities, both with 'official' projects and private commercial ventures. For small-scale farmers and livestock producers, training is likely to move beyond technical and economic considerations to encompass health-related issues as well. Thus, even in poor countries, RTAC activities will be an early step along the way toward developing a broader based Agricultural and Rural Development Extension Service.

The task of integrating projects will undoubtedly bring new management challenges. At the same time, the partnering between the national and international technical agencies (NTAC and ITAC) will bring an array of effective managerial techniques into play. These can include developing the Inspector General's *managerial audit* for integrated projects, training staff on conducting such audits, and presenting the results to decision-makers. This investment in managerial processes, when properly conducted, generates greater transparency and will be likely to gain support of the local communities involved, who will be encouraged by the prudent use of resources.

To emphasize the importance of getting things 'right, consistent and suitable' within each project, two salaried MDG workers could be posted in each village involved in the pilot program to support the families, community, and technical specialists associated with MDG & LEG initiatives.

Lever Four:
Curbing Corruption

Curbing corruption will remain an issue throughout the New Dynamic Approach I'm describing here, but specific institutions already exist that are designed to do nothing else, and these can be improved. Currently several international agencies and organizations have sufficient clout to (i) freeze accounts, (ii) return stolen money to the proper international and national sources and (iii) prosecute and imprison the 'Big Fish' violators, be they officials in the public realms and/or private sector. These Big Fish continue on many countries with impunity by hiding behind a veil of legal propriety and banking secrecy established and maintained by the Centroid Power club itself, of which they are dues-paying members. At this stage and for a limited time, the above-mentioned agencies could (and perhaps should) be coordinated under the umbrella of the International Corruption Hunters Alliance.[4] There is also considerable information currently available on major sources and patters of corruption. For instance, Tax Justice Network for Africa has been on the vanguard with investigative work on the main aspects of 'Looting Africa.'[5] Similarly, Transparency International, the global coalition against corruption has provided solid assessments on aspects of corruption including the annual Corruption Perception Index.[6] Armed with such strength in numbers, it should proceed to freeze the accounts containing 'Claw-Back' monies from a representative sampling of Big Fish. Returning the moneys to the rightful agencies would be a benefit in itself, and the action would also serve as a deterrent to corruption in other organizations.

At this stage, it would be premature to attempt an institutional reform to handle Claw-Back money. Perhaps a separate division in the UN International Criminal Court (ICC), The Hague could be created for such a purpose. Others options would include using the resources of ICC and internationals banks through the International Bank for Settlements facilities. It might also be possible to use the UN Office on Drugs and Crime and The Basel Institute on Governance - (International Center for Asset Recovery, ICAR) infrastructure to obtain evidence on Big Fish corrupter.[7]

The case of Charles Taylor at ICC reveals the difficulty of tracing stolen money and property.[8] The Mubarak and Gadhafi cases will also be very interesting.[9] Amazingly we are even seeing some minor leaks in the secure walls of fabled Swiss banking secrecy laws and institutions, with almost $1 billion having been frozen in accounts held by Gaddafi, Mubarak and Ben Ali (Tunisia) and in February 2011 of Laurent Gbagbo (Ivory Coast).[10] In the cases of Middle East and Maghreb countries, local organizations are collecting evidence of stolen fortunes and can prosecute the Big Fish in coordination with banks and international agencies. Could it be that the fortresses of

Centroid Power are weakening, or is this only a temporary feign in response to a short-lived rise in People Power?

One thing is clear: attempts to retrieve stolen funds from these Big Fish is seldom easy, and might even require regime change. After all, the individuals involved have channels of influence throughout the public and private sectors. Often major decision-makers themselves, they exercise control over people in a wide array of local institutions, extorting money for themselves, their families, and their stooges through time-honored systems of patronage that have been thoroughly integrated with modern legal and financial institutions worldwide.

Yet because they have integrated their operations with the world banking system, they, too, are susceptible to exposure and prosecution by international agencies or their own Ministry of Finance.

This process of 'Rightful Return' varies in particulars from country to country, but the following features would be most reasonable and usually present:

(i) The Big Fish is charged *in abstentia* on the basis of testimony and documentary evidence; all members of the immediate family, close relatives, and a 'circle of friends and accomplices' are likely to be included in the indictment.

(ii) Whistleblowers evidence is accepted and rewarded on an internationally agreed-upon scale.

(iii) Operational costs for the lawyers, accountants and technical specialists of the Division of Corruption and UN involved are similarly standardized.

(iv) A scale of Financial Penalties (a Fine), in addition the amount 'clawed back' from individual corruption, can be agreed upon and placed on the defendant. In instances that such amounts are available to the international banks, the banks will be required to transfer the financial penalty to the respective national Ministry of Finance or Treasury.

(v) Property resources collected in the corruption cases will be disposed of at the highest price and the money placed into an account for retrieval by the Division of Corruption; then returned to the organization and country's Treasury.

(vi) Evidence in the ('rightfully returned') clawed-back money and resources in corruption can be used for criminal and/or other determined civil legal charges.

In cases of donor projects that have been abused and pilfered, the usual procedures within the organization will be used. In most instances the national legal system, codes and practices will be used for criminal prosecutions. In cases of transnational corporate corruption, the country may use either its national jurisprudence systems or that of the corporation's 'home country.' Some countries may ask that the ICC, Division of Corruption, or some other international agencies agreed upon by the International Corruption Hunters Alliance conduct the criminal procedures against its nationals, using an agreed national framework of jurisprudence and penalties.

Another aspect of anti-corruption efforts involves the technical agencies I described above. It is essential that explicit provisos are monitored by at least the donors' procurement offices, the Ministry's Inspector General and the National Audit Board in the contracting procedures. The finance and procurement specialist's role would be to ensure timely knowledge that contracting and disbursement procedures were followed correctly and consistent with the 'streamlined processes and procedures' to emerge from the review by donors (briefly described in Lever One).

LEVER FIVE:
AN AVANT-GARDE CADRE FOR SUSTAINED ACTION

The levers of developmental aid activity that I've described above can be seen at work in the field and the halls of banks and governments today. I've suggested some points of reorganization, streamlining, and altered emphasis, but the agencies I've been referring to already exist today, at least in some fledgling approximation. The fifth and final lever I'd like to discuss is different. It doesn't really exist at present as a full-blown agency of any type. I am proposing the creation of a cadre of individuals (and organizations) whose roll will be to provide support for ongoing projects that are at risk of crashing to a halt or remaining uncompleted.

It has often been pointed out by 'development' professionals that after receiving aid for decades, some countries are worse off than they were before. This continuing 'aid dependency' leaves behind a dreaded legacy of failed projects and wealthy bureaucrats and is really little more than neocolonialism—with the burden of paying off the loans falling on generations of the most vulnerable. Some advocate for eliminating foreign aid in all its forms entirely.

One of the serious problems many programs encounter is to fund recurring operational costs at district and local levels. And 'Foreign aid,' which has already seen a decline in percentage terms for quite some time, will continue to be attacked by the reactionary forces in many countries, regardless of the fact that 'soft power,' including sustaining development initiatives, has often proven to be a more effective policy tool than military intervention.

I have suggested that funds can be increased to some degree by reducing corruption and rationalizing donor and NGO agencies. But that will not be enough. Significantly more money will be needed to sustain programs designed to reduce poverty in the years ahead. That's why I'm proposing that the means be devised, under the New Dynamic Approach, to have a steady stream of revenue available specifically designated for recurrent expenditures at the district and community levels. Alongside this financial resource would be a broadly based movement of people from all levels of society, contributing their differing skills adroitly to the needs at hand. This cadre of Avant-Garde (as I call them) would be a *broadly-based worldwide movement* of people, institutions, organizations and corporations, though the arena of active participation would be distinctly local. The question is, how is such a cadre to be established, directed, and sustained?

In some ways this movement already exists. Many people and groups are poised to extend support, in times of distress, to others from far different social-cultural environments. There are now 13,000 Civil Society Organizations (SCO) at work on such missions throughout the world today. Most of these NGOs receive funding from individuals, corporations, other NGOs and governments.[11] Following natural disasters such as the 2004 Indian Ocean tsunami and the 2010 Haitian earthquake, millions of individuals immediately donated billions of dollars.

It's true, a substantial amount of this *largesse* was hived off and landed in banks beyond the shores of the beleaguered countries in need of it. Less often reported in the headlines is the fact that medical professionals and communities often field teams of volunteers to build and provide recurrent costs for schools and health clinics in remote locales and urban slums. To mention a single example, Rotary International[12] for two decades has been among the main contributors to the successful polio vaccination programs in many countries, to the point that polio had nearly been eradicated. Religious groups, NGOs (including nonprofit humanitarian organizations)[13] and corporations[14] (such as Procter &Gamble's Children's Safe Drinking Water Program) support of Global Green grants water projects and have enjoyed longstanding volunteerism with developing countries and communities. In this spirit there are compelling reasons to formalize mechanisms for emphasizing and accelerating MDG achievements, sustaining poverty reduction and economic development of targeted districts.

It may be questioned whether formalizing such volunteerism would really be of benefit to anyone, rather than merely taking the spark out of community initiative while adding to the bureaucracy. Yet I think there would be distinct advantages to such an approach. A program of joint sponsorship or "twinning," would bring added financial clout mainly to supplement recurring costs, technical expertise, and market opportunities to local communities; and emphasize those communities in greatest need of sustained support. It would also provide a more professional approach to accounting practices, thus insuring greater transparency and accountability. Having such proactive transparency would keep a project on track and heighten trust for the sponsoring group, which in turn would lead to more confident and generous funding.

Considered in general terms, a separate ITAC Avant-Garde Division would:

(i) Establish criteria for 'adopting and twining' arrangements.

(ii) Coordinate with NTAC Division of Avant-Garde and respective Ministry of Finance in maintaining listing of the linkages between districts and Avant-Garde.

(iii) Facilitate initial communication between the districts and Avant-Garde.

(iv) Develop a proactive reporting network and communication among these adopted and twinning MDG & LEG successes.

The 'adopting and twinning sponsoring partnerships' could include: cities and communities, amateur and professional sports teams, highly paid sports and entertainment stars, universities, NGOs (all kinds), businesses (all sizes), wealthy individuals with trusts and foundations, social networking sites and religions (though tight regulations prohibiting any forms of proselytizing would be required). Criteria would be established on the *kinds* of activities the Avant-Garde could participate in and the management oversight for resources and money for each Avant-Garde group.

The Avant-Garde would collaborate with the district and villages/urban slums in preparing the annual budgets for MDG & LEG initiatives. Since the Avant-Garde would be contributing recurrent expenses, the case could be made that they could *cooperate* in any midterm and annual planning and budgeting; but decision-making would remain in the hands of local government officials, empowered community representatives, and perhaps the central government, as mentioned above. The ministry of finance would enable the

Avant-Garde to 'log-in' to see their contributions to the respective district, and use 'bypass procedures' (from Lever Two) to arrange direct transfer to the district's bank account.

Such 'twinning' arrangements between private organizations, universities, and communities involved in development projects often last for many years and open networks that lead to benefits for all parties. These might include sponsoring expanded educational opportunities such as scholarships within the country and in the sponsors' countries, supplying and maintaining specific technology, and expanding business and marketing horizons. Since this supplementary support from Avant-Garde will be to poor districts and locales under the project, most enlightened governments will recognize the advantages and encourage long-standing relationships which exceed the term of the projects, and the donors interests. Here are two examples: Imagine how horizons are opened when primary school children have communication with 'digital friends' in other countries; and how small-scale farmers can learn, for example, to improve their yield and storage of crops with modern low-cost technology, leading to increased income and savings! The success achieved by these means in reaching MDG targets and sustaining local economic growth might well inspire further involvement by individuals, churches, businesses, and other institutions.

10

Inaugurating the Pilot Project

I have described, albeit in somewhat abstract terms, a reorientation and reorganization of the developmental aid industry. I understand that transformations of this magnitude get to the very core of traditional institutions' 'high viscosity.' That's why they so seldom take place. In any case, presenting a vision for more rationally focused and efficiently coordinated system of institutions and agencies is one thing. Figuring out how such a transformation can be gotten underway is something else again. In this chapter I'm going to delve more deeply into the practical details of how to redirect and coordinate the various levers of the industry to make it work better.

I have suggested that such a transformation is most likely to succeed if it's introduced as a pilot program to be conducted in a maximum of ten countries. It strikes me that such a program will require a three-year setup period.

The first step of such a project would be to select the participants. The project would be phased into ten countries with up to ten districts with a mix of rural districts and urban slums. Additionally, for monitoring and evaluation (see point 9 below) there would be ten control districts. I would expect that up to four counties selected would fall into the class of Heavily Indebted Poor Countries with high levels of poverty and 'debt overhang' (HIPC). There are currently forty countries classified as such (twenty-nine in sub-Saharan Africa) that are eligible for special debt relief assistance from the International Monetary Fund and the World Bank due to their precarious financial position. (Since the HIPC program was started in 1996, thirty-six countries have received full or partial debt relief.[1])

The countries selected would be required to refashion their finance ministries in accordance with the guidelines I described earlier (in Lever Two).

In most instances the populations of these countries will include two categories. Conditions of near serfdom will be common in agriculture areas, while those in urban areas will abide in slums. In either case, families will be suffering a high level of food insecurity, and consider themselves lucky to have access to some level of basic healthcare and education for their children. Although all countries in the pilot will be classed as poor, some may be benefiting from advanced natural resources development (such as in the extractive mining industries) or through large-scale industrial farming. Though as described in Lever Four substantial money from contracts and tax revenues is likely to have been spirited to the international banking network and will have to be tracked down and returned for the country's development initiatives, including MDG and LEG.

In any case, most of the countries chosen will be from sub-Saharan Africa, Asia, and Latin America, though at least one should be from the Middle East/Maghreb Region.[2] The countries in the pilot will have highly inequitable systems of income distribution—a condition which won't be hard to find. All the countries in the pilot project will probably have experienced decades of highly Centroid Power, but they may differ widely in population size, culture, natural resources, economic potential, and infrastructure. By selecting a diverse array of countries, it will be easier to draw a bead on which aspects of the project are working and which should be modified or dropped altogether. The governments selected for inclusion (even those in 'post conflict' conditions) will have at least a semblance of civil administration, with central, regional and district (or similar) levels. Their infrastructure and systems will probably be rudimentary, and trained staff in virtually all sectors are likely to be scarce.

THE THREE-YEAR PREP PHASE

All of these governments will, to some degree, already be involved in development programs with international donors, and they'll be prepared to accept the conditions required by the pilot project. These conditions, in brief, are as follows:

- The nations involved will engage in a three-year preparatory phase so that each of the Levers will be functional by the time the project commences.
- The main activities during the three-year preparatory period will be to reorient budgets at the central and regions levels, prepare the projects, and distill sets of 'best practices' for systems and interventions. This having been accomplished, it will be easier to weigh the budgets for the subsequent five-year (and extended) pilot projects toward developing districts' capacities and systems, training and empowerment, and delivery of services.*
- It will commit itself to take the steps necessary to empower the people, particularly women, in the piloted districts, which will require reorienting the planning, budgeting and financing of the project initiatives toward a 'bottom-up' approach.
- It will agree to invest in the tools required to insure transparency, and to keep a lid tight on corruption.
- It will agree to share its work openly with the International Technical Assistance Center (ITAC) described in the previous chapter.

Meanwhile, an International Quality Assurance Board (IQAB) would be established to hire personnel to staff the international technical center, whose functions are detailed below. It's more enduring function would be to evaluate the effectiveness of the myriad NGOs that have proliferated so much in the past few decades that they now dispense more than 30 percent of all Official Development Assistance (ODA) foreign assistance. [3]

---

* This shift in budget-weight is discussed in greater detail below under Basic Principles of Aid Financing for the Pilot Program.

No one could deny that individual NGOs have made substantial contributions to reducing poverty. One notable example is the Bangladesh Rural Advancement Committee (BRAC) which provides basic curative and preventive health services to more than 97 million Bangladeshis.[4] Yet I suspect that Centroid Power networks often intentionally choose to work with NGOs of highly dubious standards to deliver services at district and field level, rather than investing in a sound government apparatus at that level and then funding its operations reliably. One critical factor that the Quality Assurance Board will need to consider in making judgments is whether a given NGO has participated in building the district's infrastructure as part of its program for delivering MDG and related services. Other factors would include past performance, specific skills, and proven independence from the contracting agency.

It would be useful to establish two sections under the IQAB: one for Technical Advisors and the second for NGOs. The IQAB could also support National Quality Assurance Boards (NQAB discussed below) with criteria for inclusion in preferred lists, remuneration schedules, and hiring procedures. This would be similar (as described in the previous chapter) to an Avant-Garde following ITAC guideline for 'twining' arrangements and then registering with the NTAC and ministry of finance.

The next step, and it's a big one, would be to establish the International Technical Assistance Center (ITAC) as an interface between the big money and the realities 'on the ground.' This agency will have a variety of tasks under its preview, many of which are not being shouldered by anyone today. Some would argue that as long as we're working so hard to satisfy needs and empower people at the local level, we might as well just give them the money to do with as they think best. The problem with such an approach is that some of the things needed most in villages and urban slums fall under the category of systems and infrastructure, which requires a broader focus and more extensive planning and coordination over longer time frames than individual communities can typically supply. Meanwhile, most of the locales are not ready to absorb the money and do not have their functional capacities up to speed.

The initial task of the ITAC would be to solidify an efficient 'brain-ware and knowledge-ware' infrastructure for the pilot period. There are already massive amounts of specialists' expertise and information in the field, of course.[5] The problem lies in harnessing this ever-expanding knowledge base. In this regard, The World Bank Group Strategy (October 2013) will build on its strength; reorganize and integrate its knowledge-base in fourteen global practices and 'cross-cutting' areas; and work to bring billions of dollars of private sector capital into poor countries, including fragile and conflict-affected (FCS), directed to problem solutions.[6]

Modern information technology should make the job easier. The international banks, UN system (and specialized agencies), bilateral AID agencies, private foundations, universities, and NGOs could contribute key specialists to establish the ITAC, which could operate from various points in the field. The ITAC could also contract specific projects' activities to universities and think tanks.

That having been accomplished, the ITAC would commence working on a variety of infrastructure subjects which would be used in the country projects, dialoging with the government's ministry of finance, I&C Board and NTAC, communicating with other countries and the development industry. I list here a few of the most important. Since the ITAC will be responsible to several interrelated activities, I recommend they be conducted by specialists in six sections, with fluid communication among the staff in these sections.†

---

† The sections would include: (i) IQAB (discussed earlier), (ii) planning (select the countries in the pilot and in conjunction with the country NTAC and districts, plans the project and annual budgets), manpower training, interacts with the 'macro-section' and Finance Division to prepare for the extended period, (iii) systems design (including information with linkages to managerial decisions); (iv) review literature and new technologies, (v) operations and

1 Review past projects

Conduct an independent review of projects over the last decade to determine their effectiveness and make recommendations of what should be included within a pilot country's project portfolio. (The World Bank's Independent Evaluation Group[7] may well have established suitable review protocols; and their evaluations of projects will be incorporated to the preparatory phase and pilot period.)

2 Review low-cost technologies

While computing and communication are all the rage, it's important to recall that a large body of field-level knowledge has been distilled from applicable low-cost and effective technologies in many countries, including building and construction, agriculture, water and sanitation, energy generation and usage, health care, food care and storage, transportation and finance—particularly microfinance and social entrepreneurship.[8] Advances in agriculture and its allied infrastructure deserve special attention. The portfolios of several organizations focus on specific crops (e.g. sorghum), and low-cost innovations in Africa and South Asia can bring tried and true 'best practices' (see 9 below) forward quickly in the pilot countries' districts.[9] Technologies that prove to be both technically and financially feasible for local systems services should be included in each piloted country's portfolio of projects. Those that are available locally are even better.

3 Identify Patterns of Essential Socio-cultural features

Investigate socio-cultural aspects of pilot countries and their localized populations that might have a bearing on the success of the projects. This would include power nexuses between government levels, within locales and between genders.[10]

---

management (which includes the designated Project Manager for each piloted county), and (vi) monitoring and evaluation.

4 Invest In New Technology

Most countries collect excessive amounts of data, health care information being the prime example. This is largely due to the 'silo' effect and the presence of multiple donors working independently. Accordingly, during the preparatory phase of the pilot, ITAC will review and crystallize the essential data to be collected at the different levels and determine which elements it will be essential to collect at each level. The purposes for selecting information will be based on helping decision-makers and informing the public. This streamlining process needs rigor but is eminently doable in the sectors of health, education, and agriculture—and will be welcomed by the participating countries. Whilst there will be a degree of standardization in these mini-managerial information systems, there will also be adequate flexibility to incorporate country- and district-wide differences, should these be requested by decision-makers.

This information-gathering protocol will make it easier to engage in the 'bottom-up' planning and budgeting processes the New Dynamic Approach requires. The needs' assessment from the communities will be more accurate and easier to match with the array of interventions, technological advances and 'best practices' available.

5 Develop techniques to manage the minutia of planning cycles, budgeting, monitoring and evaluating projects

During the early phases of the pilot it will be essential to (a) develop low-cost decentralized 'bottom-up' planning and budgeting processes localized at the district level and (b) establish reliable controls for evaluating its impact.[11] It is crucial not only to include such control populations in the design of each country's pilot, but also to distinguish between indicators that become significant within five years and those that require a decade or more to expose genuine differences between pilot and control areas. These are likely to include *work done or input measures* such as the percent of people having access to improved sanitation and drinking water, births attended by trained personnel, measles immunizations; and *outcome measures* like chronic malnutrition as measured by the stunting rates in under-fives, primary school attendance rates, and malaria prevalence rates.

6 PROVIDE DIRECT TECHNICAL SUPPORT FOR THE PILOTED COUNTRIES AND THEIR DISTRICTS

This would involve, among other things, helping to establish technical assistance centers on a nation and regional level in the participating countries. In Chapter 6, I outlined the main district-level functions and described how the districts would improve systems and service delivery to empower people in villages and urban slums. The piloted countries will exhibit differences in the way the central and regional levels interact with and support the districts, naturally. In the three-year prep period up to five districts and control districts in the ten countries will be selected with consultation of the ITAC and NTAC to be representative of the country's rural communities and urban slums. The experiences will be used to increase to ten districts during the five-year project and then after used to 'scale-up' to other districts.

7 DEVISE METHODS TO INTEGRATE PROJECTS BETWEEN SECTORS

An essential part of Lever Three, the Integration and Coordination Boards, (which I described in greater detail in the last chapter) will involve the international technical team (ITAC) working with the pilot country's national team to *integrate* MDG & LEG projects *within sectors and among sectors*. The key here is to select from interventions that have achieved impressive results under similar conditions elsewhere (see i and iii above). Examples within the health sector could include combining water and sanitation with multi-services community-based maternal and child health activities. Another example would be to combine subsidized seed, fertilizer and pesticides with low interest credit/loans for food production and an expanded nutritional service that might include micronutrients for children and expectant mothers, and school gardens at primary schools. No doubt the Millennium Village Project [12] will provide further examples of multi-sector interventions that can be reviewed and assessed for possible inclusions as well.

In short, both the international and nation technical bureaus will have an expanded brief to integrate activities from within and between sectors. They will be able to bring down barriers and eliminate the 'silo' effect created by isolated and autonomous departments pursuing uncoordinated agendas. In time, they will be able to determine why some World Bank initiated Sector Wide Approach projects (SWAp) succeed and others fail.[13]

8 REVIEW AND IMPROVE TRAINING SYSTEMS

Investment in basic technical, managerial and administrative training will be an essential ingredient in any MDG and LEG project initiative. Beyond the specific results of any given project, huge benefits are likely to be gained by families and communities as they learn more from both formal and non-formal trainings about local empowerment, farming, health, education and small business.

9 MONITOR AND EVALUATE A GIVEN COUNTRY'S PILOT PROJECTS AND 'BEST PRACTICES' PROJECTS WORLDWIDE

This section has two main briefs. (i) In line with the project's formulation, establish M&E protocol with distilled information to be integrated into the planning, budgeting, operations and managing the project in each piloted country. This includes incorporating 'rigorous impact evaluation' methodology. Clemens and Demombynes identify multiple approaches of impact evaluation, including "differences-in-differences, regression discontinuity, random control trials (RCTs) and propensity-scores and other forms of matching"— with techniques discussed by Gertler et. al.[14] (ii) With an eye toward cost-effective field-oriented evaluation methods to improve the network among the piloted countries; such ongoing evaluation with worldwide scope will keep the short-list of 'best practices' up-to-date and easily accessible to others. Selection of the 'best practices' are determined using impact evaluation techniques and analyses (mentioned above), possibly control groups, differences-in differences, or periodic review to identify practices that would replace the current 'best practice.' Where necessary, care will be taken to adapt 'best practices' to be accepted in differing social-cultural environments. For example, the courageous work on sustainable environmental development by the 2004 Noble Peace Laureate Wangari Maathai (deceased, September 2011) and her organization, The Green Belt Movement, continues to have huge positive near and long-term impact on, among others, significantly reducing land degradation and empowering women throughout Africa and the world.[15] Other African organizations specialize on incorporating multi-sector and sustainable features for small-holders and communities.[16]

A Three-Year Initiating Phase

As the above discussions indicate, there will be much to accomplish during the three-year preparatory period to re-align the various Levers involved as they pertain to the Pilot Project. Here are highlights of the respective agencies' focus and outputs.

LEVER ONE: INTERNATIONAL ORGANIZATIONS

Year 1: Establish the IQAB and ITAC together with processes and procedures, select countries for pilot project. Review, consolidate and update project financial management processes and procedures focused on reducing corruption. Begin analysis and discussions to streamline UN and related agencies portfolios and personnel. (Note: This streamlining work will continue during the prep-period and throughout the five-year project. It is expected that savings from streamlining these agencies will be 'plowed-into' the project during implementation phases. Select appropriate district level modality with linkages to central, regional and field levels, with manpower training plans.

Year 2: Begin working on agenda items and work with the pilot country's NTAC (Lever 3) to prepare the project. Develop low-cost 'bottom-up' planning and budgeting methods for district and villages/urban slums. Select appropriate district level modality with linkages to central, regional and field levels, with manpower training plans.

Year 3 : Project prepared including the first year activities and budget. Then accelerated approval processes with World Bank and piloted countries.

LEVER TWO: STRENGTHEN AND BRING GREATER TRANSPARENCY TO THE NATIONAL MINISTRIES OF FINANCE

Year 1: Assess laws and procedures to reduce corruption and direct transfers to districts, and design initial plan to strengthen 'corruption watch' and direct transfer to piloted districts.

Year 2: Design and approve laws and protocols for further clamp down on corruption and direct transfer from within country and without (including funds from Avant-Garde) to piloted districts; approve 'carry over' funds provisions for following year of approved budgeted activities.

Year 3: Trials in direct transfers to districts with accountability procedures and processes; work with World Bank and Lever 3 (I&CB) to receive all essential approvals as one of the countries in the pilot project; work with Lever 4 (curbing corruption) with the aim to gain resources from Big Fish to be used for expanding the pilot project.

LEVER THREE: NATIONAL INTEGRATION & COORDINATION BOARD

Year 1: Establish the NQEB and NTAC, together with processes and procedures; and select districts and 'control districts' for pilot project.

Year 2: Coordinate with ITAC for project identification and preparation; and train district officials and empowered councils from districts, their villages and slums.

Year 3: Project prepared including the first year activities and budget. Then accelerated approval completed with ministry of finance and World Bank.

Lever Four: Curbing Corruption

Year 1: Continue working with network (Stolen Asset Recovery Initiative)

Year 2: Devise processes and work with trials for one or two pilot countries to retrieve money from Big Fish.

Year 3: Initial results in the complicated process—this continues throughout the five-year pilot with targeted Big Fish and the money returned to the respective countries' treasury.

Lever Five: the Avant-Garde

Year 1: Establish (international and national for piloted countries); criteria, processes and procedures for the Avant-Garde; together with software to track money to the districts and information access from Avant-Garde in full coordination of ministry of finance.

Year 2: Continue the work of Year 1.

Year 3: Establish trial Avant-Garde for one or two piloted countries.

Basic Principles of Aid Financing for the Pilot Program

It is envisioned the pilot project would be designed and have the multiple funding sources, including other bilateral donors and agencies and some financial support from the host government. With the pilot projects initiated in the countries, sufficient flexibility is built-in for annual planning and budgeting along the lines discussed above. Within three years of the pilot, the technical agencies should be up and running; and deep into planning for the extended pilot programs in pursuit of Millennium Development Goals and LEG. Here are three main principles that I have come up with, based on my own field work and a review of the literature.

Principle One Understanding there are differences in countries sources of finances derived from various donors and their national resources and efforts; and there are multiple budgets for investments and recurring costs. First, let's consider the totality of all financing directed for 'development' MDG and LEG project initiatives. Second, for convenience, let's consider two levels, (i) the central, including the region and (ii) all districts (given variability among districts). Third, when estimating costs (for these two levels) separate three broad composition of expenditure (a) physical infrastructure; (b) managerial 'systems' and management functions (which includes accounting, financial reporting and auditing); and (c) recurrent operational expenses.

To be consistent with all discussed above in the New Dynamic Approach, I'd see a plan where the percentage of all costs in an *indicative budget* of the initial phase of "typical" project over the five-years shift from the central/region to districts allocated as follows. The central/regions have allocated 60 percent in year one, 40 percent by year three, and 25 percent by year five. Thus, the amount of total project costs for all districts would be 40 percent in year one, 60 percent in year three, and 75 percent in year five.

Most poor countries with aid programs find that most of the aid money involved goes to personnel emoluments rather than actual services delivery. This is unfortunate. It's part of the problem the New Dynamic Approach is designed to address. The table below represents my best guess as to what the proportions of a "typical" five-year pilot project might be, year by year. You will see that with the passage of time the composition of expenditure shifts from physical infrastructure (schools, health facilities, agriculture/water, transport/roads, local energy generation and distribution) to the operations (training, salaries and related personnel costs, books, medicines and vaccines, seeds and appropriate usage of fertilizer, and selecting local economic growth initiatives).

Indicative Budget Separations between Main Classes of Expenditures in Initial Phase of Project

Year	Operations	Management	Infrastructure
1	30 %	25 %	45 %
2	35 %	25 %	40 %
3	45 %	20 %	35 %
4	50 %	15 %	35 %
5	60 %	15 %	25 %

A key element in any project's success is whether contracts for physical infrastructure are awarded locally or not. When they are, a 'multiplier effects' kicks in. Pumping money into local areas via employment and purchasing has been a proven tool for LEG. When members of moderate and extremely poor families are employed on infrastructure projects, they find themselves able to save a little money (accumulate capital), in turn, providing them with opportunities to pursue agricultural related and other commercial activities, which also helps to lift them out of poverty.

A second key factor influencing any project's success is whether annual operating expenses for managing it are a part of the budget.[17] A small but important part of such expenditure (5-7 percent) should be devoted to managing the financing, contracting, disbursement and accounts/financial reporting for the project. Having such costs built into the project will make it more likely that sufficient auditing will actually take place to guard against and expose corrupt practices. As discussed in examples in other chapters (such as block grants for village level development), proactive measures that leads to transparency will safeguard against abuses and enhance a program's credibility, perhaps leading to even greater investments along the same line. Looking past the project's basic time frame and cognizant of the long history most governments face in keeping a flow of operational (annually recurring) costs after the 'life of the project,' I have intentionally added the Avant-Garde level as Lever 5, though it would be unreasonable to rely on this source of continued funding.

Principle Two One primary objective of the New Dynamic Approach will be to redirect roles, responsibilities and resources from the central to the district and village level. As discussed in Chapter 6, depending on the country these modes can be *deconcentration,* or *devolution,* where the local government has greater responsibilities and more control of the resources. In any case, it's a matter of degree. For the foreseeable future, the countries in the pilot will need central level support; however, the planning, budgeting, implementation and management including financial accountability can and should be localized at the district level, and depending on the level of infrastructure in the country, at the village level for some functions. In a gradual shift similar to the one described above, investments would be directed more heavily toward the central level in the early years of a project, and redirected gradually to the district level as the project progresses. Proportions would vary depending on the case in hand, but such a shift should be considered standard procedure and the failure of a project to exhibit such a budgetary "shape" would act as a red flag to those reviewing it.

Among the important result of this gradual shift would be greater *community participation* on decision-making committees. After all, the main emphases for Millennium Goals are on reducing poverty and improving the quality of life for the world's most vulnerable people, while simultaneously increasing local economic growth. In many rural villages, voluntary community participation is intertwined with social-cultural mores, celebratory events, and agriculture production cycles. Dealing with flooding and other natural disasters also requires serious community involvement. The same community good-will can also be used to mobilize efforts in education and health. At the core of sustained pro-active local empowerment is *genuine* Bottom-Up Planning and Budgeting; and to support the operations and aspects of management during the implementation. It's critical that projects conceived in this way receive timely funding, including some for block grants during implementation phases. (I will elaborate on local empowerment and community participation in the next chapter.)

Among the forms such community involvement might take are:
- Local non-official citizenry in rural communities, villages and urban slums could be appointed as active members of committees for planning, contracting and auditing expenditure of local project activities.
- Accounts for local projects and initiatives could be openly published for the communities review and comments.
- As computers and cell phones become more widely available, communities can learn from one another which projects and techniques work and which don't. This open sharing or experiences may have an impact in further curtailing corruption.

Principle Three The financial underpinnings of a given project must be coordinated and not overlapped among the development agencies involved. The expertise of the technical agencies (the ITAC and NTAC) I described a moment ago will make such coordination easier, as will the availability of a limited number of 'best practices' for the districts and locales with separate sector and then integrating activities among multiple sectors. Such coordination will result in far less duplication in training and services, hence a huge cost savings when compared to the current scattershot system.

Overview of advantages/benefits

It is my belief that such a reorientation of agencies will result in more effective programs and less waste. Key MDG target indices will be met more rapidly, local economic development will accelerate, and programs will find it easier to sustain themselves.

Yet mid-term monitoring the pilot project will undoubtedly

expose initiatives that have not borne fruit. Thus begins the process of planning for the project's extended period with assistance from the International Regional Development Bank Systems network, including World Bank, Asian Development Bank, African Development Bank, and Inter-American Bank. At the same time, senior decision-makers in international development agencies under the UN and EU, and countries with bilateral development assistance portfolios, could conduct open forums to be determine a streamlined organization framework for: (i) the development funds to be consolidated ‡ with (ii) projects to be designed and (iii) implemented, with appropriate managerial tools and decision-making structure. Given the all encompassing reach of Centroid Power, the pragmatic issue is to insure that consolidated funds will work within the New Dynamic Approach.

Further Evidence in Support of the New Dynamic Approach

I have provided examples through the discussion of specific projects that anticipate some of the innovations contained in the New Dynamic Approach. Another source of encouraging information comes from The Commission on Growth and Development (which I briefly summarized in Chapter 4) and will focus on selected points that are congruent with the New Dynamic Approach.

This Commission was established in April of 2006, for the purpose of conducting a high-profile examination of the policies and strategies that underlie rapid and sustained economic growth and poverty reduction. Its extensive deliberations resulted in a report published in December 2010: *The Growth Report: Strategies for Sustained Growth and Inclusive Development.* [18]

In its report the Growth Commission advocates, on the basis of its study of past successes, market-oriented strategies alongside continued public sector investment and support. It differs from earlier

---

‡ The Global Fund to Fight AIDS, Tuberculosis and Malaria, an international financial institution which has committed $22 Billion in 150 countries will provide lessons learned. http://www.theglobalfund.org/en/ and Jeffrey Sachs, 'Pool resources and reinvent global aid', Financial Times, September 20, 2010.

strategies in that *it places emphasis of economic growth, from which other health and educational goals are presumed to follow*. While this is not precisely the approach I'm advocating, some of the report's findings do dovetail closely with the New Dynamic Approach.

For example, the commission argues that growth is a necessary, if not sufficient, condition for broader development, because it enlarges the scope of opportunities for individuals to be productive and creative. "The growth of GDP may be measured up in the macroeconomic treetops," the report asserts, "but all the action is in the microeconomic undergrowth, where new limbs sprout, and dead wood is cleared away."

The report goes on to argue that "…leadership requires patience, a long planning horizon, and an unwavering focus on the goal of inclusive growth." I couldn't agree more. "Experience suggests that strong, technocratic teams, focused on long-term growth, can also provide some institutional memory and continuity of policy. This stability and experience can be particularly valuable during political upheavals, because new systems of collective decision making can take a long while to bed down and function efficiently." Once again, well put.

The commission also notes that successful programs often emphasize infrastructure development over the long term: "No country has sustained rapid growth without also keeping up impressive rates of public investment—in infrastructure, education, and health. Far from crowding out private investment, this spending crowds it *in*. It clears the way for new industries to emerge and raises the return to any private venture that benefits from healthy, educated workers, passable roads, and reliable electricity." Echoing the dreary history I've been describing in these pages, the section concludes: "Unfortunately, we discovered, infrastructure spending is widely neglected."

The report emphasizes the importance of educating girls, thus providing them greater opportunities for their lives and their predominant role in breaking generational poverty. These and other nuggets of wisdom lend further credence to the principles upon which my New Dynamic Approach is based. However, the extended timeframe of the pilot I'm advocating, and the benefits to be derived from the creation of technical boards and increased corrupting control, may make it possible to effect sweeping change in the landscape, far beyond anything described or envisioned by the Growth Commission.

'Yellow Light' for the New OECD Initiatives

The Fourth High Level Forum on Aid Effectiveness[19] organized by the Development Co-operation Directorate (DCD-DAC) of OECD (Korea, December 2011) focused once again on creating environments and institutions to increase development funding, with special focus on the MDG's, and coordinating aid among donors whilst building solid partnerships with recipient countries.

The evidence suggests that aid funding has peaked—a fact that, along with rising criticism of aid effectiveness from both donors and developing countries, wonderfully concentrated the minds of those who prepared the final report, "Busan Partnership for Effective Development Co-operation."[20] The report distills initiatives for OECD, donors and recipient countries in these challenging years ahead. As expected, the document reads as 'top-down' (with selected exceptions I will point out) and has a wide brief with many platitudes. Here are a few of the initiatives it suggests.

- Noting the major changes in emerging economies, the initiatives include greater South-South cooperation and encourages nations to spur economic growth from their own resources. It also stresses greater emphasis on regular monitoring of quantitative targets, and further expand the role of Civil Society Organizations (read NGOs).
- It provides a set of activities for the private sector that constitutes a major departure from OECD's ODA portfolio. Many advocates of aid will no doubt share my view that the private sector has been over emphasized, to the point of undermining

sustained poverty reduction. Phrases such as "…develop innovative financial mechanisms to mobilize private finance for shared development goals" will set off 'alarm bells' for many field-oriented development specialists. [21]

In the end, it all begins to sound very much like a not-so-subtle return to the famed Washington Consensus we discussed in Chapter 4. The private sector already has a longstanding involvement in ODA aid development projects. We may be encouraged by the socially responsible initiatives of certain private companies, some of which were outlined as *avant-garde* activities. And I am a strong advocate for private sector initiatives for LED, which usually is stimulated and sustained though public sector projects mainly focused on "public goods" and financing. However, when private interests set policy and promote private investments in countries with authoritarian governments, where regulation is weak and oversight virtually non-existent, it's easy to imagine the overwhelming majority of the surpluses being spirited away by Powers Elites' to the Swiss banks and beyond.

• In the positive column, the document does present interrelated germane points on the need to build government systems and effective institutions, which in turn reinforce the development of co-operative initiatives. Reference is also made to accelerating "our efforts to achieve gender equality and the empowerment of women." The report also refers to importance of transparency, accountability, and up-to-date information management systems.

• ODA will remain a dominate force in development aid, regardless of the separate sovereign and transnational corporate investments. [22] As I noted, the Development Co-operation Directorate's document is very much 'top-down' Centroid Power driven and certainly not as nuanced with reality as the Commission on Growth and Development. As ODA is seriously concerned about "aid effectiveness" the first priority is to make existing resources deliver sustained results to reduce poverty. To focus on *hustling for more money within the existing architecture and operating system is hardly a way to engender greater "aid efficiency."* That being said, the essence of the New Dynamic System and pilot I have presented would be a natural fit, if the more progressive elements within Development Co-operation Directorate and ODA become strong advocates among their peers for strengthening the foundation of the pyramid.

11

How will the New Dynamic Approach be Sustained?

Having mulled over these ideas at length, I am acutely aware that the most crucial job in establishing a successful program is to create a healthy working environment, sound leadership, and a sensible incentive structure that will motivate those involved to "get with the program." Of course, those individuals, corporations, and loyal political 'hacks' who benefit enormously from the Centroid approach aren't likely to walk away quietly into the night. On the contrary, they will use whatever means they have at their disposal to hold tight to their control over funds, orbits, and populations.

Yet I am also well aware of the large number of dedicated professional on the staff of various international and national development agencies, including the UN. The key issue is: to locate these individuals for leadership roles in administration and technical aspects for the New Dynamic Approach.

Can we expect to change 'human nature'? No. But we can change institutional culture, by developing a clear and commanding vision of the job to be done, recruiting individuals who have demonstrated the technical skill and moral fiber to contribute to that grand enterprise, and designing remuneration schedules based on both personal enterprise and results.

New Leadership for a New Era

Under the New Dynamic Approach, leaders need to concentrate on getting solid teams of integrated technical specialists together, who would then collaborate with local and regional officials to develop practical initiatives. Of paramount importance is that the leadership for the New Dynamic Approach understand rural communities and urban slums as well as the latest 'knowledge ware' and technologies. They must be willing to cajole decision-makers and their staffs to updated their managerial tools. The numerous layers of information shufflers we often encounter in development agencies would be reduced, and the VIP status granted to leaders would be tempered by a recognition of how well their organizations have succeeded in 're-righting' the Pyramid. Ceremonial events and expense-account international conferences would become far more rare.

After all, talk is cheap. Developing a cadre of dedicated professionals is difficult. Here are some principles to guide the process.

We have all witnessed the tremendous outpouring of genuine People Power from all strata of populations in different countries; and most recently in the Middle East and Maghreb and the Occupy Movements in the cities and small town in more prosperous countries in the West. The crucial issue that these events raise is how to affect transformational change by *'keeping the pressure on'* the leadership and on decision-making processes, rather than "transforming" a nation into yet another version of the regime that's been left behind. The development industry is less dramatic than revolt in the streets, but the issues are similar, because the obstacles and enemies are the same: Overweening Centroid Power utterly free of oversight or accountability. But in the world of economic development, there are several countervailing 'loci' of power and sources of finance for projects that would create independent oversight and dialogue panels with leadership. These can be amalgams of selected countries and Avant-Garde funding, multinational agencies, and national projects. Similarly, investigative journalists and scrupulous academics also have a part to play in inaugurating a new paradigm for leadership.

It is essential to regard *local empowerment* as a main linchpin of the New Dynamic Approach, and not merely a slogan, development babble, or a throwaway line of Centroid Power, as it has been in many countries for the last fifty years. To be effective, such empowerment will require serious assessments of conditions on the ground, as it were, to ensure the empowerment initiated actually works toward the benefit of local residents.

It seems to me that to be effective, local empowerment will require a *'social contract'*, or a *'partnership in support of self-reliance'*. A wide spectrum of people would become involved for their communities in districts, rural areas and urban slums, and their efforts would be nurtured by the various organs of official disbursement and expertise I've been describing. Villagers would take responsibility for the respective activities in which they become involved: funding and technical support would be supplied through donor and government projects (ITAC & NTAC) with supplemental support from the Avant-Garde. Though investment and operational costs may be hard to come by as the world economy lurches this way and that, local people who daily face scarcity will endeavor to squeeze maximum benefit out of all resources that do come their way—trust me on this one. Some of them will be paid. In any case, they will provide a wealth of local experience and insight to any project, and the schools, health centers, and MCH services (for example) that they help to build will be *"theirs,"* and not the NGO's contracted by the government.

Local empowerment must extend beyond executing projects to planning them. Here, too, insights developed on the local level can prove invaluable. Such a partnership between aid professionals and villagers is also likely to increase transparency and reduce corruption. It will spark an appetite for wider knowledge and complementary skill development. Locals are likely to know the specifics of what needs to be done; the professionals are likely to have a better grip on the best ways to get things done. Such constructive interaction ensures the local 'buy-in' and a genuine sense of 'local ownership.'

In case my encomium on the benefits of "local empowerment" still strikes you as somewhat vague and idealistic (a bad combination) let me give you a few examples of the forms such empowerment have already taken. Empowering individuals and families through microcredit loans to women in Bangladesh through the Grameen Bank has enabled millions of women to incrementally expand their farm and other local enterprises – with over 90 percent repayment rates. Over the recent decades Grameen Bank has broadened its focus and is adding several productive and service commercial enterprises. [1]

We have briefly discussed the Bangladesh Rural Advancement Committee (BRAC) whose activities include microcredit and social partnership, providing basic curative and preventive services to about 44 percent of the Bangladesh population.[2] Also, the above-mentioned Green Belt Movement engages in many of the 'best practices' featured in the UN civil society website directly benefits women and children by focusing on specific sustainable environmental features such as reducing land degradation and providing access to NGO type sponsored health facilities.[3]

Cornell University's Mann Library maintains The Essential Electronic Agricultural Library (TEEAL), a unique 'knowledge-ware' service for institutions worldwide, consisting of a full-text and searchable database of articles from 200 high-quality research journals in agriculture and related sciences. Such up-to-date data can be invaluable help to researchers planning projects in far flung places.[4]

In San Gabriel, Mexico PepsiCo is conducting a pilot initiative to empower 300 farmers in the local area by providing credit to buy potato seed, fertilizer, crop insurance and equipment. This is a totally commercial approach which benefits PepsiCo, as they buy all the crops, but the farmers receive the income, and it gives them a viable alternative to the violent and dangerous business of running drugs to the US.[5] Grameen Bank's link with Danone Yoghurt into a 'social business enterprise' commercially benefits the local dairy farmers a ready market and Danone's market expansion.[6]

New cost-effective applicable technologies (some very 'low-tech') are continually being invented and improved upon. Here are a few examples. Oxfam international is working with a company, environmental products of Minnesota, Inc. to develop filtration systems to provide healthy drinking water for African communities plagued by fluorosis, a bone wasting condition caused by high mineral content of water in the region.[7]

Compatible Technologies International, an NGO with over a thirty-year track record, works with researchers to develop and provide a portfolio of innovative low-cost practical tools to increase food supply and clean water for rural poor people in dozens of countries.[8] Indigenous grain storage structures in India and Mali addresses villagers' storage and waste reduction needs during the part of the yearly cycle when there foodstuffs are unavailable and the prices are high at the market.[9] A recent technology with far reaching applicability to localizing energy production which can be harnessed for local energy distribution is Easy Energy Systems, Inc. The company has now made their large scale ethanol manufacturing at an appropriate size and that uses local waste from agricultural products, and affordable.[10] Eight19, a Cambridge, UK, company, has begun marketing an innovative plastic solar cell system for household use and for recharging cell phones in Kenya, Malawi, and Zambia; it can be paid for with a scratch-card through mobile phones at about half of the typical monthly cost. For several years groups in India have been producing low-cost innovations incorporating 'needs assessment' from villagers and people providing services at field level. The point being: as such technologies and 'knowledge-ware' prove workable, they can be brought forward through ITAC and incorporated to a village or urban slum environment for community and family usage.

Examples that Empower People

The local empowerment which interests us in the pilot project, and more generally in the New Dynamic Approach, is slightly different from the above examples. Specifically it involves Official Development Assistance (ODA) usually termed foreign aid. Examples of people and communities being empowered to participate in genuine (and sustaining) 'bottom-up planning' and implementation of projects and annual budgets are few and far between, unfortunately. Foreign assisted projects have, in the past, incorporated findings 'from the ground' to some extent, usually in the design phase, but Centroid Power does not have a 'proactive mode' of community support. A subclass of local empowerment however exists under the rubric of 'community participation.'

In the Indonesian stories I related in Chapter 3, the village-based primary health care initiative called Posyandu provided a variety of MCH services, leveraged from traditional community institutions. Its district and health center staff with women in their villages weighed babies, offered immunizations, dispensed high-dose vitamin C, and provided nutritional education and family planning services, among other things.[11] The program was successful in tens of thousands of villages over many years, and it benefited from the direct support of a cadre of village women themselves, all volunteer. At the same time, the Indonesian government's family planning program was inter-sectoral and paid village family-planning workers, once again providing tangible support for community participation. As I mentioned earlier, during the Soeharto regime of 'guided democracy' a delicate balance was sought. The regime worked to improve health and family planning services, with the help of community participation, but without unduly disturbing the ethos of servitude within which most villagers lived. In both Malawi and Tanzania, I often saw men from the villages doing 'self-help' repairs for local water sources; but there was no public financing for these activities. Successes in community participation from other countries could be adduced, such as China's 1970s 'Barefoot Doctor' program, though such efforts have by now been clothed in a haze of legend or submerged beneath China's 'great leap forward.'[12]

In some countries' primary health care initiatives through the local health centers train community health workers (CHW) who receive minor compensation from combinations of local government and families in the village. The CHW's duties vary, though they are principally focused on maternal and child health (as noted in Chapter 8). CHWs activities also sometimes include dispensing basic medicines to villagers for set prices and using these funds to 'stock up' from the local health center. The CHW's also support the health centers by referring mothers and children, when necessary, to the local health center or closest hospital. Although WHO promotes community empowerment explicitly in its literature, a careful read reveals some rather esoteric considerations and the examples provided do not emphasize communities' direct and continual involvement in ODA type projects.[13] As I discussed in Chapter 8, modifications to the Millennium Village Project (MVP) should explicitly enhance greater empowerment of villagers in the planning, budgeting and all aspects of managing their local projects.

Returning to Indonesia in 2008 on an assignment, I had several discussions with officials at the Ministry of Finance concerning some of the features I presented in the sections on corruption and mney transfers. We explored the feasibility of getting all foreign aid and NGO monies registered in the ministry of finance, and establishing laws with detailed procedures to bypass the central level and send monies directly to the districts and sub-districts. There were differences of opinion in the various sections of the ministry of finance, needless to say, as to the merit of my suggestions. In any case, no one was much interested taking the necessary steps to implement any of them.

Yet back in 1998, following the Asian Economic Crisis and Soeharto's resignation, the World Bank in Indonesia was looking for a major 'mea culpa' in response to the well-founded criticism that massive World Bank loans were linked to the widespread corruption in the Soeharto regime. Clearly the World Bank needed an innovative, successful project to reverse the public opinion and improve its image. It was at this time that the Indonesian Kecamatan (Sub-district) Development Programme (KDP) got underway; it ran from 1998 to 2008.[14]

Though I describe the program in greater detail in Chapter 6, a few of the details are germane to the current topic. The KDP was run through the Ministry of Home Affairs. It provided 'block-grants' directly (e.g. importantly 'bypassing' central and regional levels) to sub-districts. About 75 percent of the average grant went to design and construct small infrastructure projects for local roads, bridges and water-related works, with an emphasis on community empowerment. The other 25 percent typically was devoted to microcredit, repayable at the market rates. During these eight years it was in operation, the KDP spent serious money—about $1.6 billion in grants and loans including Trust Funds from Dutch, Japan, Multidonor Trust Fund, DFID/UK. The program was extended to 32 provinces, 350 districts, 2600 sub-districts, and 38,000 villages (about 50 percent) throughout the archipelago.

In August 2006 the Government of Indonesia (GOI) launched the National Program for Community Empowerment (PNPM in the Indonesian language) another nation-wide effort to reduce poverty in both rural and urban locales. The rural program aims to accelerate achievement of three Millennium Development Goals: universal basic education, reduction in child mortality and improvement in maternal health.

The background to these programs, which encouraged local empowerment, may illuminate roadblocks that anyone attempting to implement similar project is likely to face—and some of the ways around them, too. Why, for instance, did it take the 1998 Asian Economic Crisis to bring Centroid Power to a point of 'near enlightenment' in acknowledging that real power lies in community empowerment? What were the finance laws that enabled the KPD project to by-pass the finance ministry? And why was the Indonesian Ministry of Finance reluctant to adopt similar fast-track financing for other foreign aid projects? It's clear that the KDP, already within the World Bank's experience (and in its files) in an essential project that the ITAC should review carefully as it ramps up its own community-based pilots. The intricacy of Indonesia's complex socio-cultural economic, administrative and financing arrangements would make such a review daunting, but all the more valuable in the end, for the same reasons and be instructional guides to many other countries.

How to involve local leaders in development projects

Developing leadership at the local level lies at the core of the New Dynamic Approach. It seems to me there are five things to keep in mind when recruiting local leaders for development programs:

(i) It's important to remain sensitive to nuances of socio-cultural behavior and economic conditions whenever you're dealing with local empowerment. People living in poverty in rural villages and urban slums often have a lifetime of fortitude and resilience at their disposal, which they would gladly direct toward participation in local affairs. But their lives are often guided by customs and courtesies that outsiders ought to familiarize themselves with as soon as possible.

(ii) In most countries, the local leadership in villages has been appointed through the existing Centroid Power mechanisms and apparatus. Yet we cannot *a priori* exclude these local leaders, since they may share our enthusiasm for enhanced local empowerment, even though they have had neither opportunities nor funds to pursue such things in the past. Further, their local networks can be an invaluable recruitment tool, putting newcomers into immediate contact with members of the community who want to participate in local projects and affairs. A well-designed program would build upon the current strength of local institutions, augmenting it with newly selected leaders who possess enthusiasm and knowledge of the community.

(iii) The women and men who do accept leadership roles in programs should be rewarded for their efforts in accordance with a 'reward structure' that's understood by the entire community. The basic rewards may include a small monthly remuneration and/or 'in-kind' features such as highly subsidized medicines to the family and school fees for their children.

(iv) Local empowerment will generate leadership and advocacy from the communities' members. They will press to ensure that as participants they are not 'docile recipients' of support, but are responsibly engaged in bettering themselves and their communities.

(v) Projects will include training in various technical aspects of a given activity. In this way knowledge is transferred to those benefiting from a program, and by the same token, community input regarding local conditions increases the likelihood that a specific technique, which sounds good in theory, is given severe tests under local conditions and will actually yield results. This results in a two way traffic of sustained 'knowledge exchange' adding vigorous capital that is shared among communities in the wider public domain of the country and among countries—as it should be. And 'what goes around comes around'. In the cases of successful low-cost technical improvements in, for example, farming and health care to be replicated in neighboring villages, and slums throughout the country with the help of the national media. Armed with success stories, individuals and families will be better able to push their local officials to participate in similar projects. The successful examples will be used by the NTAC and ITAC in other countries and districts in the worldwide network.

The other side of the Equation: Funding

It will be a formidable task to get the pilot project for the New Dynamic Approach formulated, financed, and up and running and sustaining. But the task will be made somewhat easier by the very existence of the World Bank. There are vestiges of Centroid Power within the World Bank, to be sure, but there are also modernizing forces within it. The World Bank Group Strategy (October 2013) gives a strong impression that modernizing forces are leading the way.[15] These include the advocates within the World Bank who see the institution's role as a 'knowledge center' principally to provide technical assistance to countries and their people.

As I mentioned earlier, the World Bank has developed an impressive reservoir of human capital and a world-wide information network, incorporating new technologies that can provide leadership in a wide spectrum of disciplines and cultures. Our job will be to align the best resources within that institution with the framework of the New Dynamic Approach. In the previous chapter I described how the World Bank could be creatively reshaped to contribute to the new dynamic process. Further confirmation of the World Bank's proactive posture may be seen in the new International Corruption Hunters Alliance and the Stolen Asset Recovery initiative (SARI). At the same time, it could ramp up a full-scale campaign against corrupt practices. The World Bank's preeminent position would serve to put the others in the cornucopia of international and national development agencies on notice that "business as usual" will no longer do, and agencies and businesses would be advised to adopt the New Dynamic Approach themselves, selecting appropriate leadership, professionals, and staff.

But the World Bank will need the support of a number of countries to advance the pilot project and the agenda of the New Dynamic Approach more generally. Only a small number of donor countries have come close to meeting the UN's target contributions toward Official Development Assistance (ODA). In particular the Nordic countries of Sweden, Norway, Denmark, Finland, and the Netherlands have continued to do their part, over the years, and these nations also have a good deal of experience with funding projects and developing human infrastructure and aid networks in several countries in sub-Saharan Africa and Asia. They would be more favorably disposed to this New Dynamic Approach than would the general run of participating donors, and they would act as vital allies in initiating the modifications required to move the program through the sclerotic United Nations systems and development industry.

Further Sources of Finance for the Pilot Project

I begin by presuming that until proven otherwise, the international development agencies which participate in the pilot project will have adequate resources or can reorganize their budgets so that *no major additional costs* to them are required. This is based on the understanding that administrative inputs and travel budgets can be reoriented for the pilot project. The existing resources for 'knowledge centers' and 'knowledge/brain-ware' infrastructure-based systems should be adequate to the task at hand just as they are. As a sensible strategy: first 'use what you got that works'. As discussed in the sections dealing with Lever One and Three, as a first step the ITAC and NTAC should review and inventory successful low-costs infrastructure-based system in these the key specializes and sub-specialties within the piloted countries and other examples before inventing new ones.

Financing for the New Dynamic Approach will also receive a boost from several sources, just as 'the scissors cuts with two blades.' Money will be saved through the reorganizations described in our review of the Levers, and is also likely to be added as the fruits of corruption are corralled and fed back into the program. At the same time, once the pipes of resource allocation and disbursement are 'unclogging,' less of it will evaporate as it *sloshes* at the central level, and more will arrive where it can do some good, at the district and local levels (as discussed in Chapter 10). A useful benchmark of success in this regard might be 75 percent of project investment and operational costs consistently spent at the district level and below, year after year. The Avant-Garde might have a special role to play in getting the pilot project off the ground, providing one-time start-up donations. Meanwhile, it will be of the utmost important that funds accrued through the management of natural resource contracts remain in government coffers and are directed toward worthwhile goals. Resource-rich countries in sub-Saharan Africa with widespread poverty often receive offers and investments from transnational corporations (mainly the industries of petrochemical and mining) and sovereign wealth funds. As often as not, the monies for these major purchases and/or natural resource development efforts never enters the country, due to graft and corruption.[16] The frequency and gigantic amounts of the seemingly endless financial scams is unabated.[17] Hence, the importance of coalescing and strengthening the international anti-corruption institutions during the three-year preparatory phase of the pilot project (as per Lever Four.)

The *third source of added financing* for the pilot project could be a worldwide consortium of independent foundations including wealthy individuals, organizations, corporations, foundations, and trusts that share an interest in reshaping the development industry along the lines of the New Dynamic Approach. One obvious advantage of such independent financing is that it would enable pilot project staff to focus on the work at hand by limiting the amount of bureaucratic and academic bickering from various international and national development agencies.

Then again, if the international community ever went so far as to institute something resembling the Tobin Tax, even more funds would become available.[18] In light of the difficulties faced by the G8 nations in reforming their financial services industries, such taxes will not be part of the equation for decades to come. Nonetheless, perhaps some individuals or corporations in the financial industry will become proactive contributors to the New Dynamic Approach, choosing to welcome and abide by the 'rules of the road' established by the ITAC Division of Avant-Garde.

THE WORLDWIDE ACADEMY

With more than a half-century of experience in the field in many parts of the world, I remain convinced that Centroid Power rules not only many of the countries that are bemired in poverty, but also the development industry itself. That being the case, it's clear to me that no amount of tinkering around the edges of the industry will improve its dismal record at reaching the goals which it is ostensibly dedicated to reach—to reduce poverty and foster local economic growth for the more-than three billion who subsist in squalid conditions throughout the world on a few dollars a day. But I may be wrong. I welcome any and all challenges and critiques from academicians and think-tank professionals who take the time to ponder the New Dynamic Approach I'm proposing. After all, it's an open book, and their responsibility lies in either endorsing my analyses, or improving upon them.

Let the New Dynamic Approach begin!

Are you ready for a wild and most worthy ride? Do you have the tenacity and perseverance to 'pick up the cudgels,' withstand the ceaseless onslaught of abuse, some of it not so subtle, from Centroid Power, and through your energies, values and understanding, breathe life into the New Dynamic Approach, no matter the level? Your efforts and those of your friends and colleagues may be directed at one of the Levers you have specific knowledge and/or interest in, or the whole shebang.

You may, and then again you may not, meet the beneficiaries of your efforts personally. But in any case, your continual effort will keep the movement towards the New Dynamic Approach alive. Your contribution may be to support your children's schools in making 'pen pal' contact, either postal or electronic. And it might provide support to schools in the piloted projects' districts, opening numerous options for the children abroad as well as your own.

In fact, there are unlimited ways to get involved in the New Dynamic Approach; and in doing so, you too will become a beneficiary. In this regard I certainly believe in concepts such as 'A thousand flowers bloom' and 'A thousand points of light' for leadership within the development industry, both through direct local empowerment initiatives and through the Avant-Garde. You could lobby your friends and local groups, your elected leaders, and national and international development agencies. I encourage you to become involved and stay engaged. I can guarantee it will be worth the effort. Remember: the forces of self-interested Centroid control are powerful, and at present, their minions control the destiny of the world's population. It is up to us to keep continual pressure on the decision-makers to genuinely achieve the sustained poverty reduction they have committed themselves to. Are you ready to jump into 'the tank'? I am!

Appendix: Updated status for selected Millennium Development Goals aimed at 2015

Official Developmental Assistance for the Millennium Development Goals has been increasing, and reports delivered at the September 2010 UN Summit revealed that some progress had been made in most countries toward reaching the specified targets, with five years to go.[1] Readers interested in complete details, background analyses, and updated reports of the MDG's are directed to numerous available official sites. Here, in encapsulated form, are some recent findings regarding goals 1, 4, 5, 6 and 7.

MGD1, (Target 1.C) "Halve, between 1990 and 2015, the proportion of people who suffer from hunger."

Professor Per Pinstrup-Anderson argues, in a first-class article, (from a book of academic articles describing synergies between nutrition and other MDGs), that the number of people who suffer from hunger will remain far above MDG target-levels in 2015.[2] While there was a 3 percent decline in hunger between 1991 and 2005, the food crisis of 2009 brought back the hunger rate to 15 percent, suggesting little or no progress will be made by 2015. Hunger is most critical in sub-Saharan Africa where at present trends there'll be 250 – 270 million hungry people by 2015, when the targeted numbers are 87 million. This represents an increase of 40 to 60 percent, mainly in the Democratic Republic of Congo. In East, South, and West Africa incidence of hunger remained unchanged until the food crisis. With the increase in sub-Saharan population faster than hungry people this implies progress in Target 1.C.

Estimating people suffering from hunger is far from straightforward and different methodologies and indices are used. FAO in *The State of Food Insecurity in the World 2009* (Rome)[3] presented progress in sub-Saharan Africa for the number of countries reaching four levels (reproduced in table 2.3) of the Pinstrup-Anderson's article. The most optimistic index of hungry people is MDG, in which twelve countries are on target to halve hunger by 2015, and fifteen other countries are making some progress, with five countries making no progress and seven countries seriously worsening. The International Food Policy Research Institute (IFPRI) Global Food Index (GHI) [4] is a more inclusive measure of hunger – aggregating three variables: (i) the percentage of population suffering from hunger, (ii) the percentage of children under the age of five who are underweight, and (iii) the under-five mortality rate expressed as a percentage. Using the GHI in sub-Saharan Africa, only four countries are on target to halve hunger by 2015, twenty-four countries show some progress, nine countries have no progress or show worsening, and one country is seriously worsened. Ghana is cited as an example of progress, with more than two decades of investments in agriculture resulting in sustained increases in productivity and agricultural incomes for farmers and rural communities.

Estimates of nourishment in the developing world is updated by the FAO annually in The State of Food Insecurity in the World publications. The estimates for 2010 – 2012 for chronic hunger (not getting enough food to lead active healthy lives) was revised upward from 852 to 868 million people, and for 2013, downward to 842 million people, or one of eight in the developing world. Sub-Saharan Africa remains the worst off in this regard with one in four people chronically hungry. No progress was made in Western Asia, while South Asia and North Africa have had slow progress. While the prevalence of undernourished people in the developing world decreased from 23.2 per cent (1990 – 1992) to 14.9 per cent (2010 – 2012), as noted above it is unlikely the 2015 MDG target of 12 per cent will be met. Reducing child malnutrition remains a significant challenge.[5]

MDG4 (Target 4.A) Reduce by two-thirds between 1990 and 2015 the under-five mortality rate and **MDG5 (Target 5.A)** Reduce by three-quarters the maternal mortality rate.[6]

An article in the *Lancet* (2010) using updated data and new methodology, suggested that under-five deaths were declining (7.2 million in 2011), and the rate of decline was accelerating. Maternal mortality continued to decline (in thousands) from 409 in 1990 to 274 in 2011, with 56 thousand HIV-related in 2011. The authors note that 23 countries in sub-Saharan Africa were unlikely at the present pace to achieve MGD4 before 2040.

South Asia still accounts for one-third of the worldwide deaths to children under five in 2011. The highest rates of infant mortality fall within the first month of life. Only 13 countries are on track to achieve the MDG5 by 2015.

MGD6 (Target 6.A) Halt and reverse, by 2015, the spread of HIV/AIDS and (6.B) achieve, by 2010, universal access to treatment for HIV/AIDS for all those who need it.[7]

The UNAIDS World AIDS Day Report for 2011 presents significant success on key indices. AIDS-related deaths are at their lowest level since 2005, the peak, down 21 percent the number of new HIV infections in 2010 was down 21 percent from a peak seen in 1997. Sub-Saharan Africa has seen the most dramatic improvement, with a 20 percent rise in people undergoing treatment between 2009 and 2010. UN AIDS estimates 700,000 deaths were averted last year because of better access to treatment. That result, in turn, helped reduce new HIV infections by 30 to 50 percent. Namibia, for example, increased access to treatment by 90 percent, and condom use rose 75 percent, resulting in a 60 percent drop in infections by 2010. Nonetheless, at the end of 2010, an estimated 34 million people were living with HIV worldwide, up 17 percent from 2001. This rise reflects both the large number of new infections, and growth in the population of those who previously would have died, but now have access to antiretroviral therapy. Notwithstanding the successes with antiretroviral therapy, the impact of HIV/AIDS on developing nations—their health sector, enterprise and workplaces, economy, and households—remains staggering. For example, in sub-Saharan Africa, those with HIV/AIDS receive $30 per year in public health, while the remainder of the population receives less than $10 a year. People with HIV-related diseases occupy more than half of the hospital beds and soon 60 to 70 percent of hospital expenditure in South Africa will be for patients with HIV/AIDS. Women in Africa account for 58 percent of the adults with HIV/AIDS.[8]

MDG6 (Target 6.C) Have halted by 2015 and begun to reverse the incidence of malaria and other major diseases.

Between 2000 and 2010, mortality rates from malaria fell by more than 25 per cent globally. An estimated 1.1 million malaria deaths were averted over this period, with more than half of those lives saved in the ten countries with the highest malaria burden. By 2011, 50 of 99 countries with ongoing malaria transmission were on track to reduce their malaria case incidence rates by 75 per cent by 2015. Sleeping under an insecticide-treated mosquito net is the most effective way to prevent malaria transmission. By 2011, over a third of children under five slept under insecticide-treated mosquito nets, up from less than 5 per cent in 2000. However, large disparities are found across subregions.[9] These reductions constitute solid achievements in the global fight against malaria—and as all the indices needs to be sustained.

Tuberculosis: The annual global number of new cases of tuberculosis has been slowly falling since 2006 and fell 2.2% between 2010 and 2011. In 2011, there were an estimated 8.7 million new cases, of which about 13% involved people living with HIV. Mortality due to tuberculosis has fallen 41% since 1990 and is trending to globally reach a 50% reduction by 2015. Globally, treatment success rates have been sustained at high levels since 2007, at or above the target of 85%.[10]

MGD7 (Target 7.C) Halve, by 2015, the proportion of people without sustainable access to safe drinking water and basic hygiene.[11]

The UK charity Water Aid issued a report in November 2011: "Off-track, off-target: why investment in water, sanitation and hygiene (WASH) is not reaching those who need it most". It makes for grim reading. Whilst there are of course differences among countries here are some of the overall findings. Almost 900 million people worldwide live without access to clean water. The MDG Review Summit in 2010 report concluded that while the global MDG drinking water target is on-track, due to progress in China and India in particular, large parts of the developing world remain off-track, and there is a growing disparity between regions. With 2015 approaching, the effort to provide sanitation isn't keeping up with population growth. The latest projections show that the 2015 MDG sanitation target will be missed by as many as one billion people. The poorest families, particularly the women and girls who carry the water and look after sick children, pay the highest price for the lack of progress. Diarrheal diseases are the biggest killer of children in Africa, and the second biggest killer of children in South Asia. With 88 percent of diarrhea due to inadequate WASH, this shortfall in progress is responsible for over two million deaths annually. It's the second leading cause of death of children under-five worldwide.

Acknowledgments

Since my youth I have been privileged to have had illuminating dialogues with many mentors, teachers, colleagues and friends. I would like to mention some of the people who have influenced me on my journey. Without their insights and support, this treatise would never have been written. Needless to say, I take responsibility for all of the assessments and conclusions presented in this volume, which are my own.

My uncle Roger, an esteemed lawyer, instilled in me at an early age an awareness of the unavoidable presence of realpolitik in political affairs, but also of the importance of cultivating the values of fairness and social justice. He stressed the need to establish and sustain institutional environments that would provide opportunities for individuals from all walks of life. My mother, Anne, nourished the same ideals and helped to set the international focus of my career. My brother, Marshall, has served as a sounding board for my ideas over many decades, through correspondence and dialog, helping me to hone my critique of the world's often deleterious power structures through playful but relentless conceptual jousting.

Among the many fine professors and academic colleagues I have had (some of which I will mention) I was most privileged to be guided by two quiet giants in the field of land economics—Professor Philip M. Raup of the University of Minnesota and Professor Howard E. Conklin of Cornell University. Both scholars were adept at underscoring the importance of field work, delineating the tools and techniques to conduct it, and the methodologies required to analyze the results properly. After decades in the field, I found the wide-ranging conversations with these two men no less enlightening that I had as a graduate student. Various remarks these gentlemen made have echoed in my head throughout the subsequent decades. Among others, from Dr. Raup, "Clarity of thought and precision of expression." And Dr. Conklin's great personal adage: "Do you really want to get in a fur-lined groove and wiggle?"

The '60s were the halcyon years of American education. At the University of Minnesota, Professor Oswald Brownlee approved my admission to the Economics Department and Dr. Edward Coen (Professor of International Trade, Economic Department) took an interest in my graduate education; my friend Dr. Willis Anthony (Anthony Farms) spoke on my behalf to Professor Sherwood O. Berg, Head of the Department of Agricultural Economics and kindly referred me to Professor Raup who generously provided me an assistantship on his Minnesota land tenure project. In recent years I've been delighted to renew acquaintanceship with professors from the same department, Wesley Burt Sundquist and Dale C. Dahl. At Cornell the Head of the Department of Agricultural Economics, Professor Glenn Hedlund followed by Bernard Stanton, ran a seemingly smooth department of stallions in the finest of Cornell's traditions; Professor David J. Allee was on the cusp (or avant-garde) of resource economics. Also, my early assistantship with Professor Daniel G. Sisler and occasional memorable luncheon conversations with the renowned statistician on agricultural market prices, retired Professor Frank. A. Pearson, gave me a solid understanding of the department's traditions. The insights from these gentlemen were highly beneficial to me throughout graduate school.

Also at Cornell, Professor Jaroslav Vanek (Economics Department, macroeconomic theory) and Professor Peter J. McCarthy (Statistics Department) invariably provided a fine mix of rigor and humor in their unforgettable hour-and-a-half lectures, as did the many students who brought their dogs to lectures—another exceptional Cornell tradition. The friendship of fellow graduate students endures throughout life even though communication may be on hold for decades. For me these include, among others, Thomas A. Wilson (the late Milk Marketing Administrator for New York New Jersey),

Dr. Donald R. Nicholson (retired, Milk Marketing Administrator for the Central Federal Order), the late Professor Ralph d'Arge (Resource Economics at the Universities of California, Riverside; and Wyoming), Professor Thomas O'Brien (retired, Head of School of Management, University of Massachusetts, Amherst).

The cultural jolt of my first tropical work in Tanzania at the University of Dar es Salaam was blunted by Professor Simon Mbilini (from Cornell and in the Economic Research Bureau), Professor Ian Livingston (Head, Economic Research Bureau, no relation to the famed East and Central Africa explorer, David), Dr. Adolfo Mascaranous (Bureau of Resource Assessment and Land Use Planning), Professor J. E. Phythian (Mathematics Department) and Dr. E. O. Landgreen (Statistics Department). The fieldwork in Nzega District (distilled in Chapter 3) could not have been done without the students from the Bureau of Land Use Planning and the daily full support and insights provided Elias Kwelukilma (Village Executive Officer, Igunga), David Mgama and the many farmers, livestock owners in Nzega District and families in Igunga. I contracted hepatitis and during the first month I received first-class care from the staff at Kalunda Hospital, Tabora. Later I spent a month of recovery and was welcomed at the Swiss Capuchin monastery and Diocese of Mahenge in Ulanga District, Morogora Region by Father Superior Wolfram and the other fathers and brothers. Father Wolfram's leadership style was among the best I've witnessed. Among others, this was exemplified by the numerous community development projects—agricultural, infrastructure, and education—that the Swiss 'Caps' had initiated and sustained for decades in the communities of Ulanga District. I was pleased to visit several of these with Father Wolfram.

My introduction to the British National Health Service, while researching their operations, was facilitated and supported by many academicians, medical, healthcare and staff, including Professor John Ashford (University of Exeter), Dr. John Preece (General Practitioner, Exeter), Professor James Scott and Dr. David Jenkins, M.D.

(Department of Obstetrics, University of Leeds), Dr. David Pole (Head Economist, National Health Service, London) and David J. King (District Administrator, Exeter Health Care District). Each and every one provided me with magnificent learning opportunities. I am most indebted to Philip K. Tonkin (Exeter, County Devon) whose friendship, guidance, and generous insights over decades, perhaps more than most, kept my interests in poverty and economic development alive.

My immersion to Asian culture during my assignments in Indonesia was more dramatic than that of Tanzania had been a decade earlier, in part because it was simultaneous with my entrance into two humongous bureaucracies, the World Health Organization and the Indonesian Ministry of Health, which at that time was on the frontier of establishing a strong primary health care initiative. The Bureau of Health Planning, where our WHO team was posted, was near the 'tip of the spear.' Dr. Desmond Nugent, M.D. (Head of WHO Jakarta) provided experienced leadership. No one could ask for more loyal and supportive collegial team members than Dr. Haydee Lopez, M.D. and Fernando Sadek, both of whom provided me the essential background for public health and tropical medicine, and encouraged me to explore Indonesia's public finance in the health sector in depth.

I would like to thank and pay tribute to several Indonesians for their special contributions to their country and to my professional growth. As often happens, some of their valued contributions were not fully recognized at the time, but bore fruit years later. [Note: In Indonesia, dr. designates medical doctors.] In the Bureau of Health Planning, the past head, dr. Hapsara, past directorate heads, Azis la Sida, dr. Sriati da Costa, dr. Sodiono; also in the Ministry of Health, dr. Julie Sulianti Soreoso, M.D. (past director of health research), dr. Bahrawi (past inspector general), dr. Bennie Kawanaga (past inspector of development, Office of the Inspector General). dr. Brotowasisto (past head of bureau of planning and director general, Medical

Care), Mr. Soeripto (past head engineer and Asian Development Bank project head, directorate general of Medical Care), dr. Abdul Sorenro (secretary, Directorate of Community Medicine). I especially recognize Professor Dr. Soekirman, Ph.D. (professor emeritus of nutrition, Bogor Agricultural University and at BAPPENAS (Indonesian Ministry of Planning) past Deputy Minister of Human Development, including health, nutrition, education, population, women's affairs and other social affairs) for his forward foci and initiatives on all poverty and development issues. I learned a tremendous amount from 'Pak' Soekirman throughout our working years together and in ensuing conversations. My friend and colleague, Johan Arief's loyalty is unmatched as we continue to dialogue on the wide range of Indonesian and economic development subjects using e-and digital devices. Invariably, Johan's information and insights are crisp, well-founded, and otherwise 'spot-on.'

During my years working on World Bank projects, I became acquainted with many talented and well-informed colleagues, reinforcing my sense of the World Bank as a genuine 'center of excellence in knowledge' that I have proposed to utilize more fully in the pilot project described in Chapters 9–11. In Indonesia I worked with and alongside Dr. Bernard Lesie, M.D. (past senior public health specialists and medical director for World Bank personnel), Dr. David d'Ferranti, President of Results for Development (previous senior economist, then Director of Health Sector Research and finally director of Latin America and the Caribbean office) and Nick Prescott (senior health economist). In the early years of health sector financing, these colleagues supported and encouraged me to continue digging away with the collection and analysis of financing information and other potentially sensitive issues. Dr. Charles (Ok) Pannenborg, M.D. (senior public health specialist) invited me to participate on projects in Malawi and Nepal in health sector financing and health systems design. Irrespective of the complex environment and issues, Dr. Pannenborg's breadth and depth of knowledge in public health and family planning, together with his straightforward management style, encouraged creative and realistic assessments and recommendations for the involved countries and their institutions. The work in Malawi for designing a 'cost recovery' system for the state-supported health services (described in Chapter 3) was done at the request and under the supervision of Dr. David d'Ferranti, whose leadership was crucial when dealing with this highly sensitive subject.

In Ghana I greatly benefited from the support, openness, and insights of Dr. Moses Adibo, M.D. (project director, Ministry of Health), Dr. K. A. Enyimeyew, M.D. (project team member and district chief medical officer, Ministry of Health), Mr. Isaac Ewun-Tohma (controller and accountant general), Mr. S. E. K. Anipa (chief economic planning officer for health, Ministry of Finance and Economic Planning) and Dr. Richard Osborn, team project expert. The field research conducted throughout Ghana for hospitals, health centers and in the communities could not have been done without our Ghanaian team, Dr. Henry Jackson (Economics Department, Legon University), and Anthony Chinebauh, the health and medical staffs—and above all, the many individuals and farmers we were fortunate enough to meet and interview.

In Malawi, on the World Bank missions and 'cost sharing study' described in Chapter 3 I was privileged to work with many Malawian officials in the Ministries of Health, Home Affairs, and Finance. Each gave generously of their time, expertise, background information and insights, thus contributing mightily to the successful reports. Mr. R. P. Dzanjalimodzi (principal secretary, Ministry of Health) clearly outlined the issues in cost-sharing and supported all activities for the study and Mr. R. F. Kavinga (Ministry of Finance) and Chairman of the Steering Committee for the Cost Sharing Study. Frank R. Mwambaghi (principal health planning officer) was the ideal counterpart; he devoted major time and attention to me and our work; thus, enabling greater understanding and many nuances to be included. Mr. R. Khikoja (head, Accountant General Office, Ministry of Finance) generously met me on several occasions to clarify facets and procedures necessary to include in the cost-sharing study. Without the detailed knowledge he provided I would have missed several key elements. Our team members who added their specialized expertise for the cost-sharing study were Dr. P. H. van Kessel, M.D, Ph.D. (obstetrician and gynecologist, Loon op Zand, The Netherlands) and Mr. Yaw Abu-Bohene, (economist, Accra, Ghana). During the field trips with Frank Mwambaghi, we met many Malawians in health facilities and in their rural communities. I'm indebted to them for their forthright discussions on the very sensitive issues of poverty and health systems which they must all continue to endure.

My work in the Hashemite Kingdom of Jordan was part of a USAID project. I'd like to thank Dr. Willard Boynton who, as project manager for the work conducted through Westinghouse project, got me quickly up to speed on the key issues involved and facilitated the necessary contacts. I'm also most appreciative for the professional guidance and courtesies extended by the H. E. minister of health, Dr. Ziad Hamzeh, who set the stage for a systemic consideration of the health sector. I give special recognition to the Ministry of Health Directorate of Research and Planning, particularly to Dr. Mahmoud, and Dr. Abdula Hamdan, for their full participation throughout the project. I number my discussions with Brig. Dr. N. Ajlouni, head of the Royal Medical Services among the most memorable of my career. Dr. Ajlouni kindly provided his astute insights and details on the complexities of Jordan's multiple health systems. Dr. Wajih Barakat, from the Medical Syndicate, also provided details and insights; his availability and access to all in the health systems was greatly appreciated.

I appreciated the collegiality, many insights and continued support of three academic economists and pragmatists with whom I had the pleasure of working on projects and continue to have dialogues. Professor Robert N. Grosse (School of Public Health, University of Michigan) encouraged my work in Indonesia; and we worked together in Nepal on costing and financial aspects of a USAID supported

Vitamin A project. Professor Albert van der Werff (previous Head of Health Planning, Ministry of Health, The Netherlands, then Maastricht University and WHO HQ), as consultant to the WHO Indonesia health planning team, provided insightful perspectives in primary health care policy and organization; and as an independent consultant, remains a beacon of independent creativity. Professor David Bloom (Global Health and Population, School of Public Health, Harvard University) was in charge of the Palestinian Authority health sector project; he generously provided keen insights, guidance and support on many technical and administrative issues during the period in which I led our teams in Ramallah and Gaza.

There were other serendipitous encounters which created meaningful friendships. Whilst growing up our neighbors, Dr. Paul and Charlotte (CC) Finley were off to London's Hammersmith Hospital for a year. Dr. Finley most generously discussed my matriculation at the London School of Economics with the LSE's admissions director, which led to one year of study abroad at an early age, which had a profound effect on my subsequent career. Whilst in Singapore I consulted with Dr. Steven Goh on a small matter; immediately there was 'super karma' and Dr. Goh almost unwittingly and most generously clarified for me many culturally-related issues and differences between the East and West. We too, resume the paragraph in which we left off at each reunion, which unfortunately have become too infrequent.

In my current suburban neighborhood I had the pleasure of meeting Marlene LaMoure Urbach, Doug Guild, and Kent Anderson at different times and circumstances—Marlene with her background in medicine and business; Doug's expertise in human resources and software, and Kent with his astute pragmatic focus, each being interested in the economy and current affairs (domestic and international). They have been valuable friends and astute critics of most of the material in this book. The dialogues I have enjoyed with Marlene, Doug, and Kent, along with my brother, Marshall, have helped me to drop the bureaucratic jargon and convey my ideas and constructs more clearly and crisply. After decades, I met up again with a friend from college days, Ted Weinberg, a local businessman proactive in support of social justice worldwide. I have benefitted from Ted's encouragement and insights with enjoyable phone calls and queries throughout the lengthy period of research and writing. Fortunately, digital devices have facilitated stimulating discussions with my friend, Taylan Bâli (Department of Economics, Ankara University) on economics and development, during which we covered a wide range of subjects including theory, policy, statistics, and practical aspects of policy implementation. I am most appreciative to Marilyn Coulter, a senior bank manager, concerned citizen and avid reader with wide interests, for generously reading this manuscript and providing astute and incisive feedback.

Once again, a huge stroke of serendipity delivered a great gift. On a frigid winter day, while I was having coffee klatch with Marshall, we met an old family friend, Norton Stillman, owner and publisher of Nodin Press. I later met with Norton and shared with him a chapter outline of the book. After reading the outline, Norton, with his experience, wisdom, and interest in the subject, requested I meet John Toren, who edits most of the books he publishes. John has an interest in and is well read in poverty and economic development, and after he studied the initial scree, we met and he asked me to expand the chapters of that early draft. Though I have written professionally for decades, have been published in refereed journals, and been paid for completing assignments which invariably included written reports, it soon became clear, to my chagrin, that my usual formal and 'official' style needed an editor to bring things into better focus. I commend John for his masterful approach, over a lengthy haul, in providing guidance, asking pertinent questions, seeking examples and, in turn, shining a clearer light on the many complex issues involved. In time, with his help, my more relaxed writing style began to emerge.

Some writers find that the epicurean life-style enhances their thought processes. And yes, the observation of the English gentleman Thomas Hook is as pertinent today as it was in 1841: "Overindulgence at table is the curse of colonial life." I was there! However, I have found that a radical change in lifestyle has complemented the discipline of writing and the allied research. Accordingly, I am most grateful to my 'health team' who independently provided the knowledge, tools, and techniques, and motivation for me to make the 'head' and lifestyle changes. Chief amongst the 'health team' I am privileged to receive care from is Professor Gary Schwartz, M.D., of the Mayo Clinic, whose quiet and straightforward discussions, accessibility, and continued support have been the foundation of my nutrition and fitness program. Dr. Christopher Foley, D.C. (chiropractor), a Wellness specialist, accessible and provides focused guidance on a myriad of questions; and keeps me 'in the game' for the daily exercise regime. To Sonia Ostlund, my eternal appreciation, as my swimming instructor, for her persistence, utmost patience, breaking the strokes into achievable parts (together with considerable practice) proved that 'old dogs could learn new tricks.' Swimming has become the perfect complement to research and writing, especially during the brutal winter periods.

In the end, fieldwork, with its richness and reward, is not without its peril. In Sierra Leone (25 May 1997) three of Johnny Koroma's violent rebel soldiers had me at the business end of an Uzi in the outskirts of Freetown. By the narrowest of margins, my own ingenuity and some great fortune allowed me to escape with my life. In the encounter with the rebels, the survival techniques of my good German colleague Rudy (Rudiger) Mattner, and later the essential assistance of several World Bank employees, were critical to our escape in a vintage Russian helicopter which flew just above the Guinea Sea and then landed in Conakry.

Less dramatic, perhaps, is a remarkable story about being dropped off by Kahil, a retired Jerusalem primary school teacher and our driver in the Palestinian Authority health project, at the Erez Checkpoint, at which point I wheeled my bag on foot along the near half-mile 'open zone' of the Crossing to reach Israeli formalities. After completion of these I continued to walk over the Crossing to Gaza, where I was picked up by our team and driven to the office.

And then there was Turkey…an intriguing project in a fascinating land with compelling culture, which could also be an entry in another journal.

Notes

Every effort has been made to provide readers with working URL links for references from organizations and agencies. The references that do not have a working URL suggest that the organization or agency has updated the material. Readers will most likely be able to get the current URL link by searching for the title and subject presented in the reference.

Preface

1. Organization for Economic Cooperation and Development (OECD),Glossary of Statistical Terms, Official Development Assistance (ODA) http://stats.oecd.org/glossary/detail.asp?ID=6043 Source: IMF, 2003, External Debt Statistics: Guide for Compilers and Users – Appendix III, Glossary, IMF, Washington DC.

2. Peter Paul Bauer, *Dissent on Development* (Harvard University Press, 1972); *Equality, The Third World, and Economic Delusion* (Harvard University Press, 1981); Dambisa Moyo *Dead Aid: Why Aid is Not Working and How There is a Better Way for Africa* (Farrar, Straus and Giroux, 2010); William Easterly *The White Man's Burden: Why the West's Efforts to Aid the Rest Have Done So Much Ill and So Little Good* (Penguin, 2007); Paul Collier *The Bottom Billion: Why the Poorest Countries are Failing and What Can be Done About It* (Oxford University Press, 2008).

3. UN, Keeping the promise: a forward-looking review to promote an agreed action agenda to achieve the Millennium Development Goals by 2015, Report of the Secretary-General-www.ilo.org/public/english/bureau/pardev/download/mdg/a-64-665-keepingthepromise_mdgs_2010.pdf

4. Per Pinstrup-Andersen, "The African food system and human health and nutrition: a conceptual and empirical overview," Chapter 1, *The African Food System and its Interaction with Human Health and Nutrition* ed. Per Pinstrup-Andersen (Cornell University Press in cooperation with the United Nations University, 2010), p 27.

5. *The Economist*, Global Poverty, "A fall to cheer" (March 3, 2012) p 81 – 82 ; World Bank, New Estimates Reveal Drop In Extreme Poverty 2005-2010; World Bank, Provcal Net: an online poverty analysis tool.

6. *The Economist*, The world's next great leap forward "Towards the end of poverty" (June 1, 2013) p 11 and Poverty "Not always with us" (June 1, 2013) p 22 - 24 ; The World Bank, Development Economics Vice Presidency, Partnerships, Capacity Building Unit, Policy Research Working Paper 6325, (January 2013) Martin Ravallion,

"How Long Will It Take to Lift One Billion People Out of Poverty?" ; The Brookings Institute, (April 2013) Laurence Chandy, Natasha Ledlie, Veronika Penciakova "The Final Countdown: Prospects for Ending Extreme Poverty by 2030" (Washington, DC).

7. Food and Agricultural Organization, State of Food Insecurity in the World 2013; and "Global hunger down, but millions still chronically hungry."

Chapter 3

1. *Antara News*, Year ender: RI to reform its budgeting system in 201, Jakarta, (December 6, 2011).

2. *The Economist*, Briefing: The Millennium Development Goals, Global Targets, local ingenuity. (September 25, 2010): 34 – 36.

3. Stephen Nuwagira, "Lessons from Ghana's first oil journey," *New Vision*, Accra, Ghana, (December, 26, 2010).

4. Javier Blas, "Malawi 'cash-gate' corruption scandal unfolds like a thriller" *Financial Times* (November 19, 2013).

Chapter 4

1. Riddle, Roger C *Does Foreign Aid Really Work?* (Oxford University Press, 2007), pp. 31-38; Kanbur, Ravi, "The Economics of International Aid," Cornell University (Nov. 2003), www.arts.cornell.edu/poverty/kanbur/handbookaid.pdf

2. Arthur Lewis, "Economic development with unlimited supplies of labor," *The Manchester School of Economics and Social Science Studies* 22.2 (1954): 139–91; M. L. Milliken and Walt Rostow, *The Proposal: Key to and Effective Foreign Policy* (Harper and Brothers, 1957); Hollis Chenery and Alan Strout, "Foreign Assistance and Economic Development," *American Economic Review*, (1966) 56:679–733; Gunner Myrdal, *The Asian Drama (Vol. I –III)* (Twentieth Century Fund, Pantheon Books, 1968).

3. John Williamson, "What Washington Means by Policy Reform", Chapter 2, Ed. by John Williamson, *Latin American Adjustment: How Much Has Happened?* (Institute for International Economics, 1990).

4. John Williamson, "From Reform Agenda to Damaged Brand Name: A Short History of the Washington Consensus and Suggestions for What to Do Next?" Finance and Development 40, No. 3, (Sept. 2003).

5. Yergin, Daniel and Stanislaw, Joseph, *The Commanding Heights: The Battle Between Government and the Marketplace That Is Remaking the Modern World*, (Simon & Schuster; Notations edition, 1998)

6. World Bank, Poverty Net, Poverty Reduction Strategy Papers (PRSP) web.worldbank.org/WBSITE/EXTERNAL/TOPICS/EXTPOVERTY/EXTPRS/0,menuPK:384207~pagePK:149018~piPK:149093~theSitePK:384201,00.html;Bretton Woods Project, Poverty Reduction Strategy Papers (PRSPs): A Rough Guide (April 2003 revised), www.brettonwoodsproject.org/topic/adjustment/PRSP%20rough%20guide/

PRSP%20rough%20guide.pdf; Association for Women's Right's in Development, Who Has Been Assessing The Poverty Reduction Strategy Papers (PRSPs) (Dec 2, 2008); World Bank, Annual Report 2001, Lending by Themes 2002–2007; World Bank Institute, List of Thematic Groups and Leaders; Bretton Woods Project, Briefing on the World Bank's Six Strategic Themes: Minutes, Spring Meetings (April 2008).

7. Jubilee Debt Coalition, UK

8. UNDP, Human Development Report (Reports 1990 – 2011).

9. Ken Davis, "Inward FDI in China and its policy context," Columbia FDI Profiles, Vale Columbia Center on Sustainable International Investment (Oct 18, 2010): Annex Table 2 and 3.

10. Rodrik, Dani, Goodbye Washington Consensus, Hello Washington Confusion? (2006) http://ksghome.harvard.edu/~drodrik/Lessons%20of%20the%201990s%20review%20_JEL_.pdf

11. OECD, Development Assistance Committee, Shaping the 21st Century: The Contribution of Development Co-operation (Paris 1996): www.oecd.org/dataoecd/23/35/2508761.pdf

12. Per Pinstrup-Andersen, "The African food system and human health and nutrition: a conceptual and empirical overview," Chapter 1, *The African Food System and its Interaction with Human Health and Nutrition* ed. Per Pinstrup-Andersen (Cornell University Press in cooperation with the United Nations University, 2010).

13. Joseph E. Stiglitz, (2002) *Globalization and its Discontents* (A A Andrews, New York, 2002). p. 84. "…trade liberalisation accompanied by high interest rates is an almost certain recipe for job destruction and unemployment creation…Financial market liberalisation unaccompanied by an appropriate regulatory structure is an almost certain recipe for economic instability—and may well lead to higher, not lower interest rates, making it harder for poor farmers to buy the seeds and fertiliser that can raise them above subsistence. Privatisation, unaccompanied by competition policies and oversight to ensure that monopoly powers are not abused, can lead to higher, not lower, prices for consumers. Fiscal austerity, pursued blindly, in the wrong circumstances, can lead to high unemployment and a shredding of the social contract." [Note: Above quote is in Riddle, Roger C *Does Foreign Aid Really Work?* (Oxford University Press, 2007), p. 251.]; Simon Maxwell, The Washington Consensus is dead! Long live the meta-narrative! Overseas Development Institute, Working Paper 243, (January 2005).

14. Report of G7 Finance Ministers on the Köln Debt Initiative to the Köln Economic Summit, Cologne, Germany (June 1999).

15. Ibid, Ref. 2

16. Global Issues site for the G8 Summit 2005, Gleneagles, Scotland. www.globalissues.org/article/541/g8-summit-2005; Overseas Development Institute, The African Commission Report [Note: A main background document for the G8 Summit 2005.]

17. G8 Summit 2009, L'Aquila, Italy (July 2009) www.g8italia2009.it/G8/Home/News/G8-G8_Layout_locale-1199882116809_1199902080214.htm

18. WTO, Doha Development Agenda": [Note: The negotiations, implementation and development (began 2001 and remain deadlocked 2011.] www.wto.org/english/tratop_e/dda_e/dda_e.htm

19. UN, MGD Summit Sept 20-22, 2010 www.un.org/en/mdg/ summit2010/; UN General Assembly, "Report for the Summit 19," (October 2012) www.un.org/en/mdg/summit2010/pdf/outcome_documentN1051260.pdf

20. UN Economic and Social Council, Millennium Development Goals and post-2015 Development Agenda,www.un.org/en/ecosoc/about/mdg.shtml, New York, 2013.

21. UN, The Millennium Development Goals Report 2013, New York 2013 www.un.org/millenniumgoals/pdf/...2013/mdg-report-2013-english.pdf; Report Card The Millennium Development Goals, 2013, GMR_2013_Report_Card pdf.; World Bank, Global Monitoring Report 2013: Monitoring the MDGs -econ.worldbank.org/WBSITE/EXTERNAL/EXTDEC/EXTDECPROSPECTS/0,,contentMDK:23391146~pagePK:64165401~piPK:64165026~theSitePK:476883,00.html; World Bank, Prospects: Global Monitoring Report 2013: Monitoring the MDGs.

22. Dimitri Sanga, "The Challenges of Monitoring and Reporting on the Millennium Development Goals in Africa by 2015 and Beyond", The African Statistical Journal, Volume 12, May 2011 p 104 – 118; ; Claire Provost, "2013 millennium development goal progress index – get the data" , The Guardian, 29 May 2013, www.theguardian.com/global-development/poverty-matters/2013/may/29/millennium-development-goal-progress-data ; World Bank, Percentage of Countries by Global Monitoring Report (GMR) 2013 Progress Status: data.worldbank.org/mdgs/percentage-of-countries-by-gmr-2013-progress-status.

23. Center for Global Development, Millennium Development Goals, Washington, D.C. www.cgdev.org/topics/poverty/mdg ; Jonathan Karver, Charles Kenny, and Andy Sumner. 2012. "MDGs 2.0: What Goals, Targets, and Timeframe?" CGD Working Paper 297. Washington, D.C.: Center for Global Development, www.cgdev.org/content/publications/detail/1426271

24. Kanbur, Ravi, "The Co-Evolution of the Washington Consensus and the Economic Development Discourse", Cornell University (August 2008) www.arts.cornell.edu/poverty/kanbur/Co-EvolutionWashingtonConsensus.pdf; Commission on Growth and Development, The Growth Report: Strategies for Sustained Growth and Inclusive Development" World Bank, Washington, D.C. (2008) [Full information on the background and all reports of the Commission on Growth and Development are available on this site.] www.growthcommission.org/index.php?option=com_content&task=view&id=96&Itemid=169

Chapter 5

1. World Bank, About Us, Washington, D.C. web.worldbank.org/WBSITE/EX-

TERNAL/EXTABOUTUS/0, contentMDK:20101240~menuPK:1697052~pagePK:5 1123644~piPK:329829~theSitePK:29708,00.html

2. Mathew Saltmarsh, "A Bloated U, N. Bureaucracy Causes Bewilderment," *New York Times* (January 8, 2011); UN, UN Structure & Organization, http://www.un.org/en/aboutun/structure/index.shtml; UN Board of Auditors, http://www.un.org/auditors/board/reports.shtml; Riddle, Roger C, *Does Foreign Aid Really Work?* (Oxford University Press, 2007) pp. 53-54

3. Ibid. Riddle ref 2 (2007) p. 46

4. The United Nations Office at Geneva, The United Nations & Civil Society http://www.unog.ch/80256EE60057E07D/(httpHomepages)/80A3DF6327DDD70180256F040066C85C?OpenDocument

5. World Bank, How the Project Cycle Works. http://web.worldbank.org/WBSITE/EXTERNAL/PROJECTS/0,,contentMDK:20120731~menuPK:41390~pagePK:41367~piPK:51533~theSitePK:40941,00.html

6. World Bank, Sector-Wide Approaches [Note: Main aspects and benefits are summarized.]; Alternatives to the Traditional Project Approach Overview http://info.worldbank.org/etools/docs/library/48524/peter.pdf; International Development Association (IDA), A Sector-wide Approach Improves Ghana's Health Outcomes http://web.worldbank.org/WBSITE/EXTERNAL/EXTABOUTUS/IDA/0,,contentMDK:21204586~menuPK:4754051~pagePK:51236175~piPK:437394~theSitePK:73154,00.html

7. United for Sight, Selective Primary Health Care, Module 6 in Global Health History Course http://www.uniteforsight.org/global-health-history/module6; European Network on Debt and Development (Eurodad), Global Vertical Programmes: A tale of too many funds (June 26, 2008); Andrew Jack, "Population in the Family Way," *Financial Times* (Dec. 9, 2009); Ranjay Gulati *Reorganize for Resilience: Putting Customers at the Center of Your Business* (Harvard Business Press, 2010) [Note: This book highlights the poor performance of 'silo' mentality in transnational corporations with some solutions. Clearly this approach would be helpful to assess and apply in the development industry.]

8. Robert M. Gates, Remarks as Delivered by Secretary of Defense Robert M. Gates, US Department of Defense, Eisenhower Library, Abilene, KS (May 8, 2010) [Note: An interesting parallel to 'silos and multiple-tiered systems'.] http://www.defense.gov/speeches/speech.aspx?speechid=1467

Chapter 6

1. Claudia R. Williamson, "The Two Sides of de Soto: Property Rights, Land Titling and Development," *The Annual Proceedings of the Wealth and Well-Being of Nations Vol. II 2009–2010*, Beloit College, Upton Forum (2010) pp. 95–108 www.beloit.edu/upton/assets/Williamson.pgs.pdf; Hernando de Soto, *The Mystery of Capital: Why Capitalism Triumphs in the West and Fails Everywhere Else*, Random House, New York: (2000); Richard M. Ebeling, Book Review, The Future of Freedom Foundation (February 2001) http://www.fff.org/freedom/0201f.asp

2. Yoolim Lee and George Smith Alexander, India's Microfinance Clampdown May Trigger Failures, World Bank Aide Says" Bloomberg News (Nov. 22, 2010) http://www.bloomberg.com/news/2010-11-21/india-s-smaller-micro-lenders-likely-to-fail-srinivasan-says Liza Ponomarenko, A Lesson to Be Learned from India's Failing Microfinance, Microfinance Africa (July 3, 2011) http://microfinanceafrica.net/news/a-lesson-to-be-learned-from-india%E2%80%99s-failing-microfinance/; David Roodman, *Due Diligence: An Impertinent Inquiry into Microfinance* (Center for Global Development, Washington. D.C., 2011) http://www.cgdev.org/content/publications/detail/1425809/

3. World Bank, Starting a Business http://www.doingbusiness.org/methodology/~/media/FPDKM/Doing%20Business/Documents/Annual-Reports/English/DB12-Chapters/starting-a-business.pdf

4. World Bank, East Asia Decentralize – Making Local Government Work in East Asia [Note: The link is for *Indonesia*. The box on the right contains the Chapter of the report; and the site gives links to countries in East Asia.] http://documents.worldbank.org/curated/en/2005/05/6431825/east-asia-decentralizes-making-local-government-work

Roland White and Paul Smoke, East Asia Decentralizes, Chapter 1, World Bank http://siteresources.worldbank.org/INTEAPDECEN/Resources/Chapter-1.pdf

Chapter 7

1. World Bank Independent Evaluation Group, Decentralization in Client Countries – An Evaluation of World Bank Support, 1990–2007 (2008) http://lnweb90.worldbank.org/oed/oeddoclib.nsf/DocUNIDViewForJavaSearch/CB108AC5A1CACD30852574EF0050139B/$file/decentralization_eval.pdf

2. Indahnesia.com, Indonesia shifts to conquer widespread malnutrition (June 22, 2005); Roy Tjiong and Protus Tanuhandauaru, "Health reform: revitalizing Indonesia's integrated service post" *The Jakarta Post* (June 27, 2011)

3. Mongaby.com, Indonesia – The economy [Note: Derived from several country studies program sources including the US Army Area Handbook and the Library of Congress.] http://www.mongabay.com/reference/country_studies/indonesia/ECONOMY.html

4. Asian Development Bank (ADB), Community – Driven Development country profile Indonesia (2008) http://www.adb.org/news/adb-supports-indonesias-community-driven-rural-infrastructure-development http://www.adb.org/search?keyword=40247&id=40247 ADB, A Review of Community-Driven Development and its Application to the Asian Development Bank (September 2006) http://www.adb.org/Documents/Participation/Review-CDD-Application-ADB.pdf; ADB, CDD Financing & Budgeting: The Case of PNPM in Indonesia: CDD to Empower Villagers, Build Village Infrastructure, and Alleviate Poverty, http://www.adb.org/news/indonesia-project-step-poverty-reduction-drive-rural-villages http://www.adb.org/Documents/Events/2009/CDD-Rural-Poverty-Alleviation/S311-Sujana-Royat-

Camilla-Holmemo.pdf; World Bank, Community-Driven Development in Indonesia http://web.worldbank.org/WBSITE/EXTERNAL/COUNTRIES/EASTASIA-PACIFICEXT/EXTEAPREGTOPSOCDEV/0,,contentMDK:20327355~menuPK: 746774~pagePK:34004173~piPK:34003707~theSitePK:502940,00.html

5. Andrea Woodhouse, Village Corruption in Indonesia: Fighting Corruption in the World Bank's Kecamatan Development Project, World Bank (June 2002)

6. Richard Seymour and Sarah Turner, "*Otonomi Daerah:* Indonesia's Decentralization Experiment," New Zealand Journal of Asian Studies 4, 2 (December, 2002): 33-51 http://www.nzasia.org.nz/downloads/NZJAS-Dec02/Seymour-Turner.pdf

7. Tri Widodo Wahyu Utomo, "Building good governance through decentralization in Indonesia (recognizing some implementing factors in the implementation stage)", Chapter 7, *Limits of Good Governance in Developing Countries*, Edited by Hirotsune Kimura, Suharko, Aser B. Javier, Ake Tangsupvattana Gadjah Mada University Press, Yogyakarta, Indonesia (Nov. 2011) http://hdl.handle.net/2237/15868 [Note: This recent volume contains essays and case studies from Indonesia and other South East Asian countries (including Myanmar, The Philippines, Thailand, Brazil and Uzbekistan.]

8. Peter Heywood and Nida P Harahap, "Public funding of health at the district level in Indonesia after decentralization – sources, flows and contradictions," Health Research Policy and Systems (2009) 7:5 doi:10.1186/1478-4505-7-5. http://www.health-policy-systems.com/content/7/1/5

9. Taufik Rinaldi, Marini Purnomo, and Dewi Damayanti, "Fighting Corruption in Decentralized Indonesia, Case Studies on Handling Local Government Corruption," The World Bank Office, Indonesia, Jakarta (May 2007) [Note: The Local Government Corruption Study (LGCS) is a research activity of the Justice for the Poor Program.]

10. Satria Sambijantoro "Decentralization is a dangerous burden for state budget" The Jakarta Post (November 25, 2013)

Chapter 8

1. Millennium Villages Project website http://www.millenniumpromise.org/ and http://millenniumvillages.org/the-villages/ [Note: This is the website for Millennium Villages and includes the background, progress including monitoring and evaluation and the full battery of reports associated with the Millennium Promise/Millennium Villages.]

2. Edward R. Carr, "The Millennium Villages Project and African Development: Problems and Potentials" Progress in Development Studies 8, 4 (2008), pp. 333-44 http://www.edwardrcarr.com/Publications_files/Carr%20the%20MVP%20and%20African%20Development.pdf

3. Michael A. Clemens and Gabriel Demombynes, When Does Rigorous Impact Evaluation Make A Difference? The Case of the Millennium Villages," Working Paper 225, Center for Global Development, (October 2010) http://www.cgdev.org/content/publications/detail/1424496

4. Soils, Food and Healthy Communities, Research Results, Ontario, Canada and Ekwendeni, Malawi http://soilandfood.org/research-results/

5. Collaborative Crop Research Program (CCRP), http://mcknight.ccrp.cornell.edu/index.html [Note: This site has details on CCRP projects.]; 06-740: Legume best bets: Legume best bets to acquire Phosphorus and Nitrogen and improve family nutrition http://mcknight.ccrp.cornell.edu/projects/saf_cop/SAF_legume_bestbets/legume_bestbets_project.html

6. The Millennium Villages Project: The Next Five Years 2011 – 2014, Millennium Village Project, Millennium Village Project, Earth Institute, Columbia University, New York http://millenniumvillages.org/files/2011/12/MVPReport_FINAL_rev.pdf [Updated as The Millennium Villages Project: The Next Five Years 2011 – 2015 , Millennium Village Project www.**millenniumvillages**.org/uploads/.../MVP_**Next5yrs_2011**.pdf⊠ . The book uses the 2011 – 2014 volume.]

7. Ibid. ref. 6 p. 10.

8. Ibid. ref 6, p 27 and 29. Benin will use targeted multi-sector interventions in the community of 15,000 people. Under the Cameroon Millennium Development Program 50,000 peoples will be reached in two clusters of villages. Ghana will scale up northwards to reach approximately 25,000 peoples in districts of three regions with intervention starting early 2012. Liberia will continue one MV and will scale up their MVP to support the country's 166 most food insecure districts reaching approximately 2.6 million people mainly in the northern regions. Nigeria, to use its one billion in debt relief funds in 2010, conducted a baseline assessment for MDG related infrastructure investments in 113 of the poorest local government areas. Rwanda will scale up MV-type interventions and 416 administrative sectors. Tanzania aims to begin a new MV on Pemba, Zanzibar for more than 7600 people. Zambia partnering with in international mining company aims to focus on income generating activities in an existing MV for families with subsistence farming. In 2011 Kenya launched MDG scale up policy in eight Western new "Millennium Districts" and will train local government officials to help guide the growth of MDG focused activities. Comment: Kenya represents a unique and interesting approach for MVP and seems to be consistent with concepts I emphasize in this book – the need to strengthen the district level. However, details would have to be reviewed to compare the Kenya approach with my proposals in Chapter 9 - 11.

9. Michael Clemens and Gabriel Demombynes . 2013. "The New Transparency in Impact Evaluation: Lessons from the Millennium Villages Controversy." CGD Working Paper 342. Washington, DC: Center for Global Development. http://www.cgdev.org/publication/new-transparency-development-economics-lessons-millennium-villages-controversy-working

10. 2012 Millennium Promise Annual Report on the Millennium Villages Project, Millennium Promise, Note The 2012 report in in the website http://millenniumvillages.org/. (Not for quotation or circulation – data undergoing Verification).

11. GAVI, Saving children's lives – the GAVI Alliance pledging conference for immunization, Global Alliance for Vaccines and Immunization Conference, London,(June 13, 2011) http://fr.gavialliance.org/library/gavi-documents/resource-mobilisation/chair-s-summary-and-annexes/; Lisa Carty, Amanda Glassman, J. Stephen Morrison, and Margaret Reeves, GAVI's Future: Steps to Build Strategic Leadership, Financial Sustainability, and Better Partnerships, Center for Global Development (June 8, 2011) http://www.cgdev.org/content/publications/detail/1425191?utm_

12. Ibid., Ref 2, GAVI

Chapter 9

1. UNDP, Delivering as One: Case Study in Mozambique –Final Report June 2010 *erc.undp.org/evaluationadmin/downloaddocument.html?docid=4778*; David Bloom, Report Recommends New United Nations Population Fund Head Focus on Sexual and Reproductive Health, News at Harvard School of Public Health http://www.hsph.harvard.edu/news/features/coverage-in-the-media/unfpa-bloom-report/index.html; Brett Schaffer, United Nations: Urgent Problems That Need Congressional Action, The Heritage Foundation (February 3, 2011) http://www.heritage.org/research/lecture/2011/02/united-nations-urgent-problems-that-need-congressional-action

2. In the mid-1990's there were serious discussion within the World Bank on turning the institution solely into a technical advisory role. Subsequently the World Bank has distilled and projected its main focus in 'knowledge' and about 2006 referred to itself and the 'Knowledge Bank.' *The Economist,* "What the World Bank knows…and what it thinks it knows," (January 11, 2007) [Note: The 'knowledge' focus has indeed been duly incorporated in many aspects and sections of the World Bank.]

3. Hull TH, Hull VJ, Singarimbun M, "Indonesia's family planning story: success and challenge." Popul Bull. 1977 Nov; 32(6):1-5; http://www.ncbi.nlm.nih.gov/pubmed/12260296; http://www.ncbi.nlm.nih.gov/pubmed/12260296?report=abstract&format=text; Donald P. Warwick, "The Indonesian Family Planning Program: Government Influence and Client Choice," Population and Development Review, Vol. 12, No. 3 (Sep., 1986), pp. 453-490; SERO/WHO, Indonesia and Family Planning: An Overview, 2003 http://www.google.com/url?sa=t&rct=j&q=&esrc=s&source=web&cd=5&ved=0CEgQFjAE&url=http%3A%2F%2F209.61.208.233%2FLinkFiles%2FFamily_Planning_Fact_Sheets_indonesia.pdf&ei=mJLVUrmrB6rXyAG7yIGADg&usg=AFQjCNE0MuCwcdX-cAlvEpdJs4CvPF2nvQ&sig2=QatsaR4ZFHafcWHqqxsH_g&bvm=bv.59378465,d.aWc ;

4. Christine Clough, Highlights from the International Corruption Hunters Alliance Conference at the World Bank, Dec. 9, 2010, Financial Integrity & Economic Development Task Force, World Bank http://www.financialtaskforce.org/2010/12/09/highlights-from-the-international-corruption-hunters-alliance-conference-at-the-world-bank/

5. Tax Justice Network for Africa, Looting Africa: Some Facts and Figures [Note: The core themes and articles on the site: Tax Justice Network.] http://www.taxjustice.

net/cms/front_content.php?idcat=2 [Note: A separate website Tax Justice Network – Africa.] http://www.taxjusticeafrica.net/

6. Transparency International, Corruption Perceptions Index 2010 Results http://www.transparency.org/policy_research/surveys_indices/cpi/2010/results

7. UN Office on Drugs and Crime, The Basel Institute on Governance—(International Center for Asset Recovery) http://www.unodc.org/unodc/en/commissions/CCPCJ/institutes-ICAR.html

8. Doreen Carvajal, "Hunting for Liberia's Missing Millions" *New York Times* (May 30, 2010) http:// www.nytimes.com /2010/05/31/ world/ africa/ 31taylor.html?ref=global-home

9. Saleh, Peele and England, "Graft probe seeks to appease Egyptian public" *Financial Times* (February 8, 2011); MacFaequhar, Rhode and Roston, "Mubarak family wealth riches attract new focus" *New York Times* (February 12, 2011); Landon Thomas, Jr., "Libya's hidden wealth may be the next battle" *New York Times* (March 3, 2011).

10. Haig Simonian, "Swiss freeze Gaddafi, Mubarak and Ben Ali's funds" *Financial Times* (May 2, 2011)

11. Riddle, Roger C, *Does Foreign Aid Really Work?* (Oxford University Press, 2007), pp. 51-53.

12. Note: Rotary International for two decades has, with contribution and challenge grants, raised $555 million for polio vaccination program in many countries. www.rotary.org

13. Alliance for Green Revolution in Africa (Agra) http://www.agra-alliance.org/; Heifer International, www.heifer.org [Note: This is one example having many decades worldwide as a nonprofit humanitarian organization with a focused agenda on self-reliant hunger reduction with livestock linked to appropriate training and local protecting aspects of the local environment.]

14. PUR, PUR Water Filtration and P&G's Children's Safe Drinking Water Program Take Jessica Biel, Kenna and Other Cultural Influencers to Meet Those Affected by the Clean Drinking Water Crisis Before Embarking on SUMMIT ON THE SUMMIT: Kilimanjaro http://multivu.prnewswire.com/mnr/pur/41049/; Charity Tuesday: AVEDA's Earth Month Campaign, Air & Water Filter News http://www.filtersfast.com/blog/index.php/2011/04/charity-tuesday-avedas-earth-month-campaign/

Chapter 10

1. International Monetary Fund (IMF), Debt Relief Under the Heavily Indebted Poor Countries (HIPC) Initiative (March 31, 2011) http://www.imf.org/external/np/pp/eng/2011/110811.pdf; IMF Staff Paper (with World Bank) Preserving Debt Sustainability in Low-Income Countries in the Wake of the Global Crisis (April 4, 2011) http://www.imf.org/external/np/pp/eng/2010/040110.pdf; and World Bank, (HIPC) The Enhanced Heavily Indebted Poor Country Initiative http://go.worldbank.

org/85B908KVE0 [Note: These sites have access to voluminous amounts of policy, data and analytical papers/report on the HIPC Program.]

2. International Food Policy Research Institute (adapted from www.ifpri.org) [Note: This is an excellent site for all issues related to agriculture and food worldwide and country specific. For example, "The Republic of Yemen is one of the driest, poorest and least developed countries in the world. It ranks 140 out of 182 countries on the UNDP Human Development Index (2009). An estimated 42 percent of the people are poor, and one Yemeni in five is malnourished. Poverty is endemic, particularly in more remote and less accessible areas; about two-thirds of the population, including 80 percent of the country's poor people, live in rural areas and most of them depend on agriculture for their livelihoods. Agriculture is a vital economic sector, providing jobs and income in a country with an unemployment rate of 37 percent and averting migration to urban areas; population is increasing by more than 3 percent annually with Yemen having the world's fourth fastest growing population, according to a recent UNICEF report. Lack of water is a crucial issue; with government estimates that each Yemeni's average share of renewable water resources is *one-tenth* of the average in most Middle Eastern countries and *one-fiftieth* of the world average."; Also see: International Food Policy Research Institute, Yemen National Food security Strategy, Health, Nutrition and Risk Management http://www.ifpri.org/sites/default/files/publications/yemennote4en.pdf

3. UN and Civil Society http://www.un.org/en/civilsociety/; The World Bank and Civil Society http://www.un.org/en/civilsociety/index.html; Roger C. Riddle, *Does Foreign Aid Really Matter?* (Oxford University Press, 2007), especially Chapters 16 – 17; and Jude Howell, Armine Ishkanian, Ebenezer Obadare, Hakan Seckinelgin, and Marlies Glasius, The Backlash against Civil Society in the Wake of the Long War on Terror, LSE Civil Society Working Paper No 26, London School of Economics and Political Science (2006).

4. Ibid, Riddle; Ian Smillie, *Freedom from Want: The Remarkable Success Story of BRAC, the Global Organization That's Winning the Fight Against Poverty* (Kumarian Press, 2009).

5. Note: For starters the World Bank Independent Evaluation Group http://ieg.worldbankgroup.org/ should have assessment/reviews and insights on the Lessons Learned, 'what works', 'what does not' and reasons – throughout the whole 'project cycle' from an array of projects over decades, among diverse member countries that were/are in the Bank's portfolio. This should include the range of project from large civil works to human development projects and are largely involved in the MDG. Just in the subjects of agriculture, there are decades of substantive resources and research to distil from the following UN based organizations/centers: World Bank, Agriculture & Rural Development Section   http://web.worldbank.org/WBSITE/EXTERNAL/TOPICS/EXTARD/0,,contentMDK:20445210~menuPK:1307958~pagePK:148956~piPK:216618~theSitePK:336682,00.html; Food and Agricultural Organization www.fao.org. An umbrella organization Consultant Group on International Agricul-

tural Research www.cgiar.org for the following specialties: International Food Policy Research Institute www.ifpri,org; International Fund for Agricultural Development www.ifad.org/; International Livestock Research Institute www.ilri.org; International Center for Tropical Agriculture http://ciat.or; International Rice Research Institute www.irri.org. Comment: The task of ITASC working with the NTASCs is to be selective and integrate multi-sector technically sound interventions, with high likelihood these are used successfully the 'packets' can be adapted and scaled up in the piloted and other countries. Hence, high selectivity will need to be used to determine the most relevant research and field level examples from a wide spectrum of agencies/organizations and universities in the prime MDG facets of health, education and rural and urban slum development.

6. A main feature of the WBG Strategy is to harness the ever-changing knowledgebase over14 global practices and five cross-cutting areas to design and deliver customized development solutions, back by finance, knowledge and convening services. The 14 global practices include: agriculture, education, energy and extractive industries, the environment and natural resources, finance and markets, governance, macroeconomics in fiscal management, poverty, social protection and labor, trade and competitiveness, transport and ICT (information and communication technology), water as well as health, nutrition, and population, and urban, rural and social development. The five cross-cutting areas include climate change, gender, jobs, public – private partnerships, and fragility, conflict and violence. Source: World Bank Group Strategy, Development Committee (Joint Ministerial Committee of the Board of Governors of the Bank and the Fund on Transfer of Real Resources to Developing Countries), DC2013 – 0009, September 18, 2013, Washington DC.; The World Bank Group. 2014. The World Bank Group Strategy. Washington, DC: World Bank Group. License: Creative Commons Attribution (CC BY-NC-ND 3.0).; World Bank Group President Jim Yong Kim's Remarks at the Annual Meetings 2013 Closing Press Conference, Washington, DC, United States, October 12, 2013 http://www.worldbank.org/en/news/speech/2013/10/12/world-bank-group-president-jim-yong-kim-closing-press-conference; Michael Igoe, "What to expect from Jim Kim's 'global practices' plan", DEVEX.COM (9 October 2013), https://www.devex.com/en/news/what-to-expect-from-jim-kim-s-global-practices/82043

7. Ibid. see ref 5, World Bank, Independent Evaluation Group

8. Note: Here are but a few references and sites that have substantial experiences in low-cost and effective appropriate (sometimes referred to as sustainable) technology. Zoe International Development Organization (ZIDO) http://www.zoeinternationaldevelopment.org/; Development Center for Appropriate Technology http://www.dcat.net/; Pradip Gosh (Editor) and Denton Morison (Editor), *Appropriate Technology in Third World Development* (Glenwood Press, 1984); Soils, Food and Healthy Communities, Research Results, Ontario, Canada and Ekwendeni, Malawi http://soilandfood.org/research-results/; Collaborative Crop Research Program (CCRP), http://mcknight.ccrp.cornell.edu/index.html; David Roodman, *Due Diligence: An Impertinent Inquiry into Microfinance,* (Center for Global Development, Washington. D.C., 2011) http://

www.cgdev.org/content/publications/detail/1425809/

9. Consultant Group on International Agriculture, http://www.cgiar.org/impact/research/index.html; International Crop Research Institute for Semi-Arid Tropics, http://www.icrisat.org/, Dr. Gebisa Ejeta, Purdue University Agronomy Department, http://www.ag.purdue.edu/agry/Pages/gejeta.aspx; Alliance for a Green Revolution in Africa, http://www.agra-alliance.org/

10. Edward R. Carr, "The Millennium Village Project and African Development: Problems and Potentials," Progress in Development Studies 8, 4 (2008), pp. 333-44 http://www.edwardrcarr.com/Publications_files/Carr%20the%20MVP%20and%20African%20Development.pdf.

11. Michael A. Clemens and Gabriel Demombynes, When Does Rigorous Impact Evaluation Make A Difference? The Case of the Millennium Villages, Center for Global Development, Working Paper 225 (October 2010) http://www.cgdev.org/content/publications/detail/1424496

12. Millennium Promise http://www.millenniumpromise.org/; The Millennium Villages Project: The Next Five Years 2011 – 2014, Millennium Village Project, Earth Institute, Columbia University, New York, [Updated as The Millennium Villages Project: The Next Five Years 2011 – 2015, Millennium Village Project *www.millenniumvillages.org/uploads/.../MVP_Next5yrs_2011.pdf*. The book uses the 2011 – 2014 volume.]

13. Mead Over, A New Report Slams the World Bank's Support of Health Systems for Insufficient Focus on Results, Center for Global Development, http://blogs.cgdev.org/globalhealth/2010/06/a-new-report-slams-the-world-bank%e2%80%99s-support-of-health-systems-for-insufficient-focus-on-results.php; Richard Skolnik, Paul Jensen, Robert Johnson, How the World Bank and Development Partners are Failing to Improve Health Through SWAPs, Advocacy to Control TB Internationally http://c1280352.cdn.cloudfiles.rackspacecloud.com/results_swaps_report_0610_lowres.pdf; Steven J. Klees, World Bank Development Policy: A SAP in SWAPs Clothing, 2002 Current Issues in Comparative Education, Teachers College, Columbia University (May1, 2001) http://www.eldis.org/go/home&id=14918&type=Document#.UtWhUvty7FJ

14. Michael Clemens and Gabriel Demombynes . 2013. "The New Transparency in Impact Evaluation: Lessons from the Millennium Villages Controversy." CGD Working Paper 342. Washington, DC: Center for Global Development.http://www.cgdev.org/publication/new-transparency-impact-evaluation-lessonsmillennium-villages-controversy; Gertler, Paul J., Sebastian Martinez, Patrick Premand, Laura B. Rawlings, and Christel M.J. Vermeersch. 2011. Impact Evaluation in Practice. Washington, DC: World Bank.

15. The Green Belt Movement http://www.greenbeltmovement.org/; Professor Wangari Maatha http://nobelprize.org/nobel_prizes/peace/laureates/2004/maathai.html

16. Green Africa Network, Networking Rural Africa Communities and Sustainable

Development Programs http://www.greenafrica.org/; Green Africa Foundation, http://www.greenafricafoundation.org/

17. Peter, Heller, The underfinancing of recurrent development costs, Finance & Development (March 1979) http://www.petersheller.com/documents/Underfinancing_of_recurrent.pdf

18. Commission on Growth and Development, The Growth Report: Strategies for Sustained Growth and Inclusive Development, World Bank, Washington, D.C. (2008) [Note: Full information on the background and all reports of the Commission on Growth and Development are available on this site. http://www.growthcommission.org/index.php?option=com_content&task=view&id=96&Itemid=169]

19. OECD, Development Co-operation Directorate (DCD-DAC), Enabling Effective Development, The Fourth High Level Forum on Aid Effectiveness, Busan, Korea (November 29 – December 1, 2011).

20. OECD, Busan Partnership for Effective Development Co-operation, Outcome Document www.aideffectiveness.org/busanhlf4/images/stories/hlf4/OUTCOME_DOCUMENT_-_FINAL_EN.pdf

21. Ibid. ref v1, page 10.

22. *The Economist*, Briefing Africa's hopeful economies "The sun shines bright," (December 3, 2011) p 82 – 84

Chapter 11

1. Grameen Bank http://www.grameen-info.org/

2. Ian Smillie, *Freedom from Want: The Remarkable Success Story of BRAC, the Global Organization That's Winning the Fight Against Poverty* (Kumarian Press 2009)

3. The Green Belt Movement http://www.greenbeltmovement.org/; UN, Civil Society Network, Best Practices http://esango.un.org/irene/?section=2&type=2

4. Cornell University Mann Library, TEEAL, or The Essential Electronic Agricultural Library http://www.teeal.org/what-is-teeal

5. Stephanie Strom, "For Pepsi, a Business Decision with Social Benefit" *New York Times* (February 21, 2011)

6. Development Crossing, Social Business Enterprise, New Project from Grameen Bank and Danone Yoghurt (January 30, 2007) http://www.freerepublic.com/focus/f-news/1791104/posts

7. Kaitie Mintz, "Awash in ideas" *The Eden Prairie Sun-Current* (May 5, 2011)

8. Compatibility Technology International http://www.compatibletechnology.org/

9. Geeta Channal, Shobha Nagnur and Channamma Nanjayyanamath, Indigenous grain storage Structures, L E I S A I N D I A (September 2004) p. 10 http://www.agriculturesnetwork.org/magazines/india/3-post-harvest-management/indigenous-grain-

storage-structures/at_download/article_pdf; World Bank, Missing Food: The Case of Postharvest Grain Losses in Sub-Saharan Africa, Report No. 60371-AFR, prepared by staffs of World Bank, Natural Resources Institute, UK; and FAO (April 2011) http://siteresources.worldbank.org/INTARD/Resources/MissingFoods10_web.pdf

10. Easy Energy Systems, Inc. http://easyenergysystems.com/ The Economist, Technology Quarterly: Q1 2012, Monitor "Starting from scratch" (March 3, 2012) p 8 – 9; Eight19 http://www.Eight19.com. SRISTRI, Society for Research & Initiatives for Sustainable Technologies & Institutions, Honey Bee Network http://www.sristi.org/cms/en/our_network , also see CK Prahalad, *The Fortune at the Bottom of the Pyramid: Eradicating Poverty Through Profits*, Revised and Updated 5th Anniversary Edition: Pearson Prentice Hall, (2009)

11. Nursila Dewi, Posyandu: The power of women in the community's health, WHO Office Jakarta, SEARO Newsletter, REC Edition, Vol. 4 No. 2, WHO Regional Office for Southeast Asia, New Delhi (September 2011) http://www.searo.who.int/LinkFiles/RC64_HISEA.pdf

12. WHO, China's village doctors take great strides, Bulletin of WHO, Volume 86, Number 12 (December 2008)pp. 909-988 http://www.who.int/bulletin/volumes/86/12/08-021208/en/index.html; Daqing Zhang and Paul U Unschuld "China's barefoot doctor: past, present, and future" *The Lancet*, Volume 372, Issue 9653, (Nov 2008) pp. 1865 - 1867, 29 http://www.thelancet.com/journals/lancet/article/PIIS0140-6736(08)61355-0/fulltext; Lingling Zhang, Where Have All the Barefoot Doctors Gone?, asks HSPH Doctoral Student, Harvard School of Public Health, Harvard Public Health Now (February 29, 2008) http://www.hsph.harvard.edu/now/20080229/where-have-all-the-barefoot-doctors-gone-asks-hsph-doctoral-student.html "Where Have All the Barefoot Doctors Gone in Pursuing a More Equitable New Health-Care System in China?" *Young Voices in Research for Health*, Geneva, Switzerland (2007)

13. WHO, Track 1 Community Empowerment, Geneva (2008) http://www.who.int/healthpromotion/conferences/7gchp/track1/en/index.html

14. World Bank East Asia Poverty Reduction and Economic Management Unit, Combating Corruption in Indonesia - Enhancing Accountability for Development (October 20, 2003); Jin-Wook Choi "What Holds Indonesia Back? Structural Roots of Corruption and Reform", Paper presented at the 2009 Korean Association for Public Administration International Conference, University of Incheon at Songdo Campus, Korea (October 2009) pp. 22-24; World Bank, Indonesia Kecamatan Development Program http://web.worldbank.org/WBSITE/EXTERNAL/COUNTRIES/EASTASIAPACIFICEXT/EXTEAPREGTOPSOCDEV/0,,contentMDK:20477526~menuPK:502970~pagePK:34004173~piPK:34003707~theSitePK:502940,00.html ; http://web.worldbank.org/external/projects/main?pagePK=104231&piPK=73230&theSitePK=40941&menuPK=228424&Projectid=P045337 ; Syed Hussein Alatas, *The Sociology of Corruption: The Nature, Functions, Causes and Prevention of Corruption,* (Delts Oriental (Pte) Ltd, Singapore, 1975)

15. The World Bank Group. 2014. *The World Bank Group Strategy*. Washington, DC: World Bank Group. License: Creative Commons Attribution (CC BY-NC-ND 3.0).; World Bank Group President Jim Yong Kim's Remarks at the Annual Meetings 2013 Closing Press Conference, Washington, DC, United States, October 12, 2013. http://www.worldbank.org/en/news/speech/2013/10/12/world-bank-group-president-jim-yong-kim-closing-press-conference

16. *The Economist*, Briefing: China International Fund, "The Queensway syndicate and African Trade," (August 13, 2011) pp. 21-23; Human Rights Watch, Angola: Explain Missing Government Funds (December 20, 2011) http://www.hrw.org/news/2011/12/20/angola-explain-missing-government-funds; International Monetary Fund, Angola—Fifth Review Under the Stand-By Arrangement, Request for Waiver of Applicability of Performance Criteria, and Request for Modification of Performance Criteria, Staff Report; Supplement; Press Release on the Executive Board Discussion; and Statement by the Executive Director for Angola, IMF Country Report No. 11/346, Washington (December 2011). http://www.imf.org/external/pubs/ft/scr/2011/cr11346.pdf

17. Greg Palast, "Vultures feed when economies are turned into rotting carcasses" *The Guardian*, (November 16, 2011) http://www.guardian.co.uk/global-development/poverty-matters/2011/dec/20/vultures-feed-economies-carcasses; Greg Palast, "Occupy Wall Street comes home to roost with Congo's 'debt vultures'," *The Guardian*, (December 9, 2011) http://www.guardian.co.uk/commentisfree/cifamerica/2011/dec/09/occupy-wall-street-debt-vultures?INTCMP=SRCH

18. Thomas Palley, "The economic case for the Tobin tax," Published in Weaver (ed.), *Debating the Tobin Tax*, New Rules for Global Finance Coalition, Washington, (2003) http://www.thomaspalley.com/docs/articles/selected/Tobin%20Tax%20_%20New%20Rules.pdf; Going Global – East meets West – Achieves, Will The UN Collect the "Tobin Tax" ? (January 7, 2009) http://articlesofinterest-kelley.blogspot.com/2009/03/will-un-collect-tobin-tax.html; Gillian Tett, "Could Tobin tax' reshape financial sector DNA?" *Financial Times* (August 27, 2009); Lawrence Haddad, "Forget the Tobin Tax, What About a Panic Tax?" Institute of Development Studies (September 28, 2011) http://www.developmenthorizons.com/2011_09_01_archive.html

Appendix

1. UN, MGD Summit Sept 20-22, 2010; UN General Assembly, Report for the Summit (October 19, 2010) http://www.un.org/en/mdg/summit2010/pdf/outcome_documentN1051260.pdf; UN, We can end poverty 2015 millennium development goals, UN High Level Plenary Meeting of the General Assembly, 20 – 22 September 2010, New York; UN, The Millennium Development Goals Report 2010, New York, http://www.un.org/millenniumgoals/pdf/MDG%20Report%202010%20En%20r15%20-low%20res%2020100615%20-.pdf ; UNDP, Millennium Development Goals Reports, http://www.google.com/url?sa=t&rct=j&q=&esrc=s&source=web&cd=2&ved=0CDMQFjAB&url=http%3A%2F%2Fwww.un.org%2Fmillenniu

mgoals%2Fpdf%2Freport-2013%2Fmdg-report-2013-english.pdf&ei=5qvVUqmiO-OiMyAHsvIGgBg&usg=AFQjCNEQo3nMu9UQ98dzdAZ8omAxON_3uw&sig2=D-ABEPBf7aLgkBeRNuQP3A&bvm=bv.59378465,d.aWc. [Note: This site includes MDG background, country and currently available reports and publications.] UN, Keeping the promise: a forward-looking review to promote an agreed action agenda to achieve the Millennium Development Goals by 2015", Report of the Secretary-General: http://www.ilo.org/public/english/bureau/pardev/download/mdg/a-64-665-keepingthepromise_mdgs_2010.pdf. UN Millennium Development Goals Indicators, The Official UN Site for the MGD Indicators: http://mdgs.un.org/unsd/mdg/News.aspx?Ar. [Note: This site prepared and updates by the UN Statistics Division, Department of Social Affairs provides background documents and new features of MDGs.] UN, Millennium Development Goals: 2011 Progress Chart http://mdgs.un.org/unsd/mdg/Resources/Static/Products/Progress2011/11-31330%20%28E%29%20MDG%20Report%202011_Progress%20Chart%20LR.pdf; International Institute for Sustainable Development (IISD), Summary of MDG Summit 20-22 September 2010, Volume 153 Number 9 - Saturday, 25 September 2010 http://www.iisd.ca/ymb/mdg/summit2010/html/ymbvol153num9e.html; World Bank, Data Millennium Development Goals http://data.worldbank.org/about/millennium-development-goals; World Bank, eAtlas of the Millennium Development Goals, Washington, http://www.app.collinsindicate.com/mdg/en; World Bank, About Us Millennium Development Goals, Washington http://web.worldbank.org/WBSITE/EXTERNAL/EXTABOUTUS/0,,contentMDK:20104132~menuPK:250991~pagePK:43912~piPK:44037~theSitePK:29708,00.html; World Bank, Main Site of the World Bank Group, http://www.worldbank.org/; *Examples of countries MDG Reports*: Millennium Development Goals India Country Report for 2005 http://www.unicef.org/india/ssd04_2005_final.pdf; Millennium Development Goals in Ethiopia (with links to various reports over several years); http://www.et.undp.org/content/undp/en/home/librarypage/results/results/r_ethiopia.html Ethiopia MGD 2005

2. Per Pinstrup-Andersen, "The African food system and human health and nutrition: a conceptual and empirical overview", Chapter 1, *The African Food System and its Interaction with Human Health and Nutrition* ed. Per Pinstrup-Andersen (Cornell University Press in cooperation with the United Nations University, 2010), p 27

3. FAO, *The State of Food Insecurity in the World 2009: Economic Crises —Impacts and Lessons Learned*, Rome http://www.fao.org/docrep/012/i0876e/i0876e00.htm. [For up-to-date information and analysis also see:] FAO, *The State of Food Insecurity in the World 2011: How Does International Price Volatility Affect Domestic Economies and Food Security?* http://www.fao.org/publications/sofi/en/.

4. International Food Policy Research Institute (IFPRI), Global Food Index (GHI) 2011, Washington D. C. http://www.ifpri.org/book-8018/ourwork/researcharea/global-hunger-index; Overseas Development Institute Project, Ghana's Sustained Agricultural Growth, 11-07-27, http://one.org/livingproof/en/article/ghanas-sustained-agricultural-growth/.

5. Per Pinstrup-Andersen, "The Global World Food System and Related Policy Changes", Borlaug Memorial Lecture, University of Minnesota, October 14, 2013, http://symposia.appliedplantsciences.umn.edu/borlaug-lecture-2013/; FAO, The State of Food Insecurity 2013, Rome. http://www.fao.org/publications/sofi/en/, World Bank. Prospects: Global Monitoring Report 2013: Monitoring the MDGs http://econ.worldbank.org/WBSITE/EXTERNAL/EXTDEC/EXTDECPROSPECTS/0,,contentMDK:23391146~pagePK:64165401~piPK:64165026~theSitePK:476883,00.html; World Bank, Percentage of Countries by Global Monitoring Report (GMR) 2013 Progress Status Goal 1: Eradicate Extreme Poverty and Hunger http://data.worldbank.org/mdgs/percentage-of-countries-by-gmr-2013-progress-status

6. Professor Rafael Loranzo et. al., "Progress towards Millennium Development Goals 4 and 5 on Maternal and Child Mortality: An Updated Systematic Analysis", *The Lancet*, Volume 378, Issue 9797, pp. 1139 - 1165, (24 September 2011) http://www.thelancet.com/journals/lancet/article/PIIS0140-6736%2811%2961337-8/fulltext?_eventId=login; Margaret C Hogan, et.al, "Maternal mortality for 181 countries, 1980—2008: A Systematic Analysis of Progress Towards Millennium Development Goal 5", *The Lancet*, Volume 375, Issue 9726, pp. 1609 – 1623 (8 May 2010) http://www.thelancet.com/journals/lancet/article/PIIS0140-6736%2810%2960703-9/abstract#; BBC News, Millennium Development Goals on health 'will not be met', London (September, 19, 2011) http://www.bbc.co.uk/news/health-14974145

7. Bono, "A Decade of Progress on AIDS", *New York Times* (November 30, 2011); BBC News, Aids-Related Deaths 'Down 21% From Peak, says UNAids, London (November 21, 2011) http://www.bbc.co.uk/news/health-15816813; UNAIDS, *World AIDS Day Report 2011*, "*How to Get to Zero: Faster. Smarter. Better,* UN, New York [Note: For other information from UNAIDS see: Regions and Countries. http://www.unaids.org/en/regionscountries/]; Report on the Global AIDS Epidemic 2010 http://www.unaids.org/globalreport/default.htm; AIDS Outlook report 2010 http://www.unaids.org/en/resources/presscentre/featurestories/2010/july/20100713outlooklaunch/,www.unaids.org/en/media/unaids/contentassets/dataimport/pub/report/2010/2009_annual_report_en.pdf; Do Something.org The Effects of HIV/AIDS on Society http://www.dosomething.org/actnow/tipsandtools/the-effect-hivaids-society

8. World Bank, Percentage of Countries by Global Monitoring Report (GMR) 2013 Progress Status Goal 6: Combat HIV/AIDS, Malaria, and Other Diseases; http://econ.worldbank.org/WBSITE/EXTERNAL/EXTDEC/EXTDECPROSPECTS/0,,contentMDK:23159286~pagePK:64165401~piPK:64165026~theSitePK:476883,00.html

9. United Nations, The Millennium Development Goals Report 2013, New York http://www.google.com/url?sa=t&rct=j&q=&esrc=s&source=web&cd=1&ved=0CC0QFjAA&url=http%3A%2F%2Fwww.un.org%2Fmillenniumgoals%2Fpdf%2Freport-2013%2Fmdg-report-2013-english.pdf&ei=gbbVUvi8BMfT2wWU3IGIDg&usg=AFQjCNEQo3nMu9UQ98dzdAZ8omAxON_3uw&sig2=QsXEZTd-8smf9ggVHomcaw&bvm=bv.59378465,d.b2I

NOTES

10. World Health Organization, Millennium Development Goals (MDGs) Fact sheet N°290 Updated October 2013 Geneva http://www.who.int/mediacentre/factsheets/fs290/en/

11. Water Aid, Off-track, off-target Why Investment in Water, Sanitation and Hygiene is not Reaching Those Who Need it Most, Policy Report, London http://www.google.com/url?sa=t&rct=j&q=&esrc=s&source=web&cd=1&ved=0CC0QFjAA&url=http%3A%2F%2Fwww.wateraid.org%2F~%2Fmedia%2FPublications%2Fwater-sanitation-hygiene-investment.pdf&ei=w7XVUvzALYS-2AWXqYA4&usg=AFQjCNGUYFJ77t6UemuAyrfMr-L9aHPIXQ&sig2=9itpGeQW4jBsn0aO1TKFiw&bvm=bv.59378465,d.b2I ; James Melik, Poor sanitation stifles economic growth, BBC News Business, London (17 November 2011) http://www.bbc.co.uk/news/business-15552967.

Geoffrey Ferster was born and raised in Minnesota. An interest in the ways politics, economics, and culture interact eventually led him into studies at the University of Minnesota, the London School of Economics and Political Science, and Cornell University, where he earned his Ph.D. in Agricultural and Managerial Economics, with a focus on land and regional economic development. Dr. Ferster's appointments at the University of Dar es Salaam, Tanzania, University of Exeter, UK (applied health economics in the National Health Service) and with WHO in Indonesia's Ministry of Health, enabled him to work with a wide variety of professionals, bureaucrats and villagers in addressing issues from the board room to the communities. As an independent consultant to the World Bank, The Netherlands Development Co-operation, USAID, AusAID, the Harvard Institute of International Development, and UNOPS, Ferster served in Ghana, Indonesia, Jordan, Malawi, Nepal, Palestinian Authority, Sierra Leone and Turkey, further contributing to his understanding of development issues. In his first book, *The Sincere Veneer*, Dr. Ferster shares a few of these insights, along with some very practical words of advice about how the development industry can do a better job of serving that half of the world's population that lives on less than $2.50 a day. His treatise is geared for bureaucrats eager to reform the development industry, and also for a broader audience of concerned citizens and students who want to 'put a shoulder to the wheel' in this global effort.

www.gferster.com, Geoffrey@gferster.com

Made in the USA
Middletown, DE
19 July 2016